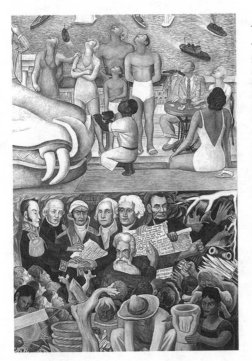

About the Cover

The cover reproduces a portion of a panel from Diego Rivera's *Pan American Unity* mural at City College of San Francisco. This is a detail from the "Elements from the Past and Present" panel. The portraits represent, from left to right, Simón Bolívar (the liberator and emancipator of Venezuela's slaves), Miguel Hidalgo y Costilla (the father of Mexican independence), José Maria Morelos y Pavón (Mexican priest, military leader, and statesman), George Washington, Thomas Jefferson, John Brown (below), and Abraham Lincoln.

Service Learning for Civic Engagement Series
Series Editor: Gerald Eisman

Available:

Race, Poverty, and Social Justice
Multidisciplinary Perspectives Through Service Learning
Edited by José Calderón

Gender Identity, Equity, and Violence
Multidisciplinary Perspectives Through Service Learning
Edited by Geraldine B. Stahly

Research, Advocacy, and Political Engagement
Multidisciplinary Perspectives Through Service Learning
Edited by Sally Cahill Tannenbaum

Forthcoming:

Promoting Health and Wellness in Underserved
Communities
Multidisciplinary Perspectives Through Service Learning
Anabel Pelham and Elizabeth Sills

RESEARCH, ADVOCACY, AND
POLITICAL ENGAGEMENT

RESEARCH, ADVOCACY, AND POLITICAL ENGAGEMENT

Multidisciplinary Perspectives
Through Service Learning

Edited by

Sally Cahill Tannenbaum

STERLING, VIRGINIA

COPYRIGHT © 2008 BY STYLUS PUBLISHING, LLC.

Published by Stylus Publishing, LLC
22883 Quicksilver Drive
Sterling, Virginia 20166–2102

Library of Congress Cataloging-in-Publication-Data
Research, advocacy, and political engagement :
multidisciplinary perspectives through service learning /
edited by Sally Cahill Tannenbaum.—1st ed.
     p.   cm.
Includes bibliographical references and index.
ISBN 978–1–57922–242–0 (cloth : alk. paper)—
ISBN 978–1–57922–243–7 (pbk. : alk. paper)
1. Service learning—California.
2. Students—California—Political activity.
3. Political participation—California.
I. Tannenbaum, Sally Cahill, 1949–
LC221.2.C2R47   2008
378.1'03—DC22   2007048783

ISBN: 978–1–57922–242–0 (cloth)

ISBN: 978–1–57922–243–7 (paper)

Printed in the United States of America

All first editions printed on acid free paper
that meets the American National Standards Institute
Z39–48 Standard.

Bulk Purchases

Quantity discounts are available for use in workshops
and for staff development.
Call 1–800–232–0223

First Edition, 2008

10   9   8   7   6   5   4   3   2   1

CONTENTS

ACKNOWLEDGMENTS

W e would like to give special thanks to colleagues both within and external to the California State University who serve on the Advisory Board for the monograph series. Debra David, Barbara Holland, Kathy O'Byrne, Seth Pollack, and Maureen Rubin continue to provide invaluable advice on the development of the current volumes and the dimensions the series will explore in the future.

This material is based upon work supported by the Corporation for National and Community Service under Learn and Serve America Grant No. 03LHHCA003. Opinions or points of view expressed in this document are those of the authors and do not necessarily reflect the official position of the Corporation or the Learn and Serve America Program.

FOREWORD

Perhaps once in a generation a movement comes along to redefine—even transform—higher education. I can point to the GI Bill of 1944, which opened the gates to a much broader population than had ever before enjoyed the opportunity to receive higher education. The civil rights struggle and the later antiwar movement galvanized students and faculty across the nation. Many of us participated directly in these movements; many more worked then, and in the years that followed, to overhaul what we perceived as an outmoded university curriculum as we struggled to open up the university to new ideas, new teaching strategies, and most of all, to underrepresented populations.

To this list, I would now add community service learning. I consider this movement in higher education as exciting as anything I have experienced as an educator. Service learning, and its central role in our goals of campuswide civic engagement and ethical education, may be the most significant development on our campuses since the curricular reforms of the 1960s. In fact, I believe that it will prove to be *the* higher education legacy of the early 21st century, and that it will have a lifelong impact on our students.

Since service learning began to take formal hold throughout the nation in the early 1990s, it has come to be seen as much more than community volunteerism linked with academic study. It is a vehicle for character and citizenship development—in short, for all that we most value in a liberal education. Through thoughtfully structured service-learning experiences, students can test and apply the values of a healthy democracy to some of the most complex and challenging issues of our time.

In recent years, higher education has begun more deliberately to pursue a historic mission: what I might call moral education—our responsibility both to our students and society. The Association of American Colleges and Universities terms this "core commitments," and calls on us to educate our students "for personal and social responsibility." This is the highest aim of liberal education. It is the culmination of our mission to service, to preparing our students with the skills and desire to contribute positively to our democratic society and to the greater world, to fostering a campus climate where speech is open, but where we can disagree—even passionately—without venom or hatred, and to ensuring that our students find in the classroom a safe and receptive environment in which to express, test, and challenge varying views.

A true liberal education encompasses far more than the breadth of knowledge and exposure to fields other than one's major that typically shape general education programs. That is certainly necessary, but liberal education transcends subject matter. Liberal education addresses both mind and heart. It is a set of experiences that give our students the tools they will need to think about complex issues and to deal with them as informed, ethical citizens. Liberal education helps our students deal with ambiguity and contradictions, helps them evaluate competing arguments and perspectives so that they will not have to fall back on the comfort—and distortion—of a binary, good/bad worldview.

Complexity characterizes our key social missions, as we seek to foster in our students respect and understanding of other cultures and viewpoints together with the skills they will need to move positively and effectively in a diverse and global society. I am most emphatically not talking about indoctrinating our students—presenting our values and asking them to take them as their own. Rather, I am talking about teaching our students *why* and *how* to think and reason about ethical and moral issues—not presenting them with answers, but developing their skills in finding their own way.

Liberal education prepares our students to act—and to do so in the context of values that take in the needs and concerns of others. Viewed in this context, the value of civically focused service learning is clear. It places our students in the arenas where ethics and efficacy need to join, where disciplinary boundaries are often irrelevant and integrative learning occurs naturally, and where students can gain a profound experience of their capacity—and responsibility—to effect positive change. As an antidote to cynicism and passivity, it is hard to top service learning.

Looking at the society into which they are graduating, our students might be excused for being cynical. From the front page to the business page to the sports section, headlines repeatedly reflect the ethical lapses of our society. This profound lack of integrity—the failure of a moral value system—is not restricted to one political party, to one religious group, to one ethnic group, or one gender group. It cuts across our society. In giving a final message to graduating students, I have asked them to seek one goal: to say no—say no to greed, say no to opportunism, say no to dishonesty, and decide that integrity—their own moral compasses—is what really matters.

If we accept that aim—and I believe we do—then service learning deserves a proud and prominent place in our curriculum. This series provides less a road map than a spur to creative course development for all faculty and administrators eager to adapt a powerful educational tool to a particular institution's nature, community, and student population.

Robert A. Corrigan
President, San Francisco State University
October 6, 2006

ABOUT THIS SERIES

Many service-learning practitioners are familiar with the comprehensive series of monographs on *Service-Learning in the Disciplines* produced and published by the American Association of Higher Education (AAHE) between 1997 and 2005 (The series is now published by Stylus Publishing, LLC). Each volume of the series focused on a specific discipline—accounting, biology, composition, and so on—and provided a rich collection of exemplary practices in service learning as constituted around a disciplinary theme. Edward Zlotkowski (1997–2002), then senior associate at AAHE and series editor for the monographs, wrote that in "winning faculty support for this [service-learning] work" it was important to recognize that faculty "define themselves largely in terms of [their] academic disciplines," and so it was logical to design a series around disciplinary themes. The AAHE series became a primary reference for faculty who were considering adopting service-learning pedagogy, and the community of service-learning practitioners have much for which to thank the editors and contributors to those volumes. Other resources that were discipline specific—such as collections of syllabi—also helped to promote service learning to the level of the widespread acceptance it enjoys today on both the national and international stages.

Over the past few years, as the civic engagement movement has gained momentum, as educators have taken on the challenge of producing graduates who are engaged civically and politically in their communities, there has been a growing reexamination of service learning as the means for producing "civic learning" outcomes, that is, the combination of knowledge, skills, and disposition to make a difference in the civic life of our communities. The ubiquitous three-element Venn diagram—three interlocking circles representing enhanced academic learning, meaningful community service, and civic learning—that defines the field of service learning at its intersection (Howard, 2001), continues to do so, but there has been a marked redirection of emphasis from academic learning to civic. Nonetheless, as John Saltmarsh points out in his 2004 white paper for Campus Compact, *The Civic Purpose of Higher Education: A Focus on Civic Learning*, service learning is "the most potent method for achieving civic learning if civic learning outcomes are a part of curricular goals" (p. 7).

In parallel to this shift in emphasis, a second, related movement within higher education, *integrative learning*, has begun to take hold. As characterized by the American Association of Colleges and Universities (AACU) in partnership with the Carnegie Foundation for the Advancement of Teaching (Huber & Hutchings, 2004), integrative learning encompasses practices such as thematic first-year experiences, learning circles, interdisciplinary studies, capstone experiences, and other initiatives to foster students' ability to integrate concepts "across courses, over time, and between campus and community life" (p. 13). These two educational reform movements—civic engagement and integrative learning—provide the motivation for the creation of the current series, *Service Learning for Civic Engagement*. Each volume of the series will focus on a specific social issue—gender and power, race and immigration, community health, and so forth—and then solicit contributions from faculty *across* disciplines who can provide insight into how they have motivated their students to engage in learning that extends beyond the boundaries of disciplinary goals. In some cases chapter contributors will be faculty within the "obvious" discipline relevant to a particular issue (e.g., women's studies faculty utilize service learning in the pursuit of knowledge on gender issues), but each volume will include multiple chapters from other disciplines as well. As each volume illustrates, when faculty step outside the normal confines of disciplinary learning, they can provide profound, transformational experiences for their students. Thus, the volume on gender issues includes examples from philosophy, psychology, ethnic studies, and more, and the volume on social justice includes contributions from communications, engineering, nutrition science, and so on.

It is also our intention to design each book as a collective whole. Each volume illustrates an array of approaches to examining a community issue, and we hope that, by exploring examples across the disciplines, faculty will be inspired to develop their own concepts for courses that combine academic and civic learning.

Over the past 10 years, service learning has enjoyed tremendous support throughout the California State University (CSU), from which most of our contributors have been recruited. The 23 campuses of the CSU form the largest university system in the country, with 405,000 students enrolled each year. Through strategic efforts and targeted funding, the CSU has created a systemwide network of service-learning offices with a center on each campus, a coordinating office at the chancellor's office, statewide conferences and initiatives, and a wide variety of service-learning courses and community-based research. In 2005 alone more than 1,800 service-learning courses provided opportunities for 65,000 students to participate. California, now one of four states designated minority-majority (i.e., a state in which a majority of the population differs from the national majority) by the U.S. Census Bureau, is rich in ethnic diversity and is home to great cities as well as vast rural areas. Virtually every societal issue challenges Californians, and our universities have pledged to use our resources to develop innovative ways to address them. It is this mixture of diversity and innovation that has created an environment for the success of service learning in the CSU represented in this series.

Gerald S. Eisman
CSU Service-Learning Faculty Scholar
July 19, 2006

References

Howard, J. (2001). *Service learning course design workbook.* Ann Arbor, MI: OCSL Press.

Huber, M. T., & Hutchings, P. (2004). *Integrative learning: Mapping the terrain.* The Academy in Transition. Washington, DC: Association of American Colleges and Universities.

Saltmarsh, J. (2004). *The civic purpose of higher education: A focus on civic learning.* Unpublished white paper for Campus Compact.

Zlotkowski, E. (1997–2002). (Ed.). *AAHE series on service-learning in the disciplines.* Washington, DC: American Association for Higher Education.

INTRODUCTION

Sally Cahill Tannenbaum

Thomas Ehrlich (2000b) describes political or civic engagement as "working to make a difference in the civic life of our communities and developing the combination of knowledge, skills, values and motivation to make that difference. It means promoting the quality of life in a community, through both political and non-political processes" (p. vi). He argues, in fact, that one of the most important roles institutions of higher education play in a democratic society is providing opportunities that help individual students recognize themselves "as members of a larger social fabric, to consider social problems to be at least partly their own, to see the civic dimensions of issues, to make and justify informed civic judgments, and to take action when appropriate" (Ehrlich, 2000a).

This monograph provides contributions from faculty across disciplines and throughout the California State University (CSU) system whose inventive approaches introduce students to political engagement through service learning. The result is a compilation of courses that are both innovative and varied. Engaged scholars from different disciplines view political engagement from distinct vantage points. Political scientists look at political engagement from a more traditional perspective. Mathematicians see the statistical implications. Economists focus on cost-benefit analysis. Business professors provide an entrepreneurial angle. Feminists consider the language implications of political engagement. One thing is clear: Political engagement is not just participation in the election process. It is much more. It involves playing an active role in what happens around us. Whether we are teaching students how to be politically engaged or giving students the tools to have civic and political voice, political engagement means becoming change agents.

This volume begins by examining courses that offer a more traditional approach to political engagement—conducting exit surveys during elections, working on political campaigns, gauging the temperament and priorities of local citizens through an annual survey, and assisting with the U.S. census.

Next, the book considers political engagement courses that lend business acumen to the civic sector—providing a cost-benefit analysis to government decisions and using a small-business model to look at addressing social issues. This section is followed with a discussion of courses that promote social activism—encouraging students to explore a local advocacy group, challenging students to embrace a cause, or rallying support for communities devastated by Hurricane Katrina. Finally, the volume looks at teachers who focus on political engagement pedagogy—garnering an appreciation of the First Amendment in journalism classes, teaching civic engagement by having students *do* civic engagement, exposing student teachers to the benefits of using service learning in a social studies methods course, and promoting children's rights through decision making in a liberal studies course.

The volume begins with a description of a program offered at San Francisco State University. Unquestionably, Corey Cook's course fits the classic description of meaningful political engagement. In "Beyond Service: Community-Based Research and Political Engagement," Cook articulates how a cadre of over 200 students conducted a massive exit survey of election day polling places and absentee voters in San Francisco in 2004 and 2005. The survey provided an evaluation of how well different groups of voters adapted to a change in the voting system, and it highlighted the critical role played by the Department of Elections in improving citizen competence with new ballot designs. In many ways, this project serves as a model for community-based research and political engagement—not only did the project help students better understand survey research methods, but it resulted in a report that informed public policy and provided guidance as it related to the implementation of electoral reform policy in a major city.

Providing college students studying Political Campaign Communication with hands-on experiences working in an election is certainly another classic example of political engagement. Sally Cahill Tannenbaum's chapter, "Communication in Political Campaigns: Bridging Theory and Practice," relates how students at California State University, Fresno, analyze and synthesize the unique characteristics of communication in elections by walking precincts, manning phone banks, and engaging in conversations with voters, consultants, and candidates. Pre- and post-oral presentations, papers, and classroom discourse provide multiple opportunities for meaningful observation, discussion, and reflection. The class format not only increases student knowledge about political campaigns, it also facilitates an awareness of the difficulties campaigns face in reaching and motivating disenfranchised populations to vote, creates an understanding of the importance fund-raising and finances play in giving voice to political campaigns, and reinforces students' beliefs in the underlying principles of a democratic society.

Amy Liu informs us about an excellent example of political engagement in her chapter, "Social Research and the Sacramento State Annual Survey of the Region." She describes how she and her colleagues enhance teaching and learning in a Research Methods in Sociology class at California State University, Sacramento, by having students conduct meaningful research. The political engagement has resulted in a yearly report titled the Sacramento State Annual Survey of the Region. The work has not only excited students about social research, it has also increased their concern about important social and political issues facing the Sacramento community, and has heightened student confidence in using social research as a powerful tool to study critical issues in our society. Finally, the annual survey has gained considerable credibility in the community and is used regularly by government and media.

Another outstanding example of political engagement that is relevant and educational is Peter Tannenbaum's chapter on the U.S. census. In "Making the Census Count: Learning, Service, and Political Engagement," Tannenbaum, a mathematics professor at California State University, Fresno, argues that the U.S. census, which is conducted once every 10 years, has a significant political, economic, social, geographical, and statistical impact. In an interdisciplinary special topics course titled Census 2000, Tannenbaum and his wife, Sally Cahill Tannenbaum, helped students understand and appreciate the significance the census plays in government policy and decision making. Students spent the first half of the course interacting with government officials and policy makers about the importance of the data collected and the challenges faced in obtaining an accurate count. In particular, students learned that groups that stand to gain the most economically and politically from being counted by the census—minorities, migrant workers, the homeless, and so on—are the groups most reluctant to do so. In the second half of the course, students worked with the local Complete Count Campaign and dozens of local nonprofit agencies to persuade historically undercounted populations to willingly be counted. Student reflection assignments as well as the final census report indicated that the political engagement was successful.

In "The Economics of Community Action: Applying Cost-Benefit Analysis to Local Public Policy," Greg Hunter recounts how service-learning projects allow students in an upper-division economics class to comprehend and synthesize the concept of cost-benefit analysis and understand how it is used for public policy decisions. Students select a local policy change that is under consideration. They investigate, generate, and present information to the community stakeholders who are coping with the policy issue. Through the service project, students learn to appreciate resource allocations, how stakeholders weigh alternatives, and attempt to choose a policy alternative that results in the greatest aggregate benefit. Hunter argues, "By learning how the cost-benefit numbers are calculated and dealing with the inherent uncertainty over these numbers, students are in a powerful position to engage in the political process in a way that is rarely used by the average citizen" (p. 79). He suggests that in providing information that the community partner needs, the students play the role of analyst and interpreter. "The result is a more informed community, which lays the foundation for better policy" (p. 79).

Richard L. McCline and Gerald Eisman of San Francisco State University provide an interesting spin on political engagement. In "Selected Case Examples of Service Learning in Business: Social Entrepreneurship in Action," they present a particularly creative and successful program that addresses social issues by combining community service learning with good business practices, with a specific focus on the many ways that government and business intersect. They go on to explicate how students can become change agents in their communities by applying business skills to traditionally social issues. They illustrate their point by citing a number of specific projects carried out by the Ohrenschall Center for Entrepreneurship. Each example demonstrates how community service learning combined with business acumen offers unique and useful solutions to social issues. Through the process, students begin to appreciate the benefits of approaching social issues with an entrepreneurial spirit, and also come to better understand the complex nature of the public sector and the challenges that confront those hoping to mitigate social problems.

In "Communicating Community: Engaging Silicon Valley Through Student Activism," Anne Marie Todd and Deanna L. Fassett describe how students in a Social Movement Communication course at San José State are transformed through their experiences examining social activism. Todd and

Fassett argue that studying protests, social movements, and dissent "can provide students with an understanding of democratic participation" (p. 106). Relying on their own experience to frame course material, students are asked to observe and analyze the activities of a local advocacy group. The activist experience provides students with an experiential understanding of the fundamental role social activism plays in a democracy. Journals, portfolios, and reflection papers document the impact. The in-depth exploration of activism increases student political and communication knowledge and leads to students embracing activist values. Students also report gaining comfort and confidence participating through political engagement. Todd and Fassett write that students discover their power to effect social change and begin to embrace an increased sense of social responsibility. The authors also describe their own sense of satisfaction knowing that what they have provided is a venue for students to find their own mode of civic and political engagement.

Activism is also the focus of Natalie Wilson's Introduction to Women's Studies class at California State University, San Marcos. In "The Politics of Service Learning in Introduction to Women's Studies: Addressing Social Injustices Through Activism and Political Engagement," Wilson shows how students in her course explore existing power structures and examine the disparities between privileged and oppressed groups. Wilson advocates for a communal, interactive classroom atmosphere where students are introduced to feminism as a social theory and a social movement. Active citizenship and political engagement are woven into every class discussion. Students work in groups on a semester-long Activism Project. "In keeping with third wave feminism's emphasis on everyday activism," Wilson explains, "the project takes a broad conception of activism and is grounded in the belief that activism and effective engagement come in many forms" (p. 141). Generally, student groups focus on a social ill. Following extensive research, they take action and make presentations on their issue of concern. Wilson concludes that the experience is transformative and "sparks a dedication to continuing civic engagement" (p. 142).

Scott Myers-Lipton takes political engagement to a national level in his sociology class at San José State. Inspired by the public works programs of the Great Depression and the Mississippi Freedom Summer of 1964, Myers-Lipton and his Social Action students established the Gulf Coast Civic Works Project—a project designed to employ 100,000 residents from the region devastated by Hurricane Katrina to rebuild their community. What began as a relatively modest undertaking has expanded into a national project. In January 2007, more than 100 students from 15 colleges met on the Gulf Coast for a week-long awareness campaign titled "Louisiana Winter." The campaign was followed by an April summit attended by students from 43 colleges and universities. Their ultimate goal—the passage of federal legislation to fund a $3.9 billion effort to restore the Gulf Coast by hiring the individuals affected by the massive hurricane. Suffice it to say that work described in the chapter "Using Service Learning to Change Social Structure: The Gulf Coast Civic Works Project" by Myers-Lipton serves as an inspiration to all of us on the power and possibilities of political engagement.

In "Media Mentors: Nurturing Democratic Ideals Among High School Journalists," Linda Bowen discusses the symbiotic relationship California State University, Northridge, mentors have developed with high school journalism students. Bowen suggests that in deliberating with high school students about issues surrounding the First Amendment, college students are forced to reflect on the critical roles journalists play in promoting a healthy democracy. She argues that "maintaining the freedoms espoused in the First Amendment has always depended on an informed citizenry that values the democratic ideals fostered by vibrant public debate and dissent" (p. 165). She describes how the service experience helps budding journalists better appreciate the ethics and attitudes about the responsibilities inherent in the watchdog role of the Fourth Estate. As a result of their work, students learn to appreciate the important positions journalists play in helping citizens synthesize and interpret the social, political, economic, and cultural events that happen each and every day.

One of the unique aspects of Mary Kirlin's Introduction to Government at California State University, Sacramento, is her teaching pedagogy. Kirlin's students learn civic/political engagement by *doing* civic/political engagement. In her chapter, "An Unconventional Approach to Civic Skill Development and Service Learning," Kirlin argues that adults are civically and politically engaged for three reasons: They are motivated to participate, they are connected to the network of decision makers, and they have the civic skills necessary to contribute. Similarly, she contends, students learn engagement through a political model that calls for participation and practice. Kirlin's assignment is purposely unscripted. She places students in groups and asks them to work on a problem that they believe "needs to be fixed." Her unorthodox approach challenges students to learn about civic and political engagement by doing civic and political engagement. Kirlin suggests that values and dispositions should be taught *after*, rather than *before* students have participated in a positive civic engagement experience. She writes, "the process of internalizing and valuing something develops over time and with experience" (p. 185).

In her chapter "Developing Teachers' Ability to Share Leadership," Kristeen L. Pemberton describes her work with student teachers in a social studies methods course at San José State University. Pemberton's objective is to provide future teachers opportunities to experience political engagement on a personal and professional level. Pemberton writes, "There is a need to provide opportunities for teacher candidates to reflect on the changing contexts in which they will be teaching children" and "to investigate their potential as teachers to become agents of change" (p. 198). She argues that teachers must recognize and identify the role they play in socializing students and building good citizens. She challenges her students "to recognize and identify with social and political inequities, to participate in planning and implementing ways to rectify them, and to demonstrate self-efficacy as a result of their political engagement with the community" (p. 201). Student testimonials and anecdotes document the impact of her pedagogy. Her students report that using service learning to teach a standards-based social studies curriculum is not only practical but powerful.

Finally, in "Service Learning That Engages Students in the Implementation of Children's Right to Participate in Community Decision Making," Kim Knowles-Yánez relates how she teaches the facilitation of children's rights in decision making through political engagement. Knowles-Yánez, an associate professor of urban and regional planning in the liberal studies department at California State University, San Marcos, incorporates her rights-based approach in a Children and the Environment course. She explains that the basic course concept is "guided by the principle that every child has a right to participate in decisions that affect his or her life" (p. 217). In the course, college students work with children on environmental issues. They are given an opportunity to think about the political rights of children and to help children actuate those rights. Through the process, Knowles-Yánez contends, the college students begin to examine their own political rights. Knowles-Yánez argues that the activity reaffirms and creates new knowledge of democratic practices for university students.

In many ways, it is fitting that this volume ends with a chapter on how one professor empowers her students to empower their students through political engagement. Isn't that what political engagement is supposed to do? Isn't that one of our primary roles as educators? Fortunately, the faculty who have so eloquently shared their expertise and inspired us in this book have heeded the words of John Dewey, "The trouble . . . is that we have taken our democracy for granted; we have thought and acted as if our forefathers had founded it once and for all. We have forgotten that it has to be enacted anew in every generation."

References

Dewey, J. (1980). Democracy and education. In J. A. Boyston (Ed.), *The collected works of John Dewey, 1882–1953: The middle works, 1899–1924* (Vol. 9, p. 135). Carbondale: Southern Illinois University Press.

Ehrlich, T. (2000a). Civic engagement in Measuring Up 2000: The state-by-state report card for higher education from http://measuringup.highereducation.org/c ommentary/priorcommentarydir.cm?filenameThomasEhrlich.cfm&myyear =2000

Ehrlich, T. (Ed.). (2000b). *Civic responsibility and higher education*. Phoenix: Oryx Press. (ERIC Document Reproduction Service No. ED439659)

Activity/Methodology Table: Research, Advocacy, and Political Engagement

Chapter	Discipline	Service Activity	Methodology	Applications	Type of Partner	Size of Class
Chapter 1: Cook	Political science	Exit polling project	Community-based research	Government	Government agencies	30–50 students
Chapter 2: S. Tannenbaum	Communication	Work on political campaigns	Experiential Pre-/Postcritical analysis Reflection (oral and written)	Political science	Political campaigns, consultants	24 students
Chapter 3: Liu, Scott, Sheley, Whitlatch, Cowles, & Barajas	Political science Sociology	Conduct annual regional survey through questionnaire development, data collection and analysis, report writing and distribution of results	CATI (Computer assisted telephone interview) Needs assessment Program evaluation Opinion polls Surveys	Political science Environmental studies Ethnic studies Communication Social science Liberal studies	University public relations office Government policymakers Community leaders Media outlets	20 students

(continues)

**Activity/Methodology Table: *Research, Advocacy, and Political Engagement*
Continued**

Chapter	Discipline	Service Activity	Methodology	Applications	Type of Partner	Size of Class
Chapter 4: P. Tannenbaum & S. Tannenbaum	Interdisciplinary (math/communication)	Designed outreach campaigns Organized community events Facilitated media exposure	Fieldwork Public education Pre-/Postcritical analysis Reflection (oral and written)	Social science	Community nonprofits Schools Media outlets	25 students
Chapter 5: Hunter	Economics	Conducted cost-benefit studies	Field work Pre-/postanalysis Needs assessment	Community stakeholders Public policy makers	Social science Public policy	25–30 students
Chapter 6: McCline & Eisman	Business Entrepreneurship	Public agencies	Social entrepreneurship Experiential	Small businesses	Public policy Social issues	15–20 students

Chapter	Discipline	Service Activity	Methodology	Applications	Type of Partner	Size of Class
Chapter 7: Todd & Fassett	Communication studies	Advocacy groups	Discourse analysis Critical reflection	Nongovernmental organizations Unions Student groups Community groups	Social movements Communication	30 students
Chapter 8: Wilson	Women's studies	Activism project Student discussion leadership program	Activism-based learning Peer learning Critical feminist pedagogy Field research Reflection (oral, written, group, individual)	Social justice	Various groups	25–40 students
Chapter 9: Myers-Lipton	Sociology	Advocacy Social action projects	Critical reflection Action	Social Sciences	Homeless Alliance Workers Rights Consortium Global awareness groups	30–45 students

(continues)

Activity/Methodology Table: *Research, Advocacy, and Political Engagement*
Continued

Chapter	Discipline	Service Activity	Methodology	Applications	Type of Partner	Size of Class
Chapter 10: Bowen	Journalism	Mentoring high school journalism/news media students	Critical reflection Self-assessment Pre-/postsurvey analysis Qualitative content analysis	Mass communications Media studies Education	High school and middle school journalism classes	6–12 students
Chapter 11: Kirlin	Political science/public administration/public policy	Addressed campus problems	Problem identification Strategy development Civic skill development Presentation skills	Social sciences	No formal partner, students identify problems they want to tackle and work with whomever is necessary to address the problem.	18 students

Chapter	Discipline	Service Activity	Methodology	Applications	Type of Partner	Size of Class
Chapter 12: Pemberton	Teacher education	Teaching state content standards through community-related projects generated by student teachers and their pupils	Backward design Freirean pedagogy Generative approach	Student teaching Social studies	K-8 classrooms and their communities	30 students
Chapter 13: Knowles-Yánez	Liberal studies	Community action research with children	Problem identification Critical analysis Planning Action Reflection	Education Social science	Elementary or middle school	30–40 students

CONTRIBUTORS

Manuel Barajas (chapter 3) is assistant professor of sociology at California State University, Sacramento. (mbarajas@csus.edu)

Linda Bowen (chapter 10) is assistant professor of journalism at California State University, Northridge. (linda.s.bowen@csun.edu)

Corey Cook (chapter 1) is assistant professor of politics at University of San Francisco. (cdcook2@usfca.edu)

Robert A. Corrigan (Foreword) is the president of San Francisco State University. (president@sfsu.edu)

Ernest Cowles (chapter 3) is director of the Institute for Social Research and professor of sociology at California State University, Sacramento. (cowlese@csus.edu)

Gerald S. Eisman (series editor, chapter 6) is the acting director of the Institute for Civic and Community Engagement at San Francisco State University. (geisman@sfsu.edu)

Deanna L. Fassett (chapter 7) is associate professor of communication studies at San José State University. (dfassett@sjsu.edu)

Greg Hunter (chapter 5) is associate professor of economics at California State Polytechnic University, Pomona. (gwhunter@csupomona.edu)

Mary Kirlin (chapter 11) is associate professor of public policy and administration at California State University, Sacramento. (kirlinm@csus.edu)

Kim Knowles-Yánez (chapter 13) is associate professor of urban and regional planning at California State University, San Marcos. (kyanez@csusm.edu)

Richard L. McCline (chapter 6) is cofounder of the Ohrenschall Center for Entrepreneurship at San Francisco State University and is the James A. Joseph Professor and Endowed Chair in Small and Minority Business Enterprise at Southern University. (drmccline@msn.com)

Scott Myers-Lipton (chapter 9) is associate professor of sociology at San José State University. (smlipton@sjsu.edu)

Kristeen L. Pemberton (chapter 12) is a senior lecturer in the College of Education at San José State University. (dockhall@aol.com)

Amy Qiaoming Liu (chapter 3) is professor of sociology at California State University, Sacramento. (amyliuus@yahoo.com)

Otis Scott (chapter 3) is dean of the College of Social Science and Interdisciplinary Studies at California State University, Sacramento. (scottol@csus.edu)

Joseph Sheley (chapter 3) is provost and vice president for academic affairs at California State University, Sacramento. (sheleyj@csus.edu)

Sally Cahill Tannenbaum (volume editor, chapter 2, chapter 4) is associate professor of communication at California State University, Fresno. (sallyt@csufresno.edu)

Peter Tannenbaum (chapter 4) is professor of mathematics at California State University, Fresno. (petert@csufresno.edu)

Anne Marie Todd (chapter 7) is associate professor of communication studies at San José State University. (amt@sjsu.edu)

Frank Whitlatch (chapter 3) is associate vice president for marketing and communications at Humboldt State University (frank@humboldt.edu)

Natalie Wilson (chapter 8) is lecturer in the Women's Studies Program and the Department of Literature and Writing Studies at California State University, San Marcos. (nwilson@csusm.edu)

SECTION ONE

TRADITIONAL APPROACHES TO POLITICAL ENGAGEMENT

I

BEYOND SERVICE

Community-Based Research and Political Engagement

Corey Cook

Service-learning programs have proliferated in academia in recent years. As a mechanism for promoting community service and effective experiential pedagogy, service learning purportedly offers a diverse set of educational benefits to our students. The burgeoning literature in political science bears out much of this theory. Both quantitative and qualitative assessments suggest that the outcomes include generally improved classroom learning and greater retention of knowledge. As an avid practitioner of service learning, I have found that experiences in the community enhance the traditional academic course work and provide a richness that conventional teaching strategies lack. However, in spite of our best intentions and perhaps even our expectations, the civic value of service learning is not born out in the academic literature (Kirlin, 2002, p. 571). It seems that the "residual benefits" of service learning are not quite as prevalent as many of us would have hoped. As such, it is time to get beyond "service" as a mechanism for promoting civic or political engagement and reconsider mechanisms for engaging our students in processes of sociopolitical change. And at the risk of seeming alarmist, it is clear that time is short. A mountain of empirical evidence suggests that we are facing an unprecedented and persistent engagement deficit among our students. While employing community-based research of the type I discuss in this chapter is simply one strategy for increasing the political engagement of young people, this single project illustrates the advantages of adopting a relatively simple pedagogy with encouraging results and tremendous potential. Although our particular research program is in some ways unique, our experiences in implementing it in our courses offer important lessons for others concerned about promoting engagement of college students in processes of social change.

For the past several years, I have tried to promote civic engagement among college students on campus and in my classes. These efforts have run the gamut: from guest speakers to formal internships, and from voter registration drives and field education to day-long volunteer opportunities. One fall semester, I accompanied students from my introductory course into the community where they held nonpartisan informational voter education sessions with small groups of potential voters. These service-learning opportunities were designed to achieve traditional pedagogical objectives as well as some weakly defined and perhaps ill-conceived civic goals. In fact, because definitions of service learning vary so substantially, it is probably fair to suggest that these were weakly defined as service-learning projects (Furco, 1996). But in the fall of 2005, facing the very real sound of our tenure clocks ticking and the need to establish a compelling record of academic publication, teaching prowess, and service to the community, my colleague Francis Neely and I decided to attempt to bridge this tripartite set of expectations with a single project by implementing an ambitious community-based research project. At the outset, neither of us conceived of this exit survey of election day voters in San Francisco as a "civic engagement" much less a "political engagement" project. However, as we began contemplating the involvement of our students as community-based researchers, we stumbled onto a unique mechanism for engagement that offers considerable promise, as I discuss at length.

While service learning has received an enormous amount of attention of late in the scholarship on engaged teaching and learning, we deliberately expanded upon this pedagogical model and instead sought to explicitly promote political and civic engagement rather than service. The value of experiential education as a mechanism for learning is well established in the literature and typically rests conceptually on Kolb's seminal experiential learning cycle that "combines experience, perception, cognition, and behavior" (as cited in Rosenthal, 1999, p. 64; Brock & Cameron, 1999; Kolb, 1984). And the benefits for students are substantial. For instance, Rosenthal (1999) finds that experiential learning offers students "shared field experience [as] a basis for classroom dialogue" that makes abstract concepts come alive through higher-learning strategies (p. 68), and Hunter and Brisbin (2000) conclude that students "learn about their community, further develop some academic skills and feel that they have helped members of the community" (p. 625), all worthwhile objectives. And as our following results suggest, community-based research achieves these purposes quite effectively.

But while these studies comport with my experience, it seems that compelling evidence of additional residual benefits for students, such as civic or political engagement, is absent from the scholarly literature. In their comprehensive review, Perry and Katula (2001) note that "service appears to influence favorably citizenship-related cognitive understanding" but that concrete evidence of service learning contributing to citizenship behaviors is lacking (p. 359). Similarly, Kirlin (2002) concludes that "little evidence supports expectations that service learning encourages civic behaviors such as voting, contacting elected officials, and being active in community affairs" (p. 527) because of an essential failure to develop civic skills among our students. This result reinforces previous research that concludes from student surveys that while the act of community service "significantly enhanced" the educational experiences of students, traditional service learning "did not affect their thinking about democracy or about their role as a citizen" (Hunter & Brisbin, 2000, p. 624) and "did not change students' assessments of the value of elections, the objectives of public officials, and the attentiveness of public officials to the public" (p. 625).

Similarly, it appears from the literature in political science that simply involving students in our research is unlikely to offer more avenues for engagement. For instance, Jones and Meinhold (1999) use students enrolled in a research methodology course to conduct phone surveys as part of a community needs assessment. But based on their analysis of student surveys, these scholars conclude that in the pursuit of an underfunded research program, they had exploited "a coercible labor pool" (p. 606) and failed to achieve the promised student outcomes. Indeed, they conclude that "students do not benefit" and that no evidence exists to confirm that "experiential education makes students better citizens" (pp. 603, 605). Clearly, if civic engagement is our goal, both traditional service learning and traditional research paradigms are lacking. But before turning to a discussion of how community-based research achieves these objectives, and particularly about how our project bore this out, a discussion of civic and political engagement is in order.

A Word About Civic Engagement

Definitions of civic engagement abound, but perhaps the most expansive is that offered by Thomas Ehrlich (2000) in *Civic Responsibility and Higher Education*: "Civic engagement means working to make a difference in the civic life of our communities and developing the combination of knowledge, skills, values and motivation to make that difference. It means promoting the quality of life in a community, through both political and non-political processes" (p. vi). This definition encompasses three discrete dimensions; that it is both political and nonpolitical, that it is committed to social awareness and responsibility, and that it entails melding knowledge and skills with motivation and opportunity. And while civic engagement and service learning are potentially compatible, it is clear from this definition that they are not necessarily so. For instance, some civic engagement scholarship is organized around promoting civic competency through more traditional teaching methodologies. Skill-building activities designed to develop critical thinking or advocacy skills and the dissemination of knowledge is civic education but not through the usage of service-learning pedagogies. And much service learning is not explicitly civic. Barber and Battistoni (1993) assert that service learning is often taught as altruism and charity rather than civic responsibility, and accordingly students fail to develop a conception of citizenship grounded in social obligation because this model of service learning perpetuates notions of atomistic individualism.

Political Engagement as an Explicit Goal

While Ehrlich's definition of civic engagement applies to political and nonpolitical processes of social change, we consciously sought to engage our students in an overtly political community-based research project rather than involve them in more traditional service-learning activities because politics is an essential component of civic life. As one set of authors wonders, "can civic responsibility be taught outside the realm of polity, politics, and citizenship?" Hepburn, Niemi, & Chapman, 2000, p. 621). I would think not. But from one perspective, defining our project in terms of political engagement seems like a relatively simple choice. As professors of political science, we can safely conclude that our students gravitate naturally to the political sphere.

But on second glance, the choice is far less straightforward. In an environment colored by criticisms of "liberal professors" and dangerous undercurrents threatening academic freedom, the "politicization" of college students is viewed critically outside and inside the institution. And it turns out that the vast majority of the time, "in courses that incorporate service learning, most of the service is not in political organizations or in conjunction with [politics]" (Hepburn et al., 2000, p. 621). Indeed, these authors conclude that "in some institutions of higher education, administrators have expressed apprehension regarding service in the political realm and have hesitated to endorse programs that teach civic participation" (p. 621), thus undermining the potential effectiveness of these courses. But political engagement is crucial to a democratic polity, and the capacity of students to engage effectively in political processes must be nurtured and developed. The significance of political engagement is often illustrated by the old saw about a student working in a soup kitchen as part of a service-learning course and reflecting that she gained so much from the experience that she looked forward to continuing to work in the soup kitchen after graduating. The rub, of course, is that this service is disconnected from social change. Certainly it could be said that the student is "working to make a difference" as Ehrlich (2000, p. vi) specifies but without altering power dynamics that underlie the existing social conditions and thereby subconsciously perpetuating the social injustices she is presumably endeavoring to rectify.

And this distinction is crucial. The current generation of college students is practicing increasing volunteerism but decreasing levels of overtly political activity. They are civic minded but not politically astute. So while college students nationally are actually relatively engaged and active, this activism generally occurs outside formal politics or a context of citizenship (Andolina, Keeter, Zukin, & Jenkins, 2003).

And while our primary interests were in providing students with the requisite knowledge and skills to have an impact on political processes, we were cognizant that we needed to similarly emphasize the motivations that are required for effective civic engagement. Again, the extant academic literature provides considerable insight into the various barriers we face in increasing engagement by young people. First, young adults are significantly more likely than older ones to say that people "can't be trusted" and are "more likely to look out for themselves than to try to help each other." Generally speaking, college students are cynical. In comparison to older cohorts, they tend to exhibit enormous distrust of politicians, tend to think that political leaders are dishonest, and that government is dominated by a few narrow interests. Similarly, in one survey, most high school students could not name a single government or nongovernment public leader who had the qualities they most admired: caring about average people, consistency in beliefs, strong leadership skills, ethical values, and good communication skills (Carpini, 2000).

Second, young people have limited conceptions of citizenship as obligation. Research suggests that while the priorities of young people include family, job, and material success, citizenship is far down on the list of priorities. One study reveals that where nearly twice as many college freshmen in the 1960s considered developing a meaningful philosophy of life to be essential or very important than being well off financially, those numbers have reversed in recent years reflecting substantial "increases in materialistic values" (Astin, 1998, p. 125).

Third, research suggests that college students in particular, and young Americans in general, are not simply distrustful but also tend to be dismissive of politics as relevant to their daily lives. Only one in four young Americans (ages 15 to 24) believes that government has a major impact on one's day-to-day life. Young adults are significantly less likely than older adults to think their participation in politics would make a difference. For example, 45 percent feel their vote does not matter regardless of who wins an election (Carpini, 2000).

Not surprisingly, then, a fourth barrier is that students exhibit a minimal level of interest in public affairs. Again, Carpini uncovers research showing that only 19 percent of 18- to 29-year-olds say they follow politics and government "most of the time" compared with 51 percent of those 50 or older. Only 27 percent of today's college freshmen think keeping up with public affairs is very important, compared with 59 percent of college freshmen in 1966 (Carpini, 2000). Thus, our students tend to have low levels of political literacy and high informational deficits. For instance, a national survey reports that young adults tend not to discuss politics with friends or family, and express declining interest in serving in appointed or elected government positions (Hart Research Associates, 2004). And this rate of engagement with public affairs trails substantially behind rates of previous generations according to surveys by the Pew Research Institute (Soule, 2001).

The Futures Project (2002) shows that only 26 percent of college freshmen keep "up to date with political affairs" compared with 58 percent in 1966. On any given day, more than 40 percent of 19- to 29-year-olds watch the news on television compared with 55 percent of those 30 to 50 years old, and 65 percent of those older than age 50. Less than 20 percent of young adults read the newspaper on any given day compared with about 40 percent of those between the ages of 30 to 50, and 60 percent of those older than age 50. Newspaper readership among young adults is less than half what it was for this age group in 1965 (Carpini, 2000).

Indeed, the newly released Index of Civic Engagement suggests that on nearly every indicator of civic engagement, college-aged students lag behind (Andolina et al., 2003). What is perhaps most interesting about these data is that the authors tease out distinctive indicators of engagement and find that the largest gaps between the college-age population and older citizens are in civic indicators such as being an active member of a group, electoral indicators such as voting, and attentiveness indicators such as following news stories and public affairs. The most narrow gaps are found in indicators of "voice" including protesting, boycotting, and the like (Andolina et al., 2003). The significance of these findings is readily apparent. It is not enough to simply promote service or community involvement. Rather, it is necessary to develop what Ehrlich calls the "knowledge, skills, values and motivation" (2000, p. vi) to engage in political processes to make a difference. It was our intention, then, to address the obvious need for promoting political engagement by undertaking this ambitious project.

One compelling definition of political engagement is that it involves "the capability of citizens to engage in self-rule and encompasses behaviors and cognitions necessary for identifying political preferences, understanding politics, and pursuing interests" (Nie, Junn, & Stehlik-Barry, 1996, p. 11). This project, therefore, sought to politically engage students by generating the "knowledge, skills, values and motivation" to engage in political processes. Accordingly, rather than presenting our students with the opportunity to perform service, we instead presented our community-based research project in terms of the opportunity to influence public policy and achieve equitable governmental outcomes. The social justice element of the project and the role of scholarly research in reducing inequalities of political power infused the academic program.

Community-Based Research and Political Engagement

As is the case with service learning, community-based research suffers from a lack of conceptual precision. Fortunately, however, these diverse projects have a relatively clear set of guiding principles to distinguish community-based research from other types of participatory academic research. One set of authors defines it as "research that is conducted *with* and *for*, not *on*, members of a community" (Strand, Marullo, Cutforth, Stoecker, & Donohue, 2003, xx). These scholars denote community-based research as "a next important stage of service-learning and engaged scholarship" because it offers a "distinctive combination of collaborative inquiry, critical analysis, and social change . . . to unite the three traditional academic missions of teaching, research, and service in innovative ways" (p. xxi).

At its core, community-based research involves connecting academic investigators with community partners and students in a collaborative process to address community problems and promote social change. This distinguishes it from more conventional academic research in three ways:

- "community-based research is the systematic creation of knowledge that is done with and for the community for the purpose of addressing a community-defined need";
- "community-based research places high value on the local or experiential knowledge of community members . . . (and seeks to) produce results that can be used by the community"; and
- "the central purpose of community-based research is to produce information that might be useful in bringing about needed change." (Strand et al., 2003, pp. 11–13)

And while the pedagogical value of community-based research has not been studied systematically, there is reason to think it might offer a series of benefits for students. As "a form of experiential, community-based learning that involves students in carefully-chosen meaningful community service activities that are connected with course content" (Strand et al., 2003, p. 120) it has the potential to enhance academic learning as well as promote the knowledge, skills, and values essential for engagement by increasing interaction with the community. Indeed, one prominent sociologist considers community-based research the "highest stage of service learning" (Porpora, 1999,

p. 121). But it seems to me that the greatest value of community-based research for promoting political engagement depends on the transformative value of the research. Because the research project is intended to make a difference students see immediate returns on their experiences. Rather than having a student intern file papers or answer telephone calls, community-based research entails engaging a community change process that is enticingly immediate.

By merging the principles of community-based research with the work of Ehrlich and others, we consciously designed our element of the project to be student-learning centered, integrated fully into our academic courses rather than tangentially through extra credit or other means, and intended to produce consumable "public scholarship." We additionally informed our pedagogy with Susan Ostrander's (2004) seminal work on civic engagement. She identifies four dimensions of civic engagement pedagogy that are necessary for successful integration into academia.

- Student Learning-Centered: "The work of student civic engagement is guided by an educational philosophy of integrating community concerns into intellectual life. Community projects are largely student initiated and defined" (p. 80).
- Curriculum Transformation: Academic courses promote "inquiry and critical thinking, communication for learning and expression, awareness of broad human experience and its environments, and responsibility to selves, each other, and to community" (pp. 80–81).
- Community-Defined Priorities: "Projects mobilize community resources collaboratively with community partners to address concerns and issues in the community as identified and prioritized by the community" (p. 81).
- Knowledge Production: Faculty, students, and community partners generate public scholarship that rests "on a solid intellectual rationale that addresses and defines the intellectual project of university civic engagement. In some cases, this includes specifying researchable questions and conceptual problems and using the university as a change agent" (p. 84).

Armed with these theoretical markers, we set out to produce high-quality research, enhance classroom learning, and promote political engagement among our students.

The 2005 San Francisco Exit Poll

In the March 2002 election, San Francisco voters narrowly passed Proposition A, a ballot measure amending the city charter to dramatically alter the conduct and dynamics of local elections. The first implementation of that reform occurred in November 2004 in 7 districts of the 11-seat board of supervisors. Previously, the city used a more traditional two-round runoff system to ensure that a victorious candidate received a majority of votes cast. Ranked-choice voting attempts to achieve this same result by permitting voters to rank up to three candidates and having their vote sequentially redistributed as the lowest vote getter is eliminated from the competition, creating a more or less instantaneous runoff outcome. While such alternative voting (AV) systems are relatively common outside the United States, San Francisco became the largest American city to embark on such a significant electoral experiment. In the past several years, however, numerous local jurisdictions, including Burlington, Vermont; Ferndale, Michigan; Berkeley, California; and Oakland, California, have followed San Francisco's lead in enacting an AV system. Countless others have considered its adoption, and lawmakers in 23 states have introduced legislation mandating its usage in state elections, permitting its usage by local governments, or commissioning an evaluative study. Yet little is known about the tangible consequences of adopting such a sweeping change, particularly in a diverse metropolis like San Francisco with high numbers of limited English speakers and a wide range of education levels and political sophistication among prospective voters.

The decision to adopt an AV system is clearly not a simple one. Prior to its adoption in San Francisco, considerable debate emerged centering around whether the reform would produce less-negative, more issue-oriented, and competitive elections; enhance political participation; and save scarce public resources. But perhaps the greatest source of contention was its anticipated effect on voters. While proponents used endorsements from prominent leaders of ethnic political organizations to assert that "Proposition A will not disenfranchise language minorities," (City and County of San Francisco, 2002, p. 39), opponents argued that the more likely direct effect of its passage would be to "effectively disenfranchise language minorities and people with limited education" (p. 39). Indeed, concern about whether AV would be "confusing" to voters dominated much of the preelection discourse. Consequently, some opponents argued that these disparities might threaten the legitimacy of the election. "Because many voters will not exercise their right to rank all the candidates, only the small minority of voters who are highly organized and disciplined will exercise their rights, and it will be they, not minorities, the poor, or mainstream voters who will decide the election" (p. 45).

Because of this heightened level of concern in the community and the sudden attention given this system of counting votes in other jurisdictions, we were approached by city administrators and activists eager to study the new voting system and its impact on the electorate. No doubt the reason San Francisco State University (SFSU) was chosen to evaluate ranked-choice voting was the university's well-developed relationships with, and reputation in, the community and the strong record of success of the university's Public Research Institute (PRI) in providing high-quality applied social science and public policy research to government agencies, nonprofits, and community-based organizations throughout the Bay Area.

While we were secondarily concerned with collecting data suitable for publication in academic journals, we developed our research project in consultation with community activists and elected officials to provide cutting-edge research that would be used to inform public policy and guide the implementation of electoral reform policy in the city. Without question, embarking on a community-based research program is not a simple proposition. For scholars accustomed to complete control over their subject matter, it entails handing over much of the direction of the project to key stakeholders in the community. Because we were on an exceptionally tight deadline, we found ourselves frustrated by the lack of consensus around the wording of the survey or demographic variables to include. But at the same time, the payoff for us as academics is considerable. For instance, several of our findings pertain specifically to how election administrations conduct outreach to voters who might have limited awareness of the new ballot. And in addition to briefing local legislators with recommendations, our reports have helped to prepare other jurisdictions for the implementation challenges they face. Because they witnessed policy makers grappling with the implications of the results they helped to generate, the immediate relevance of the research to our students was enhanced. As I suggest, it is not a simple thing to promote political engagement within the confines of a 15-week course. Doing so involves nurturing the necessary skills and values of our students and creating opportunities for meaningful engagement. A well-conceptualized community-based research project fully integrated into the curriculum offers this potential.

Accordingly, we sought to engage the community in discerning whether the dire predictions of the opponents of ranked-choice voting were on target, and designed a study to consider how voters adapt to a novel voting system, because if disparities do exist in the capacity of voters to understand their voting task and effectively record their preferences, the legitimacy of local elections is potentially compromised. With this in mind, we sought to determine whether different groups of voters had fundamentally different experiences in using a voting system they had no prior experience with. And doing so required us to engage over 100 undergraduate students in three distinct courses.

The Courses and Students

Like other California State University campuses, SFSU is home to a large proportion of nontraditional students. Largely a commuter campus, the typical student is in his or her mid-20s and has attended community college. The university has a proud heritage of protest activities and advocacy of civil rights and social justice, and is recognized nationally as an institutional leader in civic engagement and community service learning (Harvard University Institute of Politics and *The Chronicle of Higher Education*, 2004). For instance, students receive notations on their transcripts for student-learning experiences, and the biennial campus voter registration project has gained attention as a best practice by the American Association of State Colleges and Universities (2006). In short, evidence suggests that SFSU is a place where students are quite a bit more civically engaged and less apathetic than the typical campus. But this engagement is usually divorced from the course work as members of the faculty self-consciously avoid "politicizing" the classroom. Accordingly, the students have little opportunity to practice political engagement on campus. This seemed like a prime opportunity to change that.

To implement a citywide exit poll, we selected three courses to draw upon for this project: two required sections of our introductory social science research methods, and an upper-division substantive course called Representation and Voting Systems, which, among other topics, considered the impact of electoral reforms on the equality of voice in the electorate. Rather than offering exit credit to participating students, we made participation in the research project a required centerpiece of the courses. The research project was integrated substantively and thematically into all three courses. Care was taken to engage students in the process rather than simply exploit their free labor. Accordingly, we were not simply concerned with the capacity of students to successfully navigate the National Institutes of Health (NIH) certification and nuances of the data collection task, but spent time breaking down the elements of the project to illustrate themes and concepts of the course. Student surveyors were trained in two ways. First, each successfully completed the NIH online accreditation program for research involving human subjects. Second, each student attended a two-hour training session. Interviewers worked in pairs and surveyed voters in six-hour shifts, standing with clipboards and interacting with voters as they exited the polling place. After completing the data collection effort, students in all three classes had an opportunity to work the resultant fruits of their labor—the data— contribute to our community report, and reflect in the courses on their participation in the project.

So Did It Work?

As noted, we had several goals in mind when implementing this community-based research project in our classes. First, we sought to produce high-quality research of use to the community that would determine whether the implementation of ranked-choice voting in San Francisco created or deepened inequalities in the voice of citizens and the perceived legitimacy of local elections. Given the amount of attention the exit poll has garnered among policy makers, members of the community, academics, and people in other jurisdictions considering the adoption of ranked-choice voting, as a piece of community-based research, clearly the project surpassed our expectations. We have participated in public hearings, communicated with members of the media in several states, and had an impact on the decision making of elected officials. But did it work as pedagogy?

At the outset of the project we had identified two principal educational goals. We sought to use the research project as a means for teaching course concepts and theories, and we sought to enhance the political engagement of our students. And we subsequently assessed the effectiveness of our pedagogy in three ways. First, through our own assessments of students' learning, we gauged the relative success of the project as a teaching pedagogy. In short, our assessment was mixed. While we found that in both contexts students seemingly grasped the concepts and theories of social science research in general, and survey research methods in particular, neither faculty member was particularly optimistic about this project as a means for enhancing civic and political engagement of our students. The reason for this is pretty simple. Recall that Ehrlich (2000) defines civic engagement as encompassing the "knowledge, skills, values and motivation" to make a difference in the community (p. vi). Unfortunately, papers, examinations, in-class oral debriefings, and other mechanisms all indicate considerable growth in knowledge and skills. However, it is unclear that *because of* the opportunity provided to our students to conduct community-oriented research, the values and motivations of our students changed appreciably. At least on the basis of our usual indicators of student learning, little evidence emerged to suggest that this particular project increased the degree to which students were engaged or changed their values and motivations.

Our second method of assessment was to collect feedback surveys of student researchers. And these offer a bit more insight. Students were asked to complete a one-page survey considering the added value of the project to their learning by keeping in mind that in future courses the project might not be included in the course. For the eight indicators we are most interested in, students were asked to report whether they agreed or disagreed on a sliding scale with a series of statements about the project. We coded answers indicating full agreement as a 10 and those indicating full disagreement as a 0 with variation between these end points. The results are shown in Table 6.1.

In our assessment survey of student participants, it seems that students appreciated the value of the study to their educational programs at SFSU. The first two measures suggest general agreement that the research project contributed to their experiences. Students gave positive evaluations, saying that they thought the project added to their learning. And the second set of four questions indicates general agreement that the project contributed to classroom learning. But our objectives regarding learning were better met than those involving civic engagement. While the means are lukewarm, though, the quantitative results suggest that students did tend to recognize a positive contribution in terms of increased political engagement. But these quantitative evaluations provide only part of the picture. For students who

TABLE 6.1
Student Researcher Quantitative Evaluations

Measure	Mean	S.D.	N
The Election Survey project . . . "overall was a valuable addition to the course"	7.42	.9	75
"overall was a valuable addition to my course work at SFSU"	7.1	3.1	75
"contributed to my understanding of social science research"	7.7	2.4	75
"helped me to understand ranked-choice voting"	6.7	2.97	6
"helped illustrate concepts and themes from the course"	7.3	2.7	75
"closely matched the topics in this course"	7.2	2.7	75
"encouraged me to learn more about local elections"	6.3	3.1	76
"made me more likely to participate in politics"	6.0	3.0	76

are already engaged in local elections, the project was unlikely to have much impact. Accordingly, much of the potential impact is obscured by such broad measures. Perhaps more notable were the qualitative evaluations we received from students.

Our third method of assessment was to offer students an opportunity to reflect broadly on their experiences in open-ended formats. Not all of these assessments were positive. We received several comments about the amount of time and effort students expended in the project. These are not at all unlike the comments I receive regularly about the excessive amounts of reading assigned for my courses. But the more substantive evaluations were quite revealing. And they suggested that this community-based research project contributed along each dimension of engagement: knowledge, skills, values, and opportunities for engagement.

On the topic of knowledge, students wrote that "it made me realize that different races and genders have all sorts of opinions about politics" and "I found out more about low income areas. . . . it made me open my eyes." Another commented that "it helped you understand the election day process. It gave you an idea of what people thought about the system." One student summed it by stating, "The election survey made me more aware and knowledgeable of the electoral process." For many students, then, this project achieved the objective of increasing student awareness and understanding of political processes.

On the topic of skills students had similarly positive reactions. Several students agreed with one who reflected, "I think it has enhanced my communication skills." And others commented on specific elements of the participatory research project, commenting, "I learned how to write survey questions" and learned how to engage the community in collective problem-solving strategies.

While I was initially pessimistic that a research project might have an impact on the values and motivations of college students, a considerable number of students proved this negativity to be misplaced. In a remark that recalled the student in the soup kitchen, one student in the research design course mused, "I hope one day I will conduct my own research project that is half as valuable as yours was," and another concluded, "It gave me a hands-on understanding of what can be done through empirical research." And several offered a variant of the student's comment, "It made me feel closer to the community." Similarly, students expressed greater motivations to be engaged politically. Several agreed with, "The project taught me a lot about elections and the importance of voting," while another suggested, "It made me more interested in politics and the election itself." One student in the representation course summed this up nicely: "[The project] was a good way for me to find out what is going on in the city. I researched a lot more as a result of the study and was very interested in seeing what the results were for the election."

Finally, several students expressed a positive reaction to the opportunity provided by community-based research. These comments included: "It is nice to be a part of something valuable," "I enjoy being able to get out there and really see what is going on," and "I was really happy to go out and do something that I know was going to help other people and study more about my community." Clearly the project affected our students, several quite profoundly, including one who decided that a career in academia would offer her an opportunity to do community work, and another who applied for employment with a local county election office. In short, the project was a win, win, win. Members of the community appreciated the opportunity to pursue a systematic analysis on which they can build future efforts to improve elections in San Francisco. As academics, my colleague and I benefited from the vigorous challenge of designing, coordinating, and fielding the study. Our interaction with our students was more varied and richer, our interaction with the community was significant and lasting. And the data collected will promote our professional development. Finally, the students benefited through enhanced learning of course concepts and many became more civically and politically engaged in the process.

Lessons Learned

While it was an enormous challenge to implement a project of this magnitude, especially with an incredibly tight timeline, it took no special skills or training on our part to engage the community in a research project designed to promote social justice and facilitate processes of sociopolitical change. Certainly at times, the many cooks made the kitchen a bit messy. And undoubtedly this is true of community-based research projects in other disciplines. My colleagues in the environmental sciences, geography, sociology, African American studies, and other disciplines who have attempted these types of projects have undoubtedly learned these lessons as well as we have. But truly anybody can do this. Lead time and planning definitely contribute to the effectiveness of the project. Had we had more, we most certainly would have constructed more robust measures for assessing student learning and engagement. Better indicators of civic engagement must be used in the assessment instrument and greater attention must be placed on this important goal in the classroom.

While there are thousands of different types of community-based research projects in the works, it seems to me that several elements of this particular project were essential to enhancing student engagement. First, the research involved actually going into the community. Interacting with the community by phone is not the same thing as walking into a neighborhood and having face-to-face contact with residents. It need not be in the context of a survey or at the depth of a six-hour shift collecting exit polls. But students need to be in the community. Similarly, a survey is not the only, and perhaps not the best, mechanism for discerning the impact of a public policy on the community or assessing community needs. And while we sought to enhance student learning about research methods, what is central in terms of bridging the research with political engagement is the immediacy of the result. That newspapers would report on their findings and policy makers would take seriously our recommendations increased student perceptions that the research project was not simply a class project but something with an intensity and immediacy to be part of a process of social change. Relatedly, it was clear from the outset that this project would have an impact on the community. It is difficult to confuse community-based research with volunteerism or altruism. While students in an internship might be exposed to processes of social change, it is unfortunately rare that they take part in, rather than simply bear witness to, these processes. By engaging the community in research, our students helped to inform an important debate in their community. And this is much more likely to enhance meaningful political engagement.

In terms of political engagement generally, we discovered that it is far easier to have an impact on students' knowledge, skills, and opportunities than it is to enhance their values and motivations. Surely several students indicated a substantial change in their values. But we as academics often shy away from teaching values in the classroom. We try to promote political engagement without being political, given the pressured environment inside and outside the institution. We often convince ourselves that the things we care about matter to our students, or should matter to our students, and we rarely make the case on why these things, like political participation, *should* matter. What's more, we frequently find ourselves careful not to proselytize to our students about political or civic engagement for fear of becoming too "political." It is no wonder why our students fail to become politically engaged while in college.

Finally, in terms of the implementation of the project within the classroom setting, we heartily recommend relaxing the typical structure of a course when including a community-based research project like this. It is necessary to reserve large blocks of time for unexpected needs. Rather than engaging in hour-long lectures, faculty should plan on entering a classroom and throwing the discussion open to questions and concerns about the project. Students will express anxiety, confusion, curiosity, and interest as the term wears on. These are opportunities where their genuine engagement can lead the learning. In the process, you will find opportunities to connect their specific questions about that project with the more general topics and concepts in the course. The nature of the material that is learned may not be as systematically organized and distributed across your usual syllabus topics, but the subjects you cover through the real and extended example of the research project will be learned well.

References

American Association of State Colleges and Universities. (2006). *Electoral voices: Engaging college students in elections: An American democracy project best practices guide.* Washington, DC: Author.

Andolina, M., Keeter, S., Zukin, C., & Jenkins, K. (2003). *A guide to the index of civic engagement.* College Park: University of Maryland.

Astin, A. W. (1998). The changing American college student: Thirty-year trends, 1966–1996. *The Review of Higher Education, 21*(2), 115–135.

Barber, B., & Battistoni, R. (1993). A season of service: Introducing service learning into the liberal arts curriculum. *PS: Political Science and Politics, 26*(2), 235–240.

Brock, K. L., & Cameron, B. J. (1999). Enlivening political science courses with Kolb's learning preference model. *PS: Political Science and Politics, 35*(3), 571–575.

Carpini, M. D. (2000). *The youth engagement initiative.* Philadelphia: The Pew Charitable Trusts. Retrieved from http://www.pewtrusts.com/misc_html/pp_youth_strategy_paper.cfm

City and County of San Francisco Voter Information Pamphlet and Sample Ballot: Consolidated and Primary Elections. (2002, March 5).

Ehrlich, T. (Ed.). (2000). *Civic responsibility and higher education.* Phoenix, AZ: Oryx.

Furco, A. (1996). Service learning: A balanced approach to experiential education. *Expanding boundaries: Service and learning.* Washington, DC: Corporation for National Service.

Futures Project. (2002). *Civic engagement: Working paper.* Retrieved from http://www.futuresproject.org/publications/Civicworkingpaper.pdf

Hart Research Associates. (2004). *Attitudes, politics, and public service: A survey of American college students.* Washington, DC: Leon & Sylvia Panetta Institute for Public Policy.

Harvard University Institute of Politics and *The Chronicle of Higher Education.* (2004, September 13). *Executive summary: Survey of college and university voter registration and mobilization efforts.* Retrieved from http://www.iop.harvard/edu/pdfs/chronicle_poll_2004_summary.pdf]

Hepburn, M. A., Niemi, R. G., & Chapman, C. (2000). Service learning in college political science: Queries and commentary. *PS: Political Science and Politics, 33*(3), 617–622

Hunter, S., & Brisbin, R. A. (2000). The impact of service learning on democratic and civic values. *PS: Political Science and Politics, 33*(3), 623–626.

Jones, L. P., & Meinhold, S. S. (1999). The secondary consequences of conducting polls in political science classes: A quasi-experimental test. *PS: Political Science and Politics, 32*(3), 603–606.

Kirlin, M. (2002). Civic skill building: The missing component in service programs? *PS: Political Science and Politics, 35*(3), 571–575.

Kolb, D. A. (1984). *Experiential learning: Experience as a source of learning and development.* Englewood Cliffs, NJ: Prentice-Hall.

Nie, N., Junn, J., & Stehlik-Barry, K. (1996). *Education and democratic citizenship in America.* Chicago: University of Chicago Press.

Ostrander, S. A. (2004). Democracy, civic participation, and the university: A comparative study of civic engagement on five campuses. *Nonprofit and Voluntary Sector Quarterly, 33*(1), 74–93.

Perry, J. L., & Katula, M. C. (2001). Does service affect citizenship? *Administration and Society, 33*(3), 330–365.

Porpora, D. V. (1999). Action research: The highest stage of service learning? In J. Ostrow, G. Hesser, & S. Enos (Eds.), *Cultivating the sociological imagination: Concepts and models for service learning in sociology* (pp. 121–133). Sterling, VA: Stylus (originally published by the American Association of Higher Education).

Rosenthal, C. S. (1999). Our experience is worth a thousand words: Engaging undergraduates in field research on gender. *PS: Political Science and Politics, 32*(1), 63–68.

Soule, S. (2001, September). *Will they engage? Political knowledge, participation, and attitudes of generations X and Y.* Paper presented at the German and American Conference on Civic Education, Pottsdam, Germany. Retrieved from www.civ iced.org/papers/research_engage.pdf

Strand, K., Marullo, S, Cutforth, N., Stoecker, R., & Donohue, P. (2003). *Community-based research and higher education.* San Francisco: Jossey-Bass.

2

COMMUNICATION IN POLITICAL CAMPAIGNS

Bridging Theory and Practice

Sally Cahill Tannenbaum

"In a democracy, political campaigns are at the center. . . . they are the beginning and ending points for political communication" (Powell & Cowart, 2003, p. 3). Political campaigns, in fact, provide an ideal laboratory for scholars and students to observe, analyze, and evaluate the many communication challenges that shape the American election process and determine election outcomes. Political campaigns also provide an opportunity for students to learn about and participate in the election process through conversation, deliberation, and service learning.

Encouraging and providing opportunities for college students to learn about and shape the political landscape is important and necessary. Unfortunately, not all college students fully value the importance of their participation in the election process. Leon Panetta, former chief of staff in President William J. Clinton's administration, states, "While college students today care deeply about certain issues such as education, civil rights, gender equity, social security, and helping low-income families, there appears to be a serious disconnect with our political system" (Leon & Sylvia Panetta Institute for Public Policy, 2004, p. 1). In fact, the Higher Education Research Institute reported that from 1966 to 2000 there was a steady decline from 60.3 percent to 28.1 percent in freshmen reports of keeping up with political affairs and discussing politics (Sax, Astin, Korn, & Mahoney, 2000). Jill McMillan and Katy Harriger (2002) suggest that student alienation is most likely because of "low efficacy, lack of political knowledge, and the feeling that politics is irrelevant" (p. 240). In fact, some have argued that there is a need to renew the connection between young voters and democracy by encouraging students to practice democracy as engaged citizens at the local level (Goodnight & Hingstman, 1997; Ivie, 1998).

Political Campaign Communication, a course that deals with the principles and importance of communication in political campaigns, is purposefully offered at California State University, Fresno, every other fall to coincide with major election campaigns. What makes the course design unique is that, in addition to the traditional lectures and readings, students meet and talk with a number of candidates and consultants and work on an ongoing, active campaign through participation in service learning. The intent of this mixture of instructional approaches is to help students gain theoretical and practical insights into the various communication aspects of elections, learn to appreciate the special characteristics and challenges of political campaigns, and acquire the experience and confidence necessary to continue to be civically involved.

From the perspective of the instructor, this course serves as a template for blending the theoretical and practical aspects of political campaigns into a seamless educational experience. Students' response to the course suggests that combining textbook learning with real-life learning does indeed have a positive effect—students appear to gain a deeper understanding of the theoretical communication concepts of elections by experiencing the day-to-day realities of political campaigning.

Opportunities to engage in conversations with candidates and political consultants give students a realistic perspective on campaign strategy and implementation that no textbook can provide. Deliberating and discussing issues as they arise during the campaign help students integrate and form opinions about communication concepts in diverse political settings. Working on a campaign by walking precincts, running phone banks, and participating in campaign events also facilitates an appreciation of the challenges and rewards of the electoral process.

This chapter has two parts. The first part describes the course design and implementation. The second part discusses the impacts the course has on the classroom dynamic and on the students themselves. Student pre- and post-campaign oral presentations, reflections, and classroom discussions will be used to document course impacts. Insights derived from teaching the course will serve as evidence of the potential benefits of using this instructional approach to teach students about communication in one of the most important aspects of the democratic process.

Course Design

Political Campaign Communication, an upper-division special topics course, was designed—as the title indicates—to examine the unique communication characteristics of political campaigns. Topics covered in the course include understanding and analyzing candidates' histories and styles, campaign messages, campaign strategy, voter analysis, campaign financing, media influence, and the impact of critical events.

What makes this course somewhat unique, and especially intriguing to students, is that the students are not studying campaigns from afar—in fact, they are given opportunities to study communication theory while simultaneously working with political experts. This happens in two ways: first, political specialists regularly share their expertise as guest lecturers in class; second, each student spends at least 15 hours of service learning working on a political campaign.

Implementation of the Classroom Component

Course topics are introduced through class lectures, in-class discussions, and readings from the textbook and periodicals. *Political Campaign Communication: Inside and Out* by Larry Powell and Joseph Cowart (2003) is used because the book is written from two perspectives: the academic's outside view of campaigns and the political professional's inside view. The book, which encourages students to take on a participant-observer perspective, is a nice fit for students studying political campaign communication theory while concurrently completing service learning by working on a campaign.

The guest speaker series provides students with unique insights into the specific issues surrounding political campaigns. Guest speakers normally include candidates (or their representatives) for the U.S. Congress, U.S. Senate, state assembly and senate, city council, regional party chairpersons, and political consultants. The observation of one student underscored the impact direct contact with candidates can have: "Until this campaign, politics appeared to be a polluted profession. Then I met important public figures that took the time to speak to me and other students with whom I worked. These people were personable, approachable, and even funny." Powell and Cowart (2003) argue that campaign practitioners "bring a blend of experience and expertise to the political arena—expertise in the fields of communication technology, strategy development, and experience in the campaign process" (p. 8). By engaging in conversations with candidates and political specialists, students begin to look at campaigns from unique vantage points and learn the practical aspects of communication in the political arena.

Drawing upon the theoretical material presented in class, the information covered in the textbook, and the service-learning field experience, each student is required to give two oral presentations—one is a pre-analysis and the second is a post-analysis of the campaign in which he or she is completing service learning. In the pre-campaign presentation, students discuss the following: candidate/issue history, candidate/issue strengths and weaknesses, opponent strengths and weaknesses, campaign game plan, campaign messages and endorsements, and campaign finances. In the post-campaign oral analysis, students are asked to provide a campaign summary and to discuss the success or failure of campaign strategies, voter analysis, use of volunteers, media influence, and the impact of critical events on the campaign.

In addition to the two oral presentations, students also write a reflection paper in which they are asked to describe their experience completing service learning on the campaign, articulate how this experience connects with the concepts discussed in the textbook and in class lectures, analyze the strengths and weaknesses of the specific campaign on which they worked, and evaluate why in their opinion the campaign was or was not a success. Most of the student commentary cited in the classroom and student impact sections of this chapter were derived from course reflection papers.

Class deliberations, both formal and informal, play a significant role in the course. These deliberations provide opportunities for students to digest, evaluate, reinforce, and challenge ideas and issues that arise during the election. Communication scholars have long appreciated the importance of having students engage in political dialogue. Murphy (1995) argues that deliberative practice "contextualizes the link between communication education and democracy" and helps "develop and broaden the communication skills of democratic citizens" (p. 75). McMillan and Harriger (2002) add,

Both the experiences gained first hand through community placements and the reading and research of secondary sources broaden the content base and enrich the quality of deliberation. What students notice is that knowledge shared through deliberation has a reflexive, synergistic quality. Because the deliberation is 'dynamic' and 'active' as Dewey (1960) noted, it deepens and enriches perspectives as it is shared and expanded upon by the group." (pp. 246–247).

Implementation of the Campaign Experience Component

The course design is very much dependent on the service-learning experience of the students working on a campaign. As we know, service learning is a form of experiential education that reflects the influence of Dewey (Moore, p. 2000). For Dewey, experiential pedagogy and epistemology were connected. "His theory of knowledge was related to and derived from his notions of citizenship and democracy" (Giles & Eyler, 1994, p. 78). "While Dewey never specifically addressed 'community service learning' as a term signifying a particular conceptual framework of education, his writings do analyze five specific areas of relevance to service learning: linking education to experience, democratic community, social service, reflective inquiry, and education for social transformation" (Saltmarsh, 1996, p. 13). In fact, a substantial body of research concludes that student participation in service learning leads to increased involvement and social commitment, citizenship, social justice, and civic responsibility (Astin, 1996; Kendrick, 1996; Melchior & Bailis, 2002; Rockquemore & Schaffer, 2000).

Students complete service learning by working on the campaign of their choice. Activities on individual campaigns vary. In some cases, students are asked to work at the campaign headquarters manning phone banks, entering data into computer banks, preparing packets for volunteers, organizing press conferences, designing Web sites, and laying out campaign strategy. In other cases, students are asked to work outside the campaign headquarters by walking precincts, working at fund-raising events, and escorting candidates to specific functions. On Election Day, some students organize precinct volunteers while others monitor voter turnout. After the election, students on smaller campaigns may be asked to help campaigns analyze election results.

Impact on Classroom Dynamic

One of the most important consequences of this approach to studying communication in political campaigns is what it contributes to the classroom dynamic. Students have a vested interest in the election. They have met candidates, they have deliberated over issues, and they have labored on campaigns. These firsthand experiences bring an added air of confidence and enthusiasm to classroom discussions and classroom presentations. Students appear self-assured in their own knowledge of campaigns and campaign issues and, as a result, are more likely to ask guest speakers provocative questions and/or challenge the positions of fellow classmates. One student observed, "The Political Campaign Class gave me educational insight into the process and allowed me to meet politicians and ask the hard questions." Students report that the course design helps them contextualize and critically examine the strategies being used by candidates in the campaign. Students suggest that the course format helps them synthesize what they are reading with what they see happening in the campaigns.

Impact on Students

While the real-life experiences have an impact on the students in many ways, four areas that students have discussed at length in previous campaigns are discussed here. In particular, this course appears to increase student knowledge about politics and elections in particular, facilitate an awareness of the difficulties campaigns face in reaching and motivating disenfranchised populations, create an understanding of the importance fund-raising and finances play in giving voice to political campaigns, and emphasize the impact participation in the election process plays in a democracy.

Knowledge About the Fundamentals of Political Campaigns

McMillan and Harriger (2002) argue, "one of the undisputed advantages of deliberation in all venues is that knowledge of the issue is increased" (p. 246). That has certainly been the case for the students enrolled in this course—student knowledge about political campaigns significantly increases. Whether it is anecdotal information shared by a guest speaker or campaign war stories shared by the students themselves, theoretical concepts surrounding political campaigns are clarified as a result of the experiences the students have in this course.

In one case, for instance, a politician who was not up for reelection but had held office at the local and state levels for several decades shared behind-the-scenes stories about campaigns with students. One story illustrated how events can be misinterpreted. The guest speaker was asked by a student why the person had openly endorsed one candidate for U.S. Congress but served as master of ceremonies for the candidate's opponent at a local fund-raiser. The guest speaker explained that the governor had called directly and personally asked the guest speaker to serve as master of ceremonies at the fundraiser. The speaker joked that, contrary to the spin on the report in the newspaper, the appearance was not an endorsement of the congressional candidate—the speaker was there solely to introduce and support the governor. The speaker candidly revealed, "In fact, I was concerned that my appearance at this event might be misconstrued by the media. But, the reality is—you don't say no to the governor—at least not if you think you might want to ask him for favors in the future." The anecdote not only served as an example of how an appearance at a fund-raiser might be misconstrued by the media or the voting public, but also illustrated an important characteristic of communication in political campaigns—interpersonal relationships complicate and affect behavior in the political arena.

Students report learning a great deal about campaign mechanics through the service learning they perform. One student reported, "I walked precincts, phone banked, did some data entry, helped with the fund-raiser, [was a] precinct runner, and escorted [the candidate] to meetings." Another said, "I worked on all kinds of different projects . . . making packets to give out to the public at different events . . . walking precincts, making copies of material, making phone calls to remind everyone to vote . . . and, on the day of the election, I signed in about a hundred last minute volunteers and then was a poll checker." A third student observed, "I learned a lot not just from making packets and calls, but also from listening and observing the process." Finally, a student, who had previously worked on several local campaigns, actually took on a leadership position. "I helped to organize and schedule all press events and also helped to prepare the candidate for events. I helped to organize all fund-raising events and learned about filing 460 candidate campaign statements and other FPPC [Fair Political Practices Commission] policies."[1]

Difficulties Reaching and Motivating Disenfranchised Populations

A second learning impact that results from the course design is a better understanding of the challenges campaigns face in motivating disenfranchised populations to vote. Disenfranchised populations, groups of voters who do not traditionally participate in the political election process, fail to vote for a number of reasons: They may feel left out of the election process or feel that they have nothing at stake (Didion, 2001). They may also be uninformed, cynical, or fearful.

Students learn that, rather than reaching out to communicate with all voters, most campaigns concentrate their efforts on populations that have a history of voting. They learn that political consultants regularly buy high-propensity voter lists that provide the name, party affiliation, phone number, and address of individuals who have voted in the last three elections. Consultants argue that these individuals will, in all likelihood, vote in the upcoming election. Consultants explain that phone banks and precinct walkers use these lists. Individuals who do not have a history of voting are often ignored (Powell & Cowart, 2003). One guest speaker illustrated this practice by citing an example from a local campaign where high-propensity voters were sent five mail pieces, approached two times by precinct walkers, and called three times by phone banks. Individuals who did not have a history of voting were ignored.

This is a particularly relevant issue for students. Most students at California State University, Fresno, are under age 24, an age group that, historically, is less likely to participate in the election process (Patterson, 1999). Students reviewed a Leon & Sylvia Panetta Institute for Public Policy survey of college students (2004). The survey found that only 19 percent of college students believed that politics was relevant to their lives and 65 percent did not believe their vote would change policy. One student commented, "As discussed in class, there are many reasons that people my age do not vote. I would have to agree with the one about not knowing who to vote for and not caring. I never voted before because I felt as if my vote did not count and I did not know who[m] I was voting for."

This issue is also relevant to the students because many of the campaigns they work on have constituencies of largely poor, minority populations (that have traditionally been disenfranchised). Discussions on why one population is more likely to be disenfranchised than another are thoughtful and provocative. Students are reminded that, historically, many of these populations were not given an opportunity to vote and, as a result, learned to express their political opinions through other means. The students are reminded that before being given the right to vote, women used pickets and demonstrations; before the Civil Rights Act passed in 1964, Martin Luther King, Jr., and his followers used marches and sit-ins; and, in order to draw attention to the rights of migrant workers, César Chávez and the United Farm Workers used hunger strikes and boycotts. Students learn that lingering distrust of the election process still persists for many of the voters in these groups. In fact, one guest speaker noted that not every American appreciates that his or her vote matters, and motivating individuals who are fearful and cynical is a challenge to political campaigns.

Robert Asen (2004) argues, "To discern how citizenship is engaged, we must turn to practice" (p. 199). He argued that campaigns must reach out to voters where they gather, where they engage in civic and public discourse. "Ronald Greene calls on communication scholars to attend to the cultural dimensions of citizenship. He encourages scholars to consider the processes by which particular subjects are marked as 'different' and denied access to civic venues" (Asen, p. 193; Greene, 2002). Students learn that rather than attending a fund-raiser that calls for a hefty donation, disenfranchised voters are more likely to gather at a neighborhood park to attend a community festival. Rather than being persuaded by listening to candidates at a political forum, disenfranchised voters are more likely to be swayed by their church minister or a precinct walker who takes the time to talk about the cracks in their sidewalk and traffic congestion around their neighborhood school.

Alternative ways to reach disenfranchised voters are discussed at length. Students recognize that slick brochures do not always persuade individuals from disenfranchised communities. In fact, they note that individuals whose primary language is not English are unlikely even to receive written political campaign materials and that many disenfranchised voters do not subscribe to a daily newspaper or news magazine. Rather than reading editorials in the newspaper, students observe, these voters are more likely to receive information about the campaign by listening to the radio as they go about completing their daily chores. In fact, as a result of learning to appreciate some of the reasons specific populations are disenfranchised, students raise awareness about these practices with the campaigns they are completing their service learning on. In past cases, bilingual students have helped canvass neighborhoods and worked on phone banks in non-English-speaking communities.

In other cases, they have helped identify appropriate venues (such as community events) to reach traditionally hard-to-reach voters. One student reflected, "I was able to work closely with the campaign consultant to develop and enforce strategies based on demographics such as race, party and age."

Students also discussed the impact of new mediums. A Harvard University Institute of Politics (2006) study noted that Facebook.com and other social networking Web sites are very popular with college students and provide new venues for political organizing (p. 9). The same institute found that individuals aged 18–24 make up 24 percent of the U.S. population, but 36 percent of the "online political citizenry." Online political citizens actively participate by visiting candidates' Web sites, participating in Web logs, and making contributions online. Students noted that, while the Internet is particularly effective in attracting young voters (Sellnow, 1998), there are still large numbers of voters who lie on the other side of the digital divide. In fact, online political citizens tend to be young, White, and come from middle- to upper-class backgrounds (Anderson, Bikson, Law, & Mitchell, 1995). Students raised concerns that increased dependence on Web sites by political campaigns may leave behind the "socially and economically disenfranchised" (Goldzwig & Sullivan, 2000, p. 53).

Importance of Fund-Raising and Finances in Political Campaigns

A third learning impact that resulted from the course design was a deeper understanding of the role fund-raising and finances play in providing voice to political campaigns. Powell and Cowart (2003) note that "Academicians . . . often bemoan the role that money plays in modern campaigns" (p. 215), but concede that fund-raising and finances play an essential element in most campaigns. Without financial resources, the communication aspect of political campaigns is severely hampered. "Money buys the means of political speech. Without money political messages cannot be tested by pollsters; advertising spots cannot be created; ad time cannot be purchased; staffs cannot be hired" (p. 216). One student observed, "To win in today's political game you must have money to pay for the cost of advertisement on television and radio, traveling, food, employees, and any other requirements of the campaign." Another student reflected, "In the world of elections, money makes a difference; it allows your voice to be heard."

Students, in fact, seemed taken aback by the amount of time and energy campaigns used to raise funds. Endorsements, especially financial ones, appeared to be essential to every campaign. One student critically observed, "The music group ABBA said it best in their 1976 hit 'Money, money, money . . . it's a rich man's world' to help characterize the importance of *money* in a campaign. In my opinion, the money it takes to run for a political office is ridiculous and encourages the infestation of the rich in this profession." A second student suggested that the campaign process be overhauled. "It seems to me that political campaigns need to be restructured. The candidates have to raise a substantial amount of money in order to stay in the race."

Students appeared particularly surprised at the role played by special interest groups. A student commented, "This aspect of it really turned me off because it seems that every donor's intention when they sponsor a candidate is to get a return of some sort back." In one congressional race, over 1 million dollars was given to a local candidate by a national partisan committee. In other races, candidates received large amounts of money from political action committees and unions. Students deliberated about how the influx of unprecedented contributions from national partisan committees affected local campaigns and argued for and against finance reform.

Without the campaign experience, it is doubtful that the students would have truly understood the significant role finances play in contemporary political campaigns. The students also appeared to appreciate that there are important practical as well as ethical implications for the way campaigns are financed.

The Role Participation in the Election Process Plays in a Democracy

Finally, the three-pronged design of this course appeared to increase awareness of the role participation in the election process plays in a democracy. Rod Hart (2000) points out that political campaigns are essential to the function of a democracy and increase our awareness of the political world. Students learned that participation made a difference. One student noted, "My overall impression of the process is that every little bit counts. This election, local and national, demonstrated how each vote counts. Many of the local races came down to a very small margin of votes." Another said,

"Volunteering for something like this is the duty of all people who enjoy the freedom of a democratic system."

Students learned to also appreciate the importance of their own participation in the process. One student reflected, "Before this class I had never been much for politics. I had never voted and I didn't even have much of an opinion on political issues, but now that I have worked on a campaign . . . I can say that I have voted, I do have an interest in politics and I do have many opinions when it comes to political issues." Another noted, "During this whole process I found myself engaging in conversations that I have never had before. . . . [I] watched the debates, which prior to this class you couldn't pay me to do." Another student said, "This semester was one that I will never forget. I never thought that I would ever get into politics let alone work on a campaign."

Students also appeared energized. One person remarked, "I find the campaign process to be invigorating and even though the work hours are endless and the pressure leaves you with a lifelong headache, when you work for something or someone that you believe in, it's all worthwhile."

Conclusion

Unfortunately, not all young voters comprehend the impact participatory politics has in shaping the political, social, and economic landscape. And, while many young voters care deeply about social issues such as civil rights and education, too many do not fully appreciate the role the election process itself has on those issues. By offering opportunities for students to participate in the election process, college instructors not only teach young voters about the political process but also *empower* students and give them voice.

In fact, in post-election conversations, students expressed appreciation for the concerted effort made by campaigns to solicit input from their generation. Students appeared encouraged that the national turnout of young voters (18 to 25 years of age) in the presidential election had increased 11 percentage points—from 36 to 47 percent—from 2000 to 2004 (Center for Information & Research on Civic Learning & Engagement, 2004). Students attributed the higher turnout to campaigns that directly targeted young voters and national outreach programs by organizations such as Rock the Vote, which registered over 3 million new young voters. In fact, in the 2006 course, students were delighted to learn that voters could register online through

Facebook.com. They were encouraged by this obvious attempt to get more young voters involved in the political process.

Student feedback certainly indicates that supplementing a political campaign communication course with opportunities to converse with political experts and complete service learning by working on a campaign helps class participants connect course theory with the practical aspects of political campaigns. This triad of instructional approaches also appears to invigorate the classroom dynamic. Students in this course appear to enjoy the competitive air of elections and express surprise at the extent to which the campaign experience energizes and motivates them. Perhaps, more important, the students come to understand the importance of giving a voice to the social and political concerns of their generation and learn to appreciate the nuances of communication in this uniquely American forum.

Note

1. California requires that all candidates or office holders who have a controlled committee and have raised $1,000 or more during a calendar year in connection with an election to office to use FPPC Form 460 to file statements.

References

Anderson, R. H., Bikson, T. K., Law, S. A., & Mitchell, B. M. (1995). *Universal access to e-mail: Feasibility and societal implications*. Santa Monica, CA: Rand Corporation.

Asen, R. (2004). A discourse theory of citizenship. *Quarterly Journal of Speech, 2*, 189–211.

Astin, A. W. (1996). The role of service in higher education. *About Campus, 1*(1), 14–19.

Center for Information & Research on Civic Learning & Engagement. (2004, September). The 2004 presidential election and young voters (fact sheet). University of Maryland, College Park. Retrieved from http://www.civicyouth.org/research/products/fact_sheets_outside.htm and http:/ www.civicyouth.org/quick/youth_voting.htm

Didion, J. (2001). *Political fictions*. New York: Knopf.

Giles, D. E., & Eyler, J. (1994).The theoretical roots of service-learning in John Dewey: Toward a theory of service-learning. *Michigan Journal of Community Service Learning, 1,* 77–85.

Goldzwig, S. R., & Sullivan, P. A. (2000). Electronic democracy, virtual politics, and local communities. In R. E. Denton, Jr. (Ed.), *Political communication ethics* (pp. 51–74). Westport, CT: Praeger.

Goodnight, G. T., & Hingstman, D. B. (1997). Studies in the public sphere. *Quarterly Journal of Speech, 83*, 351–371.

Greene, R. W. (2002). Citizenship in a global context: Towards a future beginning for a cultural studies inspired argumentation theory. In G. T. Goodnight (Ed.), *Arguing communication and culture* (pp. 97–103). Washington, DC: National Communication Association.

Hart, R. P. (2000). *Campaign talk: Why campaigns are good for us*. New York: Oxford University Press.

Harvard University Institute of Politics. (2006, April). Redefining political attitudes and activism: A poll by Harvard Institute of Politics. Retrieved from http://www .iop.harvard.edu/pdfs/survey/spring_poll_2006_execsumm.pdf

Ivie, R. L. (1998). Democratic deliberation in a rhetorical republic. *Quarterly Journal of Speech, 84*, 491–530.

Kendrick, J. R., Jr. (1996). Outcomes of service learning in an introduction to sociology course. *Michigan Journal of Community Service Learning, 3*, 72–81.

Leon & Sylvia Panetta Institute for Public Policy. (2004). *Attitudes, politics, and public service: A survey of American college students*. Retrieved from http://www.pa nettainstitute.org/surveys/surrey-2004.htm

McMillan, J. J., & Harriger, K. J. (2002). College students and deliberation: A benchmark study. *Communication Education, 51*(3), 237–253.

Melchior, A., & Bailis, L. (2002). Impact of service learning on civic attitudes and behaviors of middle and high school youth. In A. Furco & S. H. Billig (Eds.), *Service learning; The essence of the pedagogy* (pp. 201–222). Greenwich, CO: Information Age Publishing.

Moore, D. T. (2000). The relationship between experiential learning research and service learning research [Special issue]. *Michigan Journal of Community Service Learning*, 124–128.

Murphy, T. A. (1995). Deliberative civic education and civil society: A consideration of ideals and actualities in democracy and communication education. *Communication Education, 53*(1), 74–92.

Patterson, D. (1999). *Americans are giving up their freedom by not voting*. Birmingham, AL: Policy Exchange Foundation.

Powell, L., & Cowart, J. (2003). *Political campaign communication: Inside and out*. Boston: Allyn & Bacon.

Rockquemore, K. A., & Schaffer, R. H. (2000). Toward a theory of engagement: A cognitive mapping of service learning experiences. *Michigan Journal of Community Service Learning, 7*, 14–24.

Saltmarsh, J. (1996). Education for critical citizenship: John Dewey's contribution to the pedagogy of community service learning. *Michigan Journal of Community Service Learning, 3,* 13–21.

Sax, L. J., Astin, A. W., Korn, W. S., & Mahoney, K. M. (2000). The American freshman: National norms for fall 2000. Higher Education Research Institute. Retrieved from http://www.gseis.ucla.edu/heri/norms_pr_00.html

Sellnow, G. W. (1998). *Electronic whistle-stops: The impact of the Internet on American politics.* Westport, CT: Praeger.

3

SOCIAL RESEARCH AND THE SACRAMENTO STATE ANNUAL SURVEY OF THE REGION

*Amy Qiaoming Liu, Otis Scott, Joseph Sheley, Frank Whitlatch,
Ernest Cowles, and Manuel Barajas*

Soc. 102A and 102B [Social Research classes] have helped me understand all that goes into creating a valid and reliable sociological study. I have gained an appreciation for the time, effort, and true dedication it takes to successfully complete a relevant study that the public can understand. . . . I was also very proud . . . that our class played a major role in processing the information that became available to the general public. I felt that everything we have done was able to be used in real life and that made me feel really good and validated. . . . Overall this class has prepared me for researching any topic and understanding the importance of sociological studies in the world.

I really feel that the most I have learned through the duration of my academic career has been in Soc. 102A and B. It has been the most real-world applicable, most exciting, most challenging, and most wonderful experience I have gone through.

This exciting learning environment was experienced in Sociology 102A and 102B at California State University, Sacramento, in 2005 and 2006. There, students were able to combine the opportunity to learn how to conduct high-quality survey research with the opportunity to make a difference in their community. Students performed a public service role by taking their community's pulse in a manner that ultimately informed the citizenry and policy makers. Moreover, the combined research and community service opportunities provided students with skill sets that were of exceptional value in today's job market. In this chapter we describe the courses and their link to civic learning and political engagement in detail.

Learning Objectives and Outcomes of Research Methods (Sociology 102A and 102B)

Research Methods is a required course for all undergraduate majors in the California State University, Sacramento, Department of Sociology. Traditionally, our curriculum offers a systematic introduction to research methods in social sciences, especially in sociology. It focuses upon the five steps of social research and related skills in carrying out social research: (a) formulate research questions, (b) design research, (c) gather data or use existing data, (d) analyze and interpret data, and (e) report research findings.

Research knowledge and skills are often developed through practice and use, but students' ability to apply those skills is traditionally bound more to in-class exercises and less to activities outside the classroom. Consequently, those applications are not always related to each other or connected to current concerns of students or their community, while at other times, projects are too small to have any significant impact on the students and/or their community. Social research can become more tangible, relevant, and interesting to students through service-learning projects. Students can accumulate knowledge, understand the social world, and make a difference for themselves and their community simultaneously, when methods classes are designed with an emphasis on doing real research. Our methods requirement consists of two classes: Sociology 102A and Sociology 102B. The former combines lectures, class discussions, and computer labs to teach basic concepts and an understanding of the big picture of social research. Students put all that knowledge into practice during Sociology 102B.[1] In this course, we designed a service-learning project, Sacramento State Annual Survey of the Region, and integrated it into each of the steps of social research. In this way, students can apply important sociological terms and/or theories they have learned in other sociology classes to their lives and their community.

The Annual Survey of the Region

Research methods, statistics, and computers are essential tools in sociology, and students need to know when, how, and why to use them. In this way, students can explore the social world and address important social and political problems on their own. However, some students in sociology are afraid of mathematics, statistics, or computers, while many others have not had the chance to witness the power of social research in their community. To minimize students' fears of mathematics or computers, stimulate their interest and confidence in social research, maximize their potential, and better serve the university and the Sacramento region, in 2002 we created the service-learning research project for our Research Methods classes, titled Annual Survey of Public Opinion and Life Quality in the Sacramento Region. With the increased popularity and significance of the annual survey in the region, we renamed it Sacramento State Annual Survey of the Region in early 2006 to bring more name recognition to our campus.

The Sacramento region, consisting of Sacramento, Yolo, Placer, and El Dorado counties, is a major center of state politics and one of the fastest growing regions in California. However, there was no systematic poll of residents' perception of the quality of life and their opinions on important issues in the region over time when we started our annual survey in 2002. While other polls have examined the state and the Central Valley (from Redding to Bakersfield), currently ours is the only comprehensive regional survey designed to focus on residents in the Sacramento region. The survey has five objectives:

1. Increase the understanding of various social, economic, and political factors that affect the quality of life in the Sacramento region.
2. Build a comprehensive database that is capable of tracking trends and changes in the quality of life and issues of local, regional, and state importance.
3. Provide decision makers and the general public with current and objective information about the Sacramento region and facilitate public discussion and debate on issues of regional and national significance.
4. Enable policy makers, media, and the public, including students, to see the potential significance of social research in facilitating social and political engagement of the university and the community.
5. Enhance teaching and learning in sociology.

Research Topics and Questionnaire Development

We typically start to think about the topics and specific research questions in late fall, in connection with our lectures on survey, measurement, and questionnaire development. We often spend a great deal of time asking how we can make sociological research an integrated part of life in the Sacramento region and the United States. To achieve this goal, we talk with leaders and experts at the university and in the community and follow the media closely. For example, we read the *Sacramento Bee* and the *Sacramento Business Journal*. In this way, we become familiar with issues important to individuals in the region, nation, and media. We are concerned with the interests of the public as well as those of policy makers. We discuss these topics in class and welcome students' input. As students realize the connections between these issues and their own lives, they become more actively engaged in the survey questions. In the end, we often have too many questions for the survey, and have to make tough decisions selecting the final questions. This process helps students better understand how real research questions are developed, changed, and finalized, and how the process is tied to the objective of the study, the budget, and the social and political world.

The survey questions and topics included each year are structured in two parts: a core section and a specific-interest section. The core section includes key indicators of quality of life and opinions on important social, economic, political, and environmental issues in the region. The specific-interest section is designed to meet the specific needs or interests that the state, region, counties in the region, and/or other private and public sectors have in a specific survey year. The core section remains the same for each survey, while the specific-interest section may vary from year to year.

For example, housing was one of the topics included in our 2006 survey. Like other regions in the state, the average housing price in the Sacramento Metropolitan Statistical Area had increased dramatically: 112 percent from March 2001 to March 2006 (Office of Federal Housing Enterprise Oversight, 2006). In the 2006 survey we included a core question (also asked in 2002–2005) to track trends in the region's perception of affordable housing. In 2006, 77 percent of residents in the Sacramento region saw affordable housing as a problem, with 51 percent viewing it as a major concern. It was the second biggest concern in the region (after transportation), and has been one of the top concerns in the region for the past 5 years: 51 percent in 2006 (Liu & Sumati, 2006), 48 percent in 2005 (Liu & Livingston, 2005), 50 percent in 2004 (Liu & Sheley, 2004), 51 percent in 2003 (Liu & Sheley, 2003), 47 percent in 2002 (Liu, 2002).

To meet the housing needs of working families, the Sacramento County Board of Supervisors adopted an affordable housing ordinance in December 2004. The program requires developers of residential housing to designate 15 percent of new units as affordable to families that earn less than $51,000, to individuals who earn less than $13,000, and to those who are designated as low-income or extremely low-income (Sacramento Housing and Redevelopment Agency, 2006).[2] The Building Industry Association filed a lawsuit against Sacramento County in an attempt to overturn the ordinance. Shortly thereafter, a coalition of low-income citizens and affordable-housing advocacy groups filed a motion seeking dismissal of the lawsuit. The attorney general's office later joined in that motion. Local media, policy makers, residents, and community organizations paid close attention to the lawsuit. To calculate how many people in Sacramento County supported a low-income housing ordinance, our team added two affordable-housing questions to the 2006 survey. Our report (Liu & Sumati, 2006) found that a majority of the public in the region supported providing housing opportunities for families earning less than $51,000 per year (91 percent), and believed that 15 percent of new homes should be priced for low-income families (70 percent). These results were shared with the public and policy makers in June 2006. Therefore, our survey questions not only provide continuity but also flexibility in monitoring trends and changes.

This research also provides communities and leaders in the Sacramento region with an opportunity to include in the survey questions of specific interest to them. This is very important and beneficial for the region, in particular to the organizations that need the data but cannot afford to do large-scale data collection. This project fosters inclusiveness and broad-based community involvement, and serves as a key resource for local communities.

Data Collection

Our data collection typically runs from February to March, after the university's Human Subjects Review Committee approves our research proposal and the survey questions. Our study is conducted using computer-assisted telephone interviews of about 1,000 adult residents age 18 or over from randomly selected households in the Sacramento region. The survey is scientifically designed to meet standards commonly used by researchers in a variety of community surveys. To obtain high-quality data, we buy our phone numbers from commercial phone banks, and work very closely with the Institute for Social Research (ISR) located on campus. For example, in 2005, more than 20 students, together with about 10 paid interviewers, conducted the phone interviews in English and Spanish from February 15 to March 16 at ISR with an ISR supervisor to closely monitor the data collection operation.

For many students, this was the first time they had engaged in data collection in a professional setting and talked with a random sample of the population in the region. This real data collection experience allowed students the opportunity to get to know people, their community, and the true data collection process. According to the students:

> This project was very useful in showing me what social research really is and how it is conducted. You see statistics and reports on social research all the time. Things like opinion polls are pretty common, and I have always wondered how the research was conducted and who they actually polled to get the information.
>
> Our participation in the Sacramento Region Quality of Life Survey (Sacramento State Annual Survey of the Region) was especially helpful in understanding the process of social research. By actually calling participants I gained an appreciation of the amount of hard work and time that goes into surveys. I also realized that data can be easily influenced, even when we try to tightly control for this. I realize that data should not be taken for granted as being accurate and that there are many factors that alter the responses of participants.

Data Analysis and Academic Papers

Once the data are collected, we show students how to clean it and get it ready for data analysis. We often use the data for lectures and in-class lab exercises. Students are also required to use the annual survey data and/or the General Social Survey data sets to write an academic research paper. This involves arguing why their studies are important; reviewing relevant literature to come up with hypotheses; using SPSS, a widely employed statistical analysis software program to run frequencies, chi-squares, regressions, and many other analyses; interpreting and presenting the results; and forming conclusions. This is the first time many students have connected questionnaire development, data collection, data analysis, data management, and hypothesis testing in a single project and seen how sociologists examine important social issues, such as housing, transportation, inequality, and diversity in our society. This also provides students with an opportunity to

apply all their statistics and research methods skills, social theories, and sociological knowledge and to demonstrate their written communication skills,
their sociological imagination, and what they have learned at college. At the
end of the year, many students are pleasantly surprised that they are able to
carry out social research projects that are meaningful to them and to the
community.

Applied Reports and Media Strategies

In order for the public, including our students, to see the impact of social
research and the university on the community, we have made this project an
important resource for the region. To achieve this goal, we work closely with
the College of Social Sciences and Interdisciplinary Studies (SSIS) and the
university's Public Affairs Office to make our results widely available through
effective media strategies.

In each survey, we ask at least 70 questions. We have a great deal of data,
but too little time to write a full report during the middle of the semester.
Therefore we decide to focus on one topic at a time. We also work closely
with students to produce applied reports. In 2006, students in the class selected the following topics, among others, for their applied reports:

1. Attitudes toward the president and the war in Iraq
2. Support for the governor and his proposals in the Sacramento
   region
3. Perception of California State University, Sacramento in the Sacramento region
4. Perception of the Sacramento Kings basketball team and the need
   for a new arena
5. Affordable housing in the Sacramento region
6. Regional safety, flooding, and emergency responses in the Sacramento region
7. Attitude toward national security and civil liberties
8. Major issues in the Sacramento region: a five-year trend
9. Racial divide in the Sacramento region (or in the United States)
10. Class divide in the Sacramento region (or in the United States)
11. Gender divide in the Sacramento region (or in the United States)
12. Political divide in the Sacramento region (or in the United States)

For example, in 2005, working with students and other faculty, we systematically produced eight applied reports on topics that were of particular interest to the public and the media from March to November. The moment a report is completed, the campus Public Affairs Office releases it to the public and the media. Students also e-mail reports to policy makers and community organizations. We often spend a great deal of time talking with the media and policy makers. Our data is valued because it is current and relevant. We have adopted many of the strategies recommended by Gans (1989), Burawoy (2004, 2005), and Schwartz (2005) in sharing our results with the public. Because of the broad dissemination process, the quality of our research, the importance of our topics, and the collaboration with the Public Affairs Office, major newspapers, TV stations, and radio stations in the region and Northern California have reported our research. Many policy makers and local organizations have also requested our reports and used them to make informed decisions.

This project has made social research more visible on campus and in the Sacramento region. Students are intrigued by the debate generated by their research and the attention garnered from the public, the media, and policy makers. This has boosted their interest and confidence in carrying out important social research for the community, thus directly and indirectly facilitating greater social and political engagement in the region.

Assessment

Three methods are used to assess how our service-learning project has affected student learning and the social and political engagement of the university and the community. The first method is students' applied research reports and academic papers, indicating students' understanding of data analysis and their abilities and involvement in studying important social and political issues in the Sacramento region and the United States. The second comes from students' reflection papers, based on the framework provided by Howard (2001), that summarize how the classes and the survey projects have affected students' learning inside and outside classrooms. Finally, a great deal of impact on the community has resulted because of the large amount of media coverage and the wide use of our data and reports by the community.

Applied Report and Academic Papers

The service-learning project has given students a great opportunity to expand their intellectual potential. Students are required to write one academic paper with five chapters: introduction, literature review, methods, results, and conclusions. Since 2005, students are also required to use the annual survey data they have just collected to carry out a sociological study of the Sacramento region (an applied report). These two papers enable us to assess whether students know how to use the sociological knowledge and skills they have learned to examine social problems in their community and come up with sound policy recommendations. To accomplish these tasks, they are required to know all the basic skills of social research, including developing a research topic that is feasible, socially important, and scientifically relevant. A considerable amount of time is spent talking with each student before he or she decides on a topic. Students have the opportunity to rewrite the paper with detailed feedback from other students and the instructor. Some students have produced excellent papers that are used by organizations on campus and in the community. Although rewriting often doubles our workload, it gives us additional chances to work with students individually. At the end of the year, many students are amazed at what they have accomplished and are very proud of their final papers. Some are confident that they can address important social and political issues in their community, while others decide to save their papers as writing examples for applications for future jobs or graduate school. Many students have also presented their research at professional conferences, such as the California Sociological Association and the Society for Applied Sociology annual meetings. For example:

> I can say that this is the first semester I actually felt like a true sociologist. . . . Up until this point, every sociology class has been relatively the same; we read books, listen to lectures, take tests on the lectures and book, and that is it. Yes, I have gained a great deal of knowledge and information from these classes but I was never sure what I was supposed to do with all of it. In 102A [Research Methods], I was able to take this knowledge and build upon it by creating my own concepts and ideas about social issues and comparing them with previous studies. It was intellectually uplifting to be able to research a topic and choose variables that I thought are beneficial to society. . . . It was the first time I chose the topic, did the research, drew hypotheses, tested my hypotheses, and drew conclusions. It

was a chance for us, as students, to ask questions and search for answers on our own.

I am truly amazed at the way I look back over these two classes [Soc. 102A and Soc. 102B]. When I registered last summer, I expected a year full of tears, sleeplessness, and a desire to change career fields. On the contrary, I am more excited and determined about my decision to pursue a degree in sociology, being able to bring life to my studies has helped validate my career and life choice. This class has made a huge difference on my outlook in sociology.

Reflection Papers

Students write two reflection papers that have provided detailed qualitative data that indicate that many students have learned a great deal in these classes, as shown by the comments from students cited in this paper. Students have told us that the service-learning projects have expanded their understanding and appreciation of social research and sociology by carrying out a real-world research project as opposed to conducting research as an exercise only. More important, the projects have also increased students' understanding of their community, their concerns about important social and political issues facing the local community and the nation, and their social and political responsibilities. Here are a few examples of students' comments:

> This course has provided me the culminating experience in understanding Sociology. I am finally recognizing how the theory and applied research come together to form the subject of sociology. . . . It has taught me the various types of social research projects, what motives social research and the overall approach to a social science project. I have learned how the social science project can answer questions about the social world. Additionally, that the importance of these projects or studies are not confined to the academic setting but used in larger social contexts such as in the government for policy making or in the cooperate work for marketing or human resources policies.

> The knowledge of GSS [General Social Survey] and surveys in general, has changed the way I view the nightly news. When I hear statistics or opinions, I wonder how the information was gathered, what the response rate was, and whether or not the sample was random.

I think this experience [participation in the annual survey] has most affected my political learning. I now realize that everyday citizens like myself do cause changes to happen in their communities. This project has the potential to advocate changes in policies based on the opinions of citizens in our community. This project has showed me that being a part of a society is not just about paying taxes and voting, but is about each individual's personal responsibility for involvement.

Media Coverage and Community Impact

Since 2002, we have released 31 applied reports to the public. These studies are widely reported in the local media and reach a large number of residents and policy makers. These reports have allowed people in the Sacramento region, the media, and policy makers to have a much better understanding of the opinions and quality-of-life issues in the region and have promoted social and political participation.

First, our surveys are important vehicles for the public to be heard by elected government officials. For example, the Kings moved to Sacramento in 1985 and began playing basketball in a brand new facility, Arco Arena, in 1988. Eighteen years have passed since they claimed Arco Arena as their home. The owners of the Kings wanted a new arena for the team and hoped the public would help pay for it. In the past five or six years, many business leaders and government officials have indicated a desire to help the Kings build the facility, and even made several proposals. However, there was no independent survey of public opinion in the region on this important topic until we conducted our polls in 2005 and 2006. Our data indicated that advocates for a new arena needed to do much more if they hoped to gain public assistance to build it. There was a passion for the Kings, but little support for helping build a new arena. The majority of residents in the Sacramento region (59 percent) did not feel that the Sacramento Kings needed a new arena. Compared to 2005, support in 2006 actually eroded by 5 percentage points. If a new arena was to be built, very few (1 percent) wanted to use public tax dollars to pay for it, although more than one-third (34 percent) thought a combination of private and public funds was acceptable. A majority of residents (54 percent) hoped all funding would be provided by private money (Liu, Hayes, Kile, Marable, Smith, & Kafouros, 2006; Liu & Sumati, 2005). The *Sacramento Bee* reported this study on the front page on May 5, 2006, and several related stories ran later. Almost all the TV and radio stations in town discussed this topic as well. Since then, local politicians have become more cognitive of public opinion and are using this knowledge when they work with the owners of the Kings and business leaders to search for a solution to this issue.

Second, our studies have provided many organizations in the Sacramento region with important data to facilitate better discussions and debates of important issues in the Sacramento region. For example, Valley Vision is a nonprofit organization committed to a regional approach to address important regional issues, including the challenges and opportunities created by rapid growth in the region. Its membership includes representatives of business, agriculture, the environmental community, organized labor, education, utilities, government, and the nonprofit sector (http://www.valleyvision.org/about-o.html). We can see how this organization has used our data from an e-mail sent by K. Mazzei, a project manager from Valley Vision:

> I just finished reading the article in the Bee about your Quality of Life study. I went to the CSU website and downloaded the full report. This is a wonderful piece of work, and really complements a project I am working on with Valley Vision called Partnership for Prosperity. We are bringing together leaders from regional organizations and institutions (which includes the participation of the President of CSU Sacramento) to develop a long-term economic development strategy for the six-county Sacramento region. If you are interested, you can read more about this project on our website: www.valleyvision.org/partnership.
>
> Next week we are hosting a meeting with the Leadership Coalition from this project. Leadership Coalition members include the lead staff members and Board Chairs of entities like SMUD [Sacramento Municipal Utility District], UCD [University of California Davis], Sacramento Area Trade and Commerce Organization, Sac Metro Chamber of Commerce, the local Community Colleges, the Airport, etc. This meeting is designed to share the latest economic and demographic data about our region. I will also plan to share copies of your report at that meeting.
>
> I figured you would appreciate knowing how your hard work will be put to use in the region. . . . in this case, right away!
>
> Thanks so much for your timely research. (K. Mazzei. April 2005, personal communication)

Third, these studies also allow us to track trends in the region, as we have compiled many years of data. For example, our 2005 annual survey showed that despite their satisfaction with the overall quality of life in the Sacramento region and their optimistic outlook for the future, Sacramento region residents had serious concerns regarding a wide range of local issues, with traffic congestion on major roads topping their list. A large majority (92 percent) viewed traffic congestion as a problem, with 66 percent thinking it was a big problem. Traffic congestion consistently remained at the top of the Sacramento region residents' list of concerns, although the level of concern has fluctuated slightly over the past four years: 66 percent in 2005 (Liu & Livingston, 2005), 67 percent in 2004 (Liu & Sheley, 2004), 58 percent in 2003 (Liu & Sheley, 2003), 73 percent in 2002 (Liu, 2002).

More important, our data has helped many organizations develop strategies and action plans to deal with specific challenges and needs. When the Public Affairs Office at California State University, Sacramento, found that only about one-third of residents in the Sacramento region are aware of campus events open to the public, they decided to take action to improve the situation. Now when you call the university on the phone, you get all kinds of information about the campus while you are waiting for your call to go through. An ad campaign in the *Sacramento Bee* is also being used by the campus.

Conclusion

This chapter has shown that a service-learning project can significantly enrich research methods curricula in sociology. We have explored diverse methods to facilitate students' appreciation of scientific methods and statistics. One of the most effective methods we have found is students' participation in this service-learning project, Sacramento State Annual Survey of the Region. This project has allowed us to show students how to ask important social and political questions, and how to use literature review and statistical computer programs to find answers to those questions by following the steps and skills we have taught in Sociology 102A and Sociology 102B.

Participation in this research project enables students to realize that their research can affect the social and political dialogue and/or policies in the region and the nation. Since 2002, we have presented our data at local, regional, and national conferences, and our studies have been widely reported in the media, used for creative teaching, scholarly research, presentations, and theses. As the most comprehensive database for many community organizations and government agencies, these surveys are also used as a major resource in contributing to well-balanced programs, plans, and policies that enhance the quality of life on campus and in the Sacramento region. Broadly speaking, the surveys have garnered high visibility in the Sacramento region, and heightened local, regional, and statewide awareness of California State University, Sacramento. Even though students approach the research methods courses with anxiety, many have left with a heightened sense of confidence in their own ability to do social research, a profound sense of accomplishment, and a deepened understanding and appreciation for sociological research.

Notes

1. Sociology 102A is a prerequisite for Sociology 102B.
2. For more detailed information about the ordinance, please see http://www .shra.org/Content/Housing/HousingDevelopment/CountyAfford.htm

References

Burawoy, M. (2004). Public sociologies: Contradiction, dilemmas, and possibilities. *Social Forces, 82*(4), 1603–1618.

Burawoy, M. (2005). For public sociology, 2004 presidential address. *American Sociological Review, 70,* 4–28.

Gans, H. (1989). Sociology in America: The discipline and the public, 1988 presidential address. *American Sociological Review, 54,* 1–16.

Howard, J. (Ed.). (2001). *Service-learning course design workbook.* Ann Arbor, MI: OCSL Press.

Liu, A. Q. (2002). *The full report for the 2002 Annual Survey of Public Opinion and Life Quality in the Sacramento Region.* California State University, Sacramento. Retrieved from http://www.csus.edu/ssis/annual_survey.htm.

Liu, A. Q., Hayes, J., Kile, J., Marable, J., Smith, K., & Kafouros, K. (2006). Poll: Little support for building a new arena, majority think the Sacramento Kings may leave the region in three years. California State University, Sacramento. Retrieved from http://www.csus.edu/ssis/documents/final%20kings%20report%2 04.pdf

Liu, A. Q., & Livingston, B. H. (2005). Affordable housing a serious challenge: Almost half can't buy new homes and one-third forced to consider relocation. California State University, Sacramento. Retrieved from http://www.csus.edu/ssis/ annual_survey.htm

Liu, A. Q., & Sheley, J. (2003). The full report for the 2003 annual survey of public opinion and life quality in the Sacramento region. California State University, Sacramento. Retrieved from http://www.csus.edu/ssis/documents/2003fullreport finalversion.doc

Liu, A. Q., & Sheley, J. (2004). The executive summary for the regional issues for the 2004 annual survey of public opinion and life quality in the Sacramento region. California State University, Sacramento. Retrieved from http://www .csus.edu/ssis/documents/2004ExecutiveSummaryfinalversion.doc

Liu, A. Q., & Sumati, L. (2005). Poll: Public says "no" to a new arena for the Sacramento Kings. California State University, Sacramento. Retrieved from http:// www.csus.edu/ssis/annual_survey.htm

Liu, A. Q., & Sumati, L. (2006). Poll: Majority of Sacramento residents support low-income housing ordinance, Thirty percent consider relocation. California State University, Sacramento. Retrieved from http://www.csus.edu/ssis/docu ments/final%20final%20housing%20report%202.pdf

Office of Federal Housing Enterprise Oversight. (2006). Housing price increases continue, some deceleration evident. Retrieved from http://www.ofheo.gov/ media/pdf/1q06hpi.pdf.

Sacramento Housing and Redevelopment Agency. (2006). *Sacramento County affordable housing ordinance.* Retrieved from http://www.shra.org/Content/Hous ing/HousingDevelopment/CountyAfford.htm

Schwartz, P. (2005). Sociology as public practice: Toward a better utilization of research and theory. Presidential address to the Pacific Sociological Association. *Sociological Perspectives, 48*(4), 423–431.

SPSS for Windows. Release 13. 2005. Chicago: SPSS Inc.

4

MAKING THE CENSUS COUNT

Learning, Service, and Political Engagement

Peter Tannenbaum and Sally Cahill Tannenbaum

"Data! Data! Data!" he cried impatiently.
"I can't make bricks without clay."

—Sherlock Holmes, *The Adventure*
of the Copper Beeches

As a subject of academic study, the census is grossly neglected—probably because it is a once-in-a-decade event. This neglect belies the fundamental role that the census plays in our nation's life. From governmental policy (federal, state, and local) to strategic planning in business, millions of decisions that significantly affect people's lives are made based on data collected through the decennial census. Although invisible, the census is as much a part of our nation's infrastructure as highways, bridges, and power lines. Moreover, a good case can be made that participation in the census is at least as important a form of political engagement as voting. The notion that every vote counts can be illusory—in many political elections this is not the case. On the other hand, it is an inescapable political and economic reality that every completed census form counts—and it does so for an entire decade.

Notwithstanding the critical importance of the census, there is a clear absence of any formal "census education" in our secondary schools and universities. As a consequence, there is a complex web of misunderstandings among the general public about the role the census plays in people's lives. Whether because of fear, ignorance, or indifference, groups that would gain the most (both economically and politically) from being counted by the census—minorities, migrant workers, the homeless, and so on—are the ones most reluctant to do so. As a result, the decennial census is a complex, unreliable, and incredibly expensive undertaking.[1]

The conception of this project was the result of serendipity and good timing. Peter Tannenbaum is a mathematician interested in the applications of mathematics to political issues, one of which is the indirect relation between the census and presidential elections (census data determines the apportionment of seats in the House of Representatives, which in turn determines the allocation of votes to states in the Electoral College). Sally Cahill Tannenbaum is a communication scholar with interests in political persuasion and campaign communication. In addition, she is the Service-Learning Faculty Scholar at California State University, Fresno (CSUF). Some timely discussions about the census led to the realization that the census sat at the interface of the authors' common interests, and that it provided a special opportunity to create a project that had the potential to be original in scope, substantive in content, and meaningful in its contributions to the community. Eventually, this led to the creation of the interdisciplinary course described herewith.

The course INTD (Interdisciplinary) 192S: Census 2000 was developed and offered in the spring semester of 2000 as an upper-division capstone course under the aegis of CSUF's New College for Instructional Innovation. The timing of the course was critical—the course ran parallel to the 2000 census, which officially kicks off on April 1 of each decennial year.

The guiding principle behind the design of the course was to combine solid academic content (statistics, political science, communication) with a relevant and important service to the community (Fresno and adjoining counties represent some of the most undercounted regions in the United States, and the service-learning opportunities were without parallel). The evidence collected by the authors indicates that the course was quite successful in achieving these goals.

Background

Every decade the U.S. government is constitutionally required to conduct the most ambitious data collection project on the face of the earth: the national census. Between April and June of each decennial year (1980, 1990,

2000, etc.), the U.S. Census Bureau tries to "capture" every man, woman, and child living (legally or not—it's irrelevant for census purposes) in the United States and record demographic data on each individual.

The most critical piece of information collected by the census is the head count, which is the basis for the population count of cities, counties, states, and the nation as a whole. The primary uses of population counts are: (a) to apportion the 435 seats in the House of Representatives among the states; (b) to draw congressional, state, and local voting districts; and (c) to allocate federal funds (approximately $180 billion a year) that are *formula driven* to state and local agencies. (Formula-driven funds are those that are allocated on the basis of some numerical criterion, rather than on the basis of need or merit. Census population data is one of the primary inputs for the computation of formula-driven funds.) In addition to the head count, the census collects more detailed demographic data about the U.S. population, including size of households, household income, education levels, and so on. This demographic data is used primarily by business and government to make planning and strategic decisions (Anderson & Fienberg, 1999; Steffey & Bradburn, 1994).

Notwithstanding the obvious political and economic impact of the census data, the data are far from accurate. Simply put, the census faces one fundamental obstacle in obtaining accurate counts: the unwillingness of people to be counted. For the 1990 census, the estimated undercount for the entire nation was 1.6 percent, for the state of California the estimated undercount was 2.7 percent, and *for Fresno County, the undercount was 3.4 percent* (U.S. Census Bureau Public Information Office, 1990). This means that there were an estimated 25,000 people in Fresno County that the 1990 census missed.

Course Objectives

Directly bearing on the census undercount phenomenon is *census ignorance* (a lack of understanding of the role of the census in people's everyday lives), and *census anxiety* (the belief that census data can actually be used to police and enforce illegal or criminal behaviors). Census ignorance and census anxiety are pervasive, even among educated people and college students (Anderson, 1990; Choldin, 1994). Thus, an important objective of the course (the *global* objective) was to teach the students about the historical, political, so-cial, economic, geographical, and statistical issues that surround the U.S. census. In particular, the instructors wanted students to understand and ap-preciate how important an accurate population count was for the nation as a whole, and for the people of Fresno and neighboring counties in particular. This objective was taught through readings, class lectures, and discussions with guest speakers. (For the course syllabus, see Appendix A.)

The second important course objective (the *local* objective) was to en-gage the students in a critical community service by taking leadership roles in the local Census 2000 Complete Count Campaign, part of a national ini-tiative aimed at achieving a more accurate census count, concentrating on the historically undercounted populations of Fresno County (migrant work-ers, minorities, and the homeless). The estimated 25,000 people in Fresno County missed by the 1990 census represented a loss of about $20 million a year to the local community in the form of formula driven, unallocated fed-eral funds. In fact, eight major programs depend on census numbers to dis-tribute federal funding—Medicaid, foster care, Rehabilitation Services Basic Support, Child Care and Development Block Grant, Social Services Block Grant, Substance Abuse Prevention and Treatment Block Grant, adoption assistance, and Vocational Education. (PricewaterhouseCoopers Census Study, 2001).

The flip side of these numbers is that every reluctant person who could be persuaded to fill out a census form represented a gain of about $800 a year in federal funds to the community, or $8,000 over the 10-year life of the census data. Thus, a 1 percent reduction of the undercount rate in Fresno County translates into a contribution of about $6.5 million a year to the county.

In addition to becoming missionaries for the campaign and helping the census acquire a more accurate local count, students in the course also real-ized other subtle benefits—their work fostered interaction between the uni-versity and the community partners, brought outside speakers onto campus, and provided the university with opportunities to share student expertise.

To accomplish a significant reduction in the undercount rate (a 1 percent to 1.5 percent reduction was set as the target) students were taught about effective campaign and public relation strategies and asked to design and complete service-learning projects with local area nonprofit agencies (a com-plete listing of the nonprofit Community Partner Agencies is given in Ap-pendix B). An added benefit of having students work with local nonprofits was that the relationships established contributed to an important aspect of the mission of CSUF—to become a nationally recognized "engaged university."

The final goal of the course was reflection and synthesis—the instructors felt that it was critical that students effectively synthesize the information learned in the course with their service experience. This goal was accomplished by having students give oral reports during the last half of the semester. In their oral presentations, students were asked to justify the project design, identify the target population, explain project logistics and execution, report results, and reflect on the success or failure of what they had done.

Course Organization and Implementation

In the first half of the semester (January through March), the course, taught by Peter Tannenbaum, focused on two separate but complementary areas. One area of study was the census itself. Here students studied the history of the U.S. Census and the role of the modern census including its social, political, legal, and economic implications. Lectures on the resampling techniques proposed by the U.S. Census Bureau to control for differential undercount in the 2000 census were also included. The second area of study, taught by Sally Tannenbaum, dealt with issues related to organizing and directing grassroots public awareness campaigns. Areas of emphasis included strategic planning, campaign management, audience analysis, public relations, campaign finances, and outreach. Topics covered included public speaking skills, target marketing, advertising themes and modalities, creation of public service announcements, press releases, television and radio spots, and formulation of community partnerships.

In the second half of the course (March through May) students were placed with community partners to spearhead a project designated by the local Census 2000 Complete Count Campaign—a national initiative aimed at achieving a more accurate census count. Students were placed with a large variety of agencies, including 21 nonprofits; in particular, students worked with organizations that serve immigrant populations, such as the Centro La Familia, Hmong Youth Foundation, Khmer Society of Fresno, Lao Community Development, Vietnamese Association of the Central Valley, Sikh Temple, Hindu Temple, and South Pacific Islander Organization. Students also worked with government agencies that were set up specifically to address the census (such as the California Complete Count Campaign Committee and the Fresno census office), with local school districts (such as the Fresno County Office of Education and the Tulare County Office of Education), and with local radio and television stations that serve second-language populations in the Central Valley of California. Each student was expected to assume a significant role in his or her assigned community partner's "complete count" activities. (A complete list of student activities and Community Partner Agencies involved is provided in Appendix B.)

Throughout their fieldwork with the community, students were expected to keep journals detailing accounts of their activities and noting personal reflections on their experiences. During this period, the class met only once a week for the purposes of reporting back and troubleshooting. Finally, in the last few weeks of the semester, students gave oral presentations in which they provided detailed reports of the service they had completed, reflected on their own growth during the project, and evaluated whether they thought their work was a success and why. Students also turned in their journals at this time.

Course Outcomes

As discussed in the Course Objectives section on p. 55, the instructors had two different types of goals for the course: *global* objectives (to give students a solid academic introduction to a subject rarely offered in the college curriculum), and *local* objectives (to involve the students in an important local project that provided a unique contribution to their community). The successful blending of these objectives was the ultimate test of how well the course met its identity as a service-learning course.

Our claim that both global and local objectives were successfully accomplished and blended is based on the following observations and facts:

- The first global objective was to have the students become educated on the census itself. This included the historical, political, social, economic, geographical, and statistical issues surrounding the census, as well as the impact of the census on Fresno and neighboring counties—a region that is rural, ethnically diverse, and grossly undercounted. Students successfully demonstrated that they had acquired a solid knowledge on the various aspects of the census through class examinations and oral reflections.

- A second global objective was to teach the students the fundamental principles of social marketing and the general issues involved in developing a grassroots public awareness campaign that focused on (a) the importance of educating the audience about the benefits of participation, (b) the importance of maintaining confidentiality, and (c) the importance of targeting populations that would gain the most from being counted (minorities, migrant workers, the homeless, etc.). Students demonstrated a thorough understanding of the principles of social marketing through class examinations, discussions, oral presentations, and most important, through the success of their individual service-learning experiences. Many of the students in the course assumed leadership roles in their chosen community-based organizations, and, in most cases, took on the role of "census expert" within the organization. Some of the students were asked to give census presentations to community organizations, some created press releases and flyers, some were interviewed by the media, and others were involved in the training of volunteer workers. Every student designed and implemented at least one activity that incorporated the marketing strategies learned in class (see Appendix B).

- A key measure of the success of the service-learning course was how students and community agencies retrospectively felt about the service experience. On both accounts, all reports were overwhelmingly positive. In their final oral presentations—where students were required to evaluate the impact of the work they did with their assigned community agency—the two consistent themes that emerged were (a) pride in their accomplishments and contributions to the community, and (b) the quality of their learning experience. The feedback the authors received from the local community agencies regarding the contributions of the students in the course was also overwhelmingly positive.

- As the saying goes, the proof of the pudding is in the eating. The actual target of reducing the Fresno County undercount by 1.5 percent was successfully met. The final 2000 census report on Fresno County (unfortunately delivered in March 2001—almost a year after the course was over—estimated the number of undercounted individuals in the county at 3 percent, a significant improvement over the 1990 census estimated undercount of 5 percent. In fact, the census indicated that the population of Fresno County had grown by 19.8 percent from 1990 to 2000. (*California Capitol Hill Bulletin*, 2001) By no means do the authors claim that credit for the 2 percent reduction in the local undercount figures should go solely to the work of the students in the course, but there is no question that the students played a significant role in this success story.

Recommendations and Observations

Issue-oriented courses provide tremendous opportunities for combining solid academic learning with meaningful and rewarding community-service opportunities. Such courses also present unique and daunting challenges. The fundamental question seems to be whether the ultimate rewards for setting up such a course justifies the initial investment. The answer, in our opinion, is in the original planning.

Based on our experience, the following are necessary (but not sufficient) elements for the success of such a course:

1. The course should run on a semiregular basis—at least once every two years. There is too much of an initial investment in organizing and planning for a course of this type, and if the course is offered infrequently then the up-front costs do not justify the benefits. (The authors were fortunate that they received release time for planning and developing the course materials from the New College for Instructional Innovation at CSUF.)

2. Instructors should develop extensive contacts and work closely with local community-based agencies. Contact between the instructor(s) and the community-based agencies should be ongoing.

3. The proper matching of students with community-based agencies and of community-based agencies with projects is essential. Student, instructor, and agency should all be involved in the process.

4. When appropriate, instructor(s) should work in partnership with local, state, and/or federal agencies. In general, governmental agencies have resources and expertise that local community agencies cannot match. In the case of the census course, the collaboration and

resources provided by the local census office was critical to the success of the course.

Conclusion

It appears at first blush that because of its very nature as a service-learning course, this course can effectively run in conjunction only with an actual census, and thus, can be offered only once every 10 years. The authors would like to submit, however, that both theme and model are separately sustainable. A multidisciplinary course about the U.S. Census without the community service element could be offered on a regular basis, and possibly rotated around different departments (political science, economics, etc.) This course might serve as the foundation for it (Gregory, 2001). More important, the authors contend that the model of an issue-based multidisciplinary course having a community service element can be applied to many other issues of local significance. The authors believe that the fundamental global and local goals of this course are portable and can be applied to other public interest, issue-oriented opportunities such as urban planning, global warming, urban beautification and reforestation, environmental problems such as water or air pollution, and in a more general setting, to local politics and political campaigns.

Thus, the authors believe that this course can serve as a model for similar issue-oriented service-learning courses in the future.

Note

1. The total cost of the 2000 census was $6.5 billion. (Social Science Data Analysis Network, 2001).

References

Anderson, M. J. (1990). *The American census: A social history*. New Haven, CT: Yale University Press.

Anderson, M. J., & Fienberg, S. E. (1999). *Who counts: The politics of census-taking in contemporary America*. New York: Russell Sage Foundation.

California Capitol Hill Bulletin. (2001). Census finally releases state's 2000 numbers. Washington, DC: California Institute for Federal Policy Research.

Choldin, L. M. (1994). *Looking for the last percent: The controversy over census under-counts.* New Brunswick, NJ: Rutgers University Press.

Gregory, M. (2001). *After the votes are counted: A post-election guide to maintaining college student civic engagement.* Providence, RI: Campus Compact.

PricewaterhouseCoopers Census Study. (2001). Census 2000 undercount could cost state billions. Retrieved from http://govinfo.library.unt.edu/cmb/cmbp/reports/080601.pricewaterhouse/state enh.asp.htm

Social Science Data Analysis Network. (2001). Retrieved from http://www.census scope.org/

Steffey, D. L., & Bradburn, N. M. (Eds.). (1994). *Counting people in the information age.* Washington, DC: National Academy Press.

U.S. Census Bureau Public Information Office, 1990 Census Information. Retrieved from http://factfinder.census.gov/servlet/DatasetMainPageServlet?_ds_name = DEC_1990_STF1_&_program = DEC&_lang = en

Appendix A

Syllabus

INTD 192 S: CENSUS 2000
An Issue-Oriented, Multidisciplinary Service-Learning Course

SPRING 2000

Tuesdays 5:00 p.m.–7:50 p.m.
Family & Food Sciences 210

Instructors:	Peter Tannenbaum	Sally Cahill Tannenbaum
	Department of Mathematics	Department of Communication
	Peters Business Bldg., Rm. 343	Speech Arts, Rm. 36
	278-4029	278-5404
	petert@csufresno.edu	sallyt@csufresno.edu

GENERAL COURSE DESCRIPTION

INTD 192S (also listed as S SCI 192S) is a new interdisciplinary course offered for the first time during spring 2000. INTD 192S counts toward the new upper-division GE Integration requirement in area D and also satisfies the community service designation (S) approved by the university.

The subject of INTD 192S is the U.S. Census, particularly the 2000 census that will start right in the middle of the spring semester. In the first part of the course we will cover the historical, social, economic, and political implications of the census, as well as issues related to the organization and implementation of a public awareness campaign (i.e., public relations, media, grassroots organizing, the role of CBOs, etc.) One of the unique features of the course is that it also involves a substantial community service component. During the second half of the course, students will be expected to take leadership roles in organizing and implementing a communitywide effort to achieve an accurate census count in their community.

COURSE OUTLINE
Week 1
- Introduction to the course.
- General introduction to the census and its role in American life.

Week 2
- History of the U.S. Census.
- The national Complete Count effort.
- Guest speaker: Richard Flores, U.S. Census Bureau, community/government partnerships specialist.

Week 3
- Economic implications of the census.
- The "differential" undercount and its implications.
- Guest speaker: Alan Peters, chairman, Fresno County Complete Count Committee.

Week 4
- Political implications of the census.
- Redistricting and its implications.
- The apportionment of the U.S. House of Representatives.
- Guest speaker: Tom Bohigian, regional director, Sen. Barbara Boxer's Office.

Week 5
- The local scene: Complete Count efforts in Fresno and adjacent counties.
- The role of community-based organizations (CBO's).
- Guest speakers: Alice Rocha, services coordinator, Valley Catholic Charities, and Jeff Ponting, executive director, California Rural Legal Assistance.

Week 6
- Political campaigns: organization and strategies.
- Guest speaker: Carolina de Soto, Outreach coordinator, California Complete Count Committee.

Week 7
- Complete Count implementation campaigns at the national, state, and local level.
- Outreach/training activities.
- Guest speaker: Diane Berry, regional director, U. S. Census Bureau.

Week 8
- The Ins and Outs of social marketing.
- Targeting specific audiences.

- Advertising themes and modalities.
- Creating public service announcements.
- Creating press releases and TV spots.
- Guest speaker: Eva Torres, associate director, Radio Bilingue.

Week 9
- The census in the schools.
- Guest speaker: Robert Segura, outreach coordinator, Fresno County Office of Education.

Week 10
- Census data in Geographical Information Systems (GIS).
- Guest speaker: Kathy Moffitt, director, Interdisciplinary Spatial Information Systems (ISIS) Center, CSU Fresno.

Weeks 9–13
- Community service fieldwork.

Weeks 14–16
- Reflection and dicussion.
- Class presentations and reports.

GRADING

- Attendance and class participation: 10%
- Four quizzes: 20%
- Implementation Plan: 20%
- Final report: 20%
- Community Service Evaluation: 30%

SELECTED READINGS:

Anderson, M. J. (1990). *The American census: A social history.* New Haven, CT: Yale University Press.

Anderson, M. J., & S. E. Fienberg. (1999). *Who counts: The politics of census-taking in contemporatry America.* New York: Russell Sage Foundation.

Choldin, L. M. (1994). *Looking for the last percent: The controversy over census undercounts.* New Brunswick, NJ: Rutgers University Press.

Steffey, D. L., & N. M. Bradburn (Eds.). (1994). *Counting people in the information age.* Washington, DC: National Academy Press.

Appendix B

Community Partner Agencies and Corresponding Activities

Activities varied. School activities included Census Information Centers at back-to-school nights and parent meetings and rallies at 21 schools. Underrepresented populations were targeted at local events, festivals, parades, and cultural centers. Information flyers were inserted with utility bills and statements from local banks. Radio Bilingue sponsored a number of programs on the census targeting different language groups. The local Panhellenic council distributed information to 26 fraternities and sororities on the CSU Fresno campus.

Fresno Census Office
   Hired and oversaw 1,300 outreach workers
   Participated in Homeless Outreach Day
   Manned Question-and-Answer Centers
   Assisted with Enumeration
   Conducted Follow-Up Interviews

Radio Bilingue
   Participated in Mariachi Festival
   Designed and produced Public Service Announcements
   Worked Question-and-Answer Centers
   Created Computer Data Bank
   Managed Census Booth at Regional Roeding Park
   Distributed information at Cambodian New Year Festival
   Answered questions at Faith Leadership Breakfast
   Distributed materials at Media Breakfast

KBIF Radio
   Inserted Census Information into Morning Agriculture Reports
   Designed and produced Public Service Announcements for Southeast
      Asian Communities

Assemblywoman Sarah Reyes Outreach
   Provided public speakers for Town Coffees
   Helped orchestrate local events for Census 2000 Strategy Committee
   Wrote Press Releases

Area Religious/Ethnic Agencies
Provided speaker for Asian Pacific Islander Organization Conference
Presented panel at Southeast Asian Crop Production Seminar
Informed participants on Asian Bus Tour
Manned Walmart Information Booth
Distributed materials at Chicano Youth Conference
Provided speakers at Sikh Temple Events
Helped hand out information at Visalia Chinese New Year Festival
Manned Fresno Chinese Gospel Church Information Booth
Provided information booths at Hindu Temple Events
Distributed materials at Selma Flea Market
Manned table at St John's Cathedral Information Distribution
Provided speaker for Fresno Downtown Club
Delivered presentation to Kiwanis
Provided bilingual speaker to Fresno Hispanic Chamber of Commerce
Delivered bilingual speech to Manteca Town Meeting
Presented talk to Beta Alpha Psi Accounting Fraternity

SECTION TWO

PROVIDING A BUSINESS PERSPECTIVE TO POLITICAL ENGAGEMENT

5

THE ECONOMICS OF COMMUNITY ACTION

Applying Cost-Benefit Analysis to Local Public Policy

Greg Hunter

An Overview of the Discipline's Perspective

The perspective of the economics profession on social issues is captured in the Pareto Criterion (Varian, 1992), which claims that one state of society should be preferred to another if, and only if, at least one member of society in the preferred state is better off and no member of society is worse off than he or she would be in the alternative state. This partial ordering of social states is the linchpin of modern welfare economics, the study of how resource allocation mechanisms affect the well-being of society. As one might guess, the Pareto Criterion, in its purest form, does not reveal a great deal about the impact of public policy on society. It does, however, give a starting point for developing an operational criterion for evaluation. And, it also points an evaluator toward an important question that needs to be resolved before an operational criterion can be selected. Namely, how does one properly consider the well-being of an individual?

Economists have argued that only nonpaternalistic measures of individual welfare should be used in comparing social states. In essence, this principle implies that the individual is the best judge of his of her own well-being. The Hicks-Kaldor Potential Compensation Test (Head, 1974), which is the intellectual prototype of the modern cost-benefit test, combines the principle of nonpaternalism with the Pareto Criterion. The Hicks-Kaldor Potential

Compensation Test claims that one social state should be preferred to another if and only if the sum of the payments collectible from those who benefit from the preferred social state can fully compensate those individuals who suffer a loss from the preferred state, whether the payments are made or not. Modern cost-benefit analysis of public policy deals with how best to calculate the sum of benefits and costs that would potentially flow to individuals if the state of society (i.e., the distribution of resources) was changed under a particular policy alternative. Policy decisions, then, are a matter of simply choosing the alternative that creates the greatest aggregate net benefit. There are, of course, distributional equity considerations. Economists typically profess no particular skill in determining how best to distribute the gains from a policy that results in an aggregate net benefit for society. Though the discipline does argue that any time an unrealized aggregate net benefit persists there is potential for every member of society to gain by simply allowing the gain to be realized and then sharing the gain among all members.

The Class in Action

In most practical applications of cost-benefit analysis to public policy, the number of policy alternatives considered is small, which makes the task of evaluation considerably easier. And, it is this down-to-earth and thorough examination of a few well-defined alternatives against a status quo policy that provides the structure this course is built around (see Appendix A). The course has three major components that divide the term into three distinct periods. The first component of the course focuses on an understanding of cost-benefit theory and its application to a hypothetical cost-benefit problem. The second component of the course concentrates on understanding the informational needs of the community partner working with the class vis-à-vis public policies affecting the community partner and designing and implementing a cost-benefit study that meets the needs of the community partner within the constraints of the class. The last component of the course produces a written document that explains the results of the students' cost-benefit study and helps the community partner synthesize the information so that it can be used to improve decisions made by the community partner.

The Partner

From an instructor's point of view, probably the most exciting aspect of this course is the wide range of topics the class design can be applied to and the equally broad range of community organizations that can serve as partners. In the past, students have worked with two partners and I imagine they will work with many more in the future. The first partner, an organization called the Rowland Heights Community Coordinating Council (RHCCC), is a concerned citizens' group representing the unincorporated area of Los Angeles County known as Rowland Heights. The second partner, the Norwalk-LaMirada Unified School District (NLMUSD), is an organization that coordinates the budgetary, administrative, and curricular needs for 21,000 students in Los Angeles County. The common characteristic these community partners share (and one that would be shared with an ideal community partner for similar classes) is that both partners desire to deviate from a status quo policy. In the case of RHCCC, the council was debating a proposal to incorporate, forming a new city in L.A. County. The NLMUSD board of education was considering whether it should consolidate some of the 17 elementary schools in the district. In both cases, the organizations were concerned about how to characterize the impact of the proposed policy changes for community stakeholders. Coincidentally, both of these organizations were instituted to serve the public interest. As a result, the public-interest role of the partner meant that the work of the students served a large number of stakeholders within the affected communities. While having organizations that serve the public interest is not a necessary feature for this course, my experience is that public-interest organizations make ideal partners. Public institutions are particularly plentiful, easy to work with, and often in need of the type of service provided by this class.

The Students

The students in the class play the role of the partner's economic consultant. There are two aspects to the students' role: analyst and liaison/interpreter. To facilitate communication between the class and the community group and to build the students' liaison/interpreter identity, I arrange three face-to-face meetings between the class and the partner.

The first meeting is a meet-and-greet session where the students explain the general approach of cost-benefit analysis to public policy issues. The session is also an opportunity for the students to ask about the partner's in-the-trenches view of the policy proposal and its consequences. By the end of the first meeting, I am left with a clear sense that the students are beginning to understand the hand wringing that policy debates cause among stakeholders and policy makers. For example, in the case of NLMUSD, my students discovered that school consolidation was a euphemism for school closure. They also learned that premature consolidation could be very costly and lead to overcrowding—both of which are weighty issues.

The second meeting is primarily an opportunity for a progress report. At this stage, students explain the study design to the partner and ask for feedback. It is important for the partner to feel like there is some give-and-take in the design process and, more specifically, that the study design will meet the partner's needs. The meeting also sets expectations about the final product the class will deliver. It is important at this stage to set reasonable expectations that take into account the time and resource constraints of the class. Typically, the community partner will be starved for the kind of information the class is attempting to provide. However, the class is not a full-service consulting firm with an unlimited budget. In fact, in both of the cases previously mentioned, my classes were able to propose pilot studies that gave detailed outlines of how a full-blown study would be conducted, illustrate data collection methods, and explain analytical techniques.

The third meeting is scheduled for the end of the term and gives the students an opportunity to explain the results of their investigation and answer questions raised by the community partner. The meeting begins with a formal presentation by the students that summarizes the contents of their written report. Ideally, a draft of the presentation and the report is distributed to the community partner a few days before the presentation. Allowing the community partner an opportunity to review the students' penultimate draft prior to the students' presentation helps the partner formulate thoughtful questions and express any concerns about the students' findings during the last meeting. Ensuring the community partner understands what the students have done is the primary objective of this meeting.

In addition to the three meetings, the students are in frequent contact with the partner. Most of the communication between the partner and students deals with students requesting information from the partner. These information requests are typically used to help students identify and find data or to sort out details about the policy proposal that require clarification. In the case of RHCCC, for example, the students required more information on how incorporation would take place upon adoption of the proposal. Specifically, cities in L.A. County have the option to contract for public services with the county. So, before the students could begin to investigate the consequences of incorporation, they needed to know if the newly proposed city of Rowland Heights would continue to use the police and fire service currently provided by L.A. County or would need to begin building its own emergency services. In both the meetings and the extemporaneous communications, the students explain and act as facilitator for the community partner—what I refer to as the liaison/interpreter role. Behind the scenes, the class is also planning the study and carrying it out—what I refer to as the analyst role.

Analyst Survey Design

The Partner

In this model for applied cost-benefit analysis, the partner also plays two roles: information consumer and policy case study. The main benefits to the partner come from consuming the information generated by the class. To provide maximum benefit to the partner from the experience, the students and, to some extent, the instructor have to take care in explaining what the information means and what it does not mean. For example, in the case of the RHCCC, as part of its analysis, the class conducted a contingent valuation survey to demonstrate how to place a value on "local control" of public services. The results of the survey, which was taken from 54 randomly selected residents from a population of about 40,000, suggested that there would be a net benefit to incorporation. The partner was cautioned that while the results were statistically significant, one had to be careful about extrapolating because of the small sample size.

As an aside, most students are surprised—as am I—to see the reaction of decision makers once there is a number. Despite warnings and caveats, there is a tendency for the number, rather than the methodology behind the number, to become a focus of discussion. It is also interesting for me to see students analyzing the sensitivity of their number with a heightened intensity once they realize its importance to decision makers. The partner also benefits from playing the role of a real-life case study. The benefit derived from being a case study might be compared to the benefits associated with independent oversight of government. The students bring an inquisitive, innocent perspective to discussions of policy consequences and alternatives. The questions they ask and the discussions they inspire among policy stakeholders are the sort of impetus needed for good collective decision making.

The Learning Experience

The primary objective of using a service-learning pedagogy to teach applied cost-benefit analysis is to allow students the chance to develop awareness about how analysis can direct policy. This learning outcome is elegantly achieved through the interaction between the class and the community partner when students realize that the partner is deeply interested in the results of their analysis.

A secondary objective is for the students to develop awareness of the fragility of their results. This objective can be clarified by looking at the activities used in class to design and conduct the study. The first activity is a set of readings, discussions, and lectures held in class. The readings are taken from a manual authored by the Canadian Secretariat of the Treasury titled *Benefit-Cost Analysis Guide* (Treasury Board of Canada Secretariat, 1998). The manual is superb because it explains the importance of the theoretical underpinnings of cost-benefit analysis but does not dwell on them.

Students read most of the manual in preparation for their first meeting with the community partner and use it to develop a list of discussion questions for the meeting. The manual emphasizes five concepts that are essential to the second learning objective: point of view, discounting, benefit estimation, uncertainty, and choosing a cost-benefit criterion. Each of these concepts defines one of the smaller learning objectives for the class.

The point-of-view concept captures the idea that measuring costs and benefits for a group depends critically on who is included in the group—a cost from one person's point of view may be a benefit from another's. In the case of NLMUSD, the students struggled in deciding whether a teacher being laid off because of a school closure should be counted as a savings to the district or a cost to the community. Through discussion the students discovered that the answer is—it depends. If the study is being conducted from the district's fiscal perspective, then salaries are a cost. If the study is being conducted from a community perspective and the teacher lives in the community, then salaries are not necessarily a cost unless the expenditure represents an unwise use of the district's budget, given the other priorities of the community.

The students' progress toward learning the secondary objective also depends critically on the development of an appreciation for how discounting cash flows over time is accomplished. Once the general formula for calculating net present value (NPV) is presented and students begin to understand how the results of the calculation depend on the discount rate chosen by the analyst, they are in a wonderful position to lead an engaging discussion with the community partner. Typically, the pattern for the discussion is as follows: The students explain the formula and its sensitivity to the discount rate to the partner; the students then ask for guidance and discover that there is no natural choice for a discount rate. Students soon realize that the only prudent course of action is to choose a few "reasonable" rates and see how the NPV calculation changes, and then present all the results to the partner.

Through the readings, discussions, and interaction with the partner, students also become aware that benefit estimation techniques are very important. The cost-benefit manual (Treasury Board of Canada Secretariat, 1998) of the Canadian Secretariat of the Treasury provides a short overview of benefit estimation techniques and emphasizes their purpose in the typical analysis of public policy. Benefit estimation comes to the fore when policy changes have intangible impacts on a community. These intangible impacts are associated with changes in the level of a nonpriced good, typically what economists refer to as a *public good.* In the case of the RHCCC, the class determined that "local control of public services" was a public good that would be increased if Rowland Heights became incorporated. As part of the class activities, the class designs and administers a contingent valuation survey to demonstrate to the community partner how intangible benefits and costs are estimated.

The fourth component of the secondary objective is for students to understand how uncertainty affects the analysis. The service-learning pedagogy is ideal for bringing the issue of uncertainty immediately to the surface. In fact, uncertainty is so common when working with a real-life case study that most students—particularly the stronger students—need to be warned up front. Students, in conducting their analysis, will need data on costs and benefits that are hard to find and often need to be estimated. Policy proposals will have impacts on a community that take place over years and even if data for the recent past are available, the question of how to project those series forward arises. A great example comes from the NLMUSD school closure proposal. A somewhat obvious and critical parameter in school closure is the student population growth rate. Students in my class found that a relatively modest change in assumptions about the growth rate had dramatic consequence for their analysis. As with the discount rate, students in a hands-on environment discover that considering a range of reasonable parameter values is essential for getting a clear picture of how a policy change will affect a community.

The last component of the secondary objective is the choice of cost-benefit criterion. The Canadian Secretariat manual (Treasury Board of Canada Secretariat, 1998) does a great job of highlighting flaws in criteria that are commonly used (other than the NPV criterion). Once students understand the NPV criterion, they have to evaluate whether they will consider a particular proposal in isolation or take a holistic view of the community's budget. If they decide to examine a particular project in isolation, then any project with a positive NPV should receive a recommendation. However, this assumes that the community has an infinite budget or a constant opportunity cost for money. Alternatively, if the budget of the organization is fixed, then all the independent projects of the organization should be considered and ranked according to NPV, and only those projects with the highest NPV should be funded. Taking a holistic view of the budget of a community organization can be daunting and my students have not attempted it. However, in considering the issue of how to apply the NPV criterion, students begin to realize that a positive NPV does not necessarily mean that the project is the wisest use of limited funds.

The assessment of these learning objectives is fairly straightforward. The class is a veritable cornucopia of opportunities for written assignment and presentations. I assign every student discussion, leadership, and presentation responsibilities, but in a class of over 20 students I can imagine that this might be difficult.

In addition, prior to the first meeting with the community partner and immediately after the basic assigned reading from the Canadian Secretariat manual (Treasury Board of Canada Secretariat, 1998), I assign a hypothetical cost-benefit case. The case is something simple, such as considering a proposal to purchase a new durable machine for use by a business. However, by having the students complete the case, I can directly verify whether every student understands the essence of NPV, discounting, uncertainty, and point of view. I also ask every student to contribute to the design of the contingent valuation survey. In particular, all students are asked to submit a question for the survey that will help in soliciting a respondent's value for the proposed policy changes. Finally, all the students contribute to the final report that is given to the community partner. Every student is assigned a subsection of the report and editorial responsibility for another subsection. Students are graded on the quality and clarity of their subsection, as well as their editorial suggestions.

Conclusion

Using service-learning pedagogy to teach cost-benefit analysis to upper-division economics students, and those in kindred disciplines, provides students with a unique and incredibly rich set of learning opportunities. Chief among these is the opportunity to learn about the debate over numbers that precedes most policy decisions. By learning how the cost-benefit numbers are calculated and dealing with the inherent uncertainty over these numbers, students are in a powerful position to engage in the political process in a way that is rarely used by the average citizen. The service-learning pedagogy allows community partners to play the role of a case study for public policy action and the role of an information consumer. In providing information that the community partner needs, students play the role of analyst and interpreter. The result is a more informed community, which lays the foundation for better policy.

As of the writing of this chapter, the final outcomes for the two community partners mentioned, the RHCCC and the NLMUSD, have yet to be determined. In part as a result of the study conducted by the class, the RHCCC decided to pursue additional funding for a more comprehensive and detailed study of the consequence of incorporating. The NLMUSD decided to do more in-house analysis of the budgetary effects of school consolidation. For the time being, the NLMUSD has postponed any school closings. To me, it seems that both of these community partners responded in a reasonable and predictable way to the information provided by the class. In essence, the partners realized more deeply that evaluating the impact of policy changes requires time and careful consideration—the key ingredients for community political engagement.

References

Head, J. G. (1974). *Public goods and public welfare.* Durham, NC: Duke University Press.

Treasury Board of Canada Secretariat. (1998). *Benefit-cost analysis guide.* Ottawa, Canada: Author.

Varian, H. (1992). *Microeconomic analysis.* New York: Norton.

Appendix A

Economics of Community Action Syllabus

Course Objectives:

The course is designed to achieve three learning outcomes. The first is for students to achieve a practical knowledge of economic cost-benefits theory. The second is for students to understand and be able to use the method of contingent-valuation to supply the information needed to conduct a cost-benefit study. The third is for students to understand how a cost-benefit study can inform and empower a community to make good public policy decisions. The following activities are designed to help students achieve these outcomes and give students an opportunity to demonstrate their achievement.

Activities:

1. Readings, lectures, and examination on cost-benefit theory: The student will be given reading assignments and a series of lectures on cost-benefit theory. The intention of these readings and lectures is to provide the student with the knowledge required to perform a hypothetical cost-benefit calculation and critically analyze the results of the calculation.

2. Readings, lectures, and examination on the method of contingent-valuation: The student will be given reading assignments and a series of lectures on the method of contingent-valuation. The objective of these readings and lectures is to provide the student with the knowledge required to design a contingent-valuation survey and critically analyze its design.

3. Designing and performing a cost-benefit study for a community-based organization: The student in conjunction with other members of the class will design and conduct a cost-benefit study of a public policy proposal for a community partner. The elements of this study will include a contingent-valuation survey and a report analyzing the results of the survey. The objective of these activities is to provide the student with a "hands-on" experience with cost-benefit analysis. As part of this objective, the student may be expected to participate in off-campus meetings.

4. Journals: During the class the student will be expected to keep a journal. The journal will be due on the day of the final exam. The journal entries must be typed. The entries should be approximately one double-spaced page per week with 12-point font and 1-inch margins. The entries should be dated by week. For example, the student should collect all the entries made during the first week of class under the heading "Week 1."

   a. In the journal the student should reflect on the learning objectives of the course, the student's progress in achieving the objectives, a note about impediments to the objectives, and possible solutions to the impediments. For example, the student during the first week of readings should have made progress on the objective of learning about cost-benefit theory. The progress (i.e., what was specifically learned) should be noted, as well as any difficulties with achieving the objective.

   b. In addition, during those activities involving group participation the student should make a special heading under "contributions to the group." Under this heading, the student should give an assessment of the contributions he or she made to the group.

Grades: The student's grade in the class will be determined by a weighted average of the grade received in each of the learning activities listed above. The weighting will be 10% for the first objective and 5% for the second. The third activity accounts for 70% of the student's grade. The journal entries account for 15% of the student's grade.

Attendance: Participation in off-campus meetings is mandatory because it is a core element of the third learning activity. If the student must miss any of these meetings, he or she will be required to provide documentation of a substantive cause for absence. Additionally, he or she will be assigned additional work in lieu of attendance.

6

SELECTED CASE EXAMPLES OF SERVICE LEARNING IN BUSINESS

Social Entrepreneurship in Action

Richard L. McCline and Gerald S. Eisman

There are those who argue that big businesses, profiting from "economies of scale," can produce far more efficiently than small businesses. But small business is where the innovations take place. Swifter, more flexible and often more daring than big businesses, small firms produce the items that line the shelves of America's museums, shops and homes. They keep intact the heritage of ingenuity and enterprise and they help keep the "American Dream" within the reach of millions of Americans.

—U.S. Small Business Administration, http://www.sba.gov/aboutsba/history/index.html

A sharp ideological divide exists in the nation on the role of government in supporting the creation and expansion of small businesses. At its worst, government—federal, state, and local—can present a confounding and sometimes contradictory collection of regulations that restrict business owners from developing successful enterprises that expand job opportunities and create new wealth in underserved communities. At its best, government can provide precisely the incentives and opportunities to make the difference in ensuring that a new business will survive. Whichever position individuals and institutions take on the role of government in promoting entrepreneurship, there are two undeniable truths all can agree on.

First, it is undeniable that small-business creation is the backbone of economic expansion in the United States today, and has been this backbone for the past 60 years. Research has shown that the number of small businesses has soared 75 percent in the last two decades alone, and we are now widely thought to be in the "age of the entrepreneur" as many business writers have labeled the 21st century. When owners and former owners are counted, about one in four adult Americans is now or has been self-employed at some time in his or her working career (Dennis, 2004; Timmons & Spinelli, 2006).

Second, it is virtually impossible to conceive of creating or operating a business without understanding the complexities of interactions that will occur with government agencies. Beyond the regulatory authority that dictates standards for health and safety, employee hiring and treatment, health care planning, minimum wage limits, environmental protections, and employment of immigrant workers, there is the reality that government contracting is the elephant in the room. Government agency procurement represents a vast opportunity for businesses to form and expand. Who, after all, builds most highways, railroads, and airports, runs the military, and builds levees, dams, and most of the hospitals and schools?

Government-based opportunity has been at the heart of economic expansion in challenging times and in challenged communities, and both national political parties have embraced the use of these opportunities at different times. The New Deal policies of Franklin Delano Roosevelt during the Great Depression are well known. From 1935 to 1943, the Works Progress Administration, for example, provided work for 8 million Americans, constructing schools, hospitals, and airfields. Perhaps lesser known is that it was none other than Republican President Richard M. Nixon who created the Office of Minority Business Enterprise (OMBE) in 1969, raised U.S. purchases from Black businesses from $9 million to $153 million (between 1969 and 1974), and increased small-business loans to minorities 1,000 percent (What Did Richard Nixon Have to do With Today's Black Middle Class? 2005). As odd as it might seem to some, Nixon is known as the first American president to put real meaning in the concept of Black capitalism.[1] As an aside, most small- and minority-business development programs trace their roots to the landmark principles embodied under OMBE. No business student's education can be complete without an examination of the multiple roles that government plays in the success of a business enterprise. At the Ohrenschall Center for Entrepreneurship (OCE) at San Francisco State University (SFSU) we have taken up this challenge by providing service-learning and community-based research opportunities for students to learn firsthand how important and effective the relationships with government can be. In doing so, we have modeled the behavior of entrepreneurs in our own actions, looking for new opportunities to engage our students in civic learning. SFSU has long embraced a mission of social justice, and the case studies in this chapter illustrate how students can experience how government support of business can support the goal of equitable opportunity for economic development.

The Role of Small Business in the Community

Entrepreneurship is the cornerstone of a free market economy. Research has shown that more than 460 million adults around the world currently are engaged in some form of entrepreneurship (Dennis, 2004). More than 850,000 new small businesses are started each year in this country with an estimated 27 million small businesses currently operating in the United States According to the Small Business Administration, small and medium businesses have created over two-thirds of the new jobs in the last decade and a half (Chao, 2007).

The numbers regarding minority- and women-owned businesses are impressive. Minority-owned businesses in the United States number some 3.25 million, generate an estimated $495 billion in revenue, and employ nearly four million workers (Young, 2002). A report from the U.S. Small Business Administration Office of Advocacy indicates that the number of Asian-owned businesses grew by 30 percent in the 1990s to 785,000. The growth in Hispanic-owned businesses equaled this increase and now numbers 1.1 million. Not far behind were African American-owned businesses that grew in number by more than 26 percent to reach more than 780,000 firms in that same time period. (U.S. Small Business Administration Office of Advocacy, 2001a).Women-owned businesses were slightly less dramatic in their growth, reflecting a growth rate of 16 percent in the 1990s, still more than twice the 6 percent experienced by all other small businesses in the United States (U.S.

Small Business Administration Office of Advocacy, 2001b). Entrepreneurship is one of those cultural phenomena that tend to penetrate all ethnic communities and seems to be popular, irrespective of gender.

The ownership picture of California small businesses reflects the significant diversity of the state. Minority-owned firms generated more than $196.5 billion in revenue. In the state, there were more than 427,000 Hispanic-owned businesses, more than 112,000 African American-owned businesses, more than 371,000 Asian- and Pacific Islander-owned businesses, and more than 38,000 American Indian- and Alaskan Native-owned businesses in 1997. Additionally, women-owned businesses made up one-third of California businesses and generated over $138 billion in revenues. Collectively, these small businesses, which are owned by traditionally underrepresented groups, contribute some $334.5 billion to the California economy and employ more than 2.3 million Californians (U.S. Small Business Administration Office of Advocacy, 2006).

The Role of Government in Promoting Small-Business Success—the Elephant in the Room

Government is at least partly to blame for the significant abuses of monopoly capitalism that helped power the U.S. economy in the late 19th and early 20th centuries. The so-called robber barons of the Industrial Revolution were extraordinarily effective entrepreneurs who used their skills to dominate large segments of the economy. Recounting the waves of legislation that have been enacted to try to prevent the abuses of early capitalism in this country is outside the scope of this chapter (see, for example, Grey, 1998; Roper & Cheney, 2005; Scranton, 1997). Suffice it to say that the government has become a permanent partner in regulating the marketplace and attempting to provide tools that slow down the monopolistic tendencies of large business. It is this legal legacy that prevails today and allocates an important role to government to be supportive and, at times, intimately involved in helping small businesses compete in the marketplace.

The ultimate goal of these regulations is to make the playing field of business fair for small and big businesses alike. An expected additional benefit of pro-small-business legislation and subsequent regulations is to provide communities with vital role models and change agents that can identify with local populations (Cornwall, 1998). The prevailing business model of the 21st century suggests that anyone affected by a business organization is indeed a stakeholder of that organization. It is expected that pro-small-business legislation will help realign the goals of the business community with those stakeholders who are the consumers in its society. Improved competition within the business community is expected to improve the economic benefits that accrue to the consumers of business activities in the society.

It is important to note that although the motivation of the government to intervene in the marketplace on behalf of small businesses is laudable, the results of these interventions often are uneven and inefficient. As Edgcomb and Klein (2005) observed, the "if we build it, they will come" mentality among government program officers has been less effective than hoped. The management consulting firm Grant Thornton commented that 80 percent of the respondents in its survey of some 250 small businesses identified reduced government regulation as the change that would provide the biggest benefit to their individual venture (Kuratko, Hornsby, & Naffziger, 1999). This is true largely because many, if not most, small-business owners have difficulty finding the time to participate in governmental programs that are overly complex. Kuratko et al. suggest that the typical government program of management and technical assistance designed to serve small businesses only reaches about one in eight targeted businesses. Few small businesses have the resources to deal with the 65,000 pages of new or modified government regulations each year and the 50 or so different agencies with some 120,000 employees that attempt to apply these often complex rules. According to a recent survey, most small businesses with employees are open for their customers about 11 hours every day; some 6 percent are open 24 hours a day. All this makes participation in a government program very difficult to fit into an already long day, even when the benefits of the program are well understood (Baron & Shane, 2005; Kuratko et al., 1999).

As Kuratko et al. (1999), noted, "The differential effect of public policy issues on small business is becoming increasingly important as the nation looks to these businesses for continued growth and job creation" (p. 82). The dilemma of balancing a free-market-based economy with the recognition that some in the society cannot fend for themselves with any sense of fairness in outcome has open[ed] "the door for the *social entrepreneur*, that is, institutions and individuals who use the philosophy and tools of free market businesses to offset the potential for abuses (unintended or intended) that might be incurred by less-adaptive segments of the society" (p. 82).

Social Responsibility and Business Education: The OCE's Role as a Social Entrepreneur

The teaching of entrepreneurship in the majority of business schools in the United States is one of the indications of the importance of this subject to the business community and the nation at large. According to Timmons & Spinelli (2006), the number of business schools that teach at least one course in entrepreneurship has increased from 100 in the 1970s to more than 1,500 in 2004. This indicates significant institutional recognition of the importance of small business to our culture and economy.

A key element in the mission statement of the OCE at SFSU is the commitment to orient our students to a socially responsible philosophy while we share and teach the important business and behavior characteristics of successful entrepreneurs. A key component of our program is an emphasis on learning how government works.

As suggested by Sagawa and Segal (2000) and Hemingway (2005), there is a potential to pair the individual entrepreneurial spirit and institutional energy located in the university's business school (or any unit of instruction for that matter) with mission-oriented public agencies that seek to promote the common constituencies of the business school and the respected public agency. The OCE is therefore positioned as a social entrepreneur, suggesting a new and intriguing paradigm that bridges the gap between the entrepreneurial behavior and thinking patterns fostered in the classroom and the public-sector issues that beg for new and innovative thinking.

Social entrepreneurs bring that creative spark as an antecedent to the innovative practices that perhaps *frame* social issues in ways that fall outside classical, regulatory, rational models. As Roper and Cheney (2005) note, there is no inherent alienation among entrepreneurship, public policy, and market regulations. The combination of government's regulatory frame and entrepreneurship's innovative frame suggests social entrepreneurship as a potentially powerful force to the benefit of those targeted but yet underserved by existing market-leveling regulations.

The OCE consciously involves students in an extensive mix of external activities with the entrepreneurial community. A focus on *experiential learning* (e.g., internships, community service-learning projects that give academic credit for socially responsible work, and consulting support on projects related to the growth and development of the small businesses/entrepreneurial community) in combination with classroom reading and lecture work is considered to be among the best-practices element of excellent entrepreneurship programs (Gibb, 1994).

The *partnership* that characterizes the relationship between the OCE and its counterpart public entity is in reality an exchange relationship. The students exchange their business and academic skills for real-world experiences in understanding how the interface between business and government works. That knowledge-sharing process actually puts together two public assets: (a) the OCE, which is based in a publicly supported university, and (b) the particular public agency targeted by the community service activity. This collaboration works to advance issues of mutual interest to the two entities. This concept leverages public sector dollars and enhances the economic vitality of the communities served by the partnership. The students learn to appreciate how government is mission driven, and the public sector partners benefit from the results-focused orientation of participating students and faculty. Sagawa and Segal (2000) suggest that the outcome is really a *new* public good: a sense of shared responsibility among the partners for the benefit of a shared constituency.

OCE is perhaps more active and *mission driven* as an academic partner by also engaging students as advocates and consultants to help reach elements of the community who might otherwise be underserved by perhaps well-intended government programs. One important consequence of involving students in the partnership is to provide that experiential component of their education that includes giving back. Students receive stipends and/or credits for their energy and work efforts, but also see how these economic benefits to them personally can be very compatible with community benefits; these experiences of the students are designed to become real-world examples of the old saw "Doing well while doing good" that is typically the essence of social entrepreneurship.

Teaching Students How to Engage Government and Interact with Small Business Through Service Learning

Although the academic literature on small-business and government policy is sparse, a select few authors have commented on the subject. Kuratko et al. (1999) reported that Cook and Barry found that the complexity of government policy was a major problem that confronted small-business owners, and Bahls (1994) noted that government regulations were a negative factor affecting their performance. Moini (1998) commented on the lack of awareness among small-business owners of programs that might be of benefit to their business operations. Our review of the selected literature suggests that academics have infrequently explored the nexus between small business and government.

In this section, we make modest contributions to this void by highlighting specific examples of how government policies can be made friendlier to the small-business community. We also share practical examples of the OCE enacting the model of social entrepreneurship that embraces the key aspects of community service learning. In each case, the courses students enrolled in were independent study courses offered by the management department. Students conducted community-based research and were required to write summary papers and make oral presentations on their findings that became part of the compiled report. The initial screening of students was a determination of availability and interest in doing independent study work that would take place outside the classroom. Students then were selected for participation in the projects based upon an *expressed* interest in the community, enthusiasm for the effort required to meet the needs of the sponsoring agency, and a track record of academic performance. Critical for replication purposes, no special skills or experience in community-based research was required of the students. Faculty provided the initial expertise in terms of understanding the scope of work and then assumed the responsibility of teaching the students the subset of skills that were important to ensure the quality of the final product. It is the nature of community service-learning projects, in the examples presented below, that faculty take the lead and allow students to benefit from the project *both* as a learning experience and as an opportunity to assist in making a positive impact on the community targeted by the project on behalf of the sponsoring agencies. Faculty also must be careful to clarify with each agency that students typically work on a semester timeline. The initial scope of work must include a work calendar that accommodates the semester timeline and yet does not compromise the needs of the sponsoring agency. This is an important issue that must be established comfortably with the agency before the project is accepted by the faculty member.

Entrepreneurial thinking is exemplified in the innovative frame the OCE applied to issues that were in the mission of the respective public sector partner. In each case, the OCE was focused on finding ways to invigorate, inform, and improve the viability of the small-business/entrepreneurial communities.

Mini Case Number 1: Procurement at the Port of Oakland

The Port of Oakland, like most public agencies, must open all procurement contracts to public bid. The port in recent years has put out to bid billions of dollars in contract opportunities. The port is unique in that it has an entire Division of Social Responsibility that makes it possible for businesses owned by underrepresented groups (women/minority-owned business enterprises [WMBEs]) to bid on these contracts. Cornwall (1998) commented on the unique potential of WMBEs to have a broader impact on the disadvantaged communities, largely because they tend to locate in and hire their employees from these local communities. Etzioni (1993) also captured this sentiment by noting that entrepreneurs have been historically and continue to be a significant force for (re)building poor and low-income communities. Thus, the society at large has strong reasons to be invested in supporting the growth and ongoing viability of small businesses that are owned by women and minorities. WMBEs do have considerable presence in the marketplace, yet, all too often contracts go to large contractors that are oftentimes not even local, thus depleting the local economy of an infusion of capital that would, were it to stay local, be respent several times over.

The port has felt compelled to adopt policies to encourage awarding contracts to small, local businesses. For example, it provides additional points to bids that include local businesses as subcontractors on at least 10 percent of the contract. The challenge is to match primary contractors with local secondary contractors that have the capability to contribute to a large job.

For this project, the team capitalized on the student members' computer science training to help develop the Internet Bid Opportunity (IBO), a sophisticated Internet-based tool that matched small businesses with specific terms of the bid documents that were developed by the port engineering staff.

Microsoft reports that some 93 percent of small businesses use PCs, but very few have used the PC to generate business leads, and therefore small businesses often fail to appreciate the economic impact that this ubiquitous piece of technology infrastructure can have on their business.

Social sector organizations need to be aware of the "technology have-nots" that are in danger of falling out of the new economy, which is driven by Internet-based contract opportunities. These organizations benefit from the intervention of other public sector institutions (e.g., OCE) that have a commitment to bring the small-business community into the Internet age. Without such intervention, small businesses, especially those owned by minorities, which historically operate with significantly less information technology (IT) sophistication than their nonminority counterparts (Cole & Robinson, 2002; National Telecommunications and Information Administration and the Economics and Statistics Administration, 2002), are most likely to miss important contract opportunities.

In addition to the more technical contribution from the IT students, engineering students helped decompose the engineering drawing and specs into key words understood by the business owners. These key words could be searched within the contract and used to match specific qualifications of the prospective small-business contractor. Finally, the business school students who participated in this project served as liaisons to the small-business owners. They helped them develop their qualification statements, input the statements into the matching tool, and see the importance of the link between PC capabilities, in combination with Internet access, to business growth and efficiency. Nothing captures the interest of small-business owners like the chance to see new and incremental business opportunities while they sit at their own desks at any time of the day.

A primary outcome of the IBO project was the potential to have minimal *friction* (to use another Microsoft reference) in developing new business leads for small businesses in the San Francisco Bay Area specifically, and the state in general. Equally important, students had an opportunity to use their disciplinary skills to help promote business growth among an underserved component of the small-business community. Given the importance of small businesses to the California economy, project students also had a chance to see how the political process can generate well-intentioned policies that may not have an impact on the targets as envisioned (without other incremental support).

The innovative frame for the Port of Oakland project was to show how technology could assist the port and the small-business community. Equally important was framing the Internet-based tool developed by the OCE faculty/student team as a minimal cost item. The resulting tool, the IBO program, could be implemented by involved students and maintained at minimal expense under an ongoing service-learning class program—a win-win result for students, the port, and the small-business community.

Mini Case Number 2: The California Employment Training Panel

Since 1983, the State of California, through the Employment Training Panel (ETP), has administered an economic development program that supports the California economy. In particular, ETP has attempted to support California employers that must compete in the global economy by providing funds to train/retrain workers. This economic development effort is the result of collaborations between business, labor, state agencies, and educational institutions, and is funded by the Employment Training Tax, which is paid by California employers that participate in the Unemployment Insurance System.

ETP obtains its funds from a tax on every business in the state (about $7 per employee per year) and distributes around $80 million per year. Unfortunately, 95 percent of these funds go back to large companies (Kmart, Frito-Lay, etc.) because these larger firms have the staff and expertise to write the grant proposals and complete the approval process. For the calendar years 1998, 1999, and 2000, the panel authorized an average of 2.2 percent per year of all panel funds to small businesses (fewer than 100 employees) that applied directly to the panel for assistance. For small businesses of 50 employees or less the percentage of total funding was less than 1 percent per year. This is clearly an issue, given that more than 95 percent of California businesses have fewer than 100 employees and two-thirds have fewer than five employees.

Thus, ETP wanted to address the disparity between training grants and the small-business economic presence in the California economy. The task was to understand the issue behind the apparent disparity and assess the successes, problems, and other issues related to implementing a streamlined application process designed to target small businesses. ETP developed the Small Business Pilot Project, and OCE was contracted to conduct a study of the effectiveness of the pilot. Goals of the streamlined process included the following:

- increasing the number of small businesses that obtain direct contract approvals with ETP
- increasing the number of small businesses holding direct contracts with ETP

- ensuring shorter contract approval time for such contracts
- streamlining and shortening the application process
- ensuring more prompt payment of these contractors

A faculty/student team developed interview and survey protocols to conduct primary research among the targeted constituency of the pilot project. Focus groups, surveys, and interviews were developed and implemented by the team. Students were involved in every phase of the project and interfaced with government staff in detailed sessions to determine how the agency interacts with the small-business community.

The outcome of the OCE effort included the following findings: (a) an indication of what procedures shortened the contract development process, (b) determination of which procedures assisted a greater number of small employers to secure ETP funds than would have been served without the special considerations, and (c) recommendation of which of these processes and procedures can be effectively incorporated into the regular ETP development function to assist businesses of all sizes to directly access ETP funds more rapidly.

The pilot, with the empirical support from the OCE findings, has now become a standard program.

The innovative frame for the ETP project was to show the government partner the potential for small businesses to be better served by streamlining the process they are required to use to access programs sponsored by this particular partner. The OCE used the emerging theory of blue ocean strategy (Kim & Mauborgne, 2005) to eliminate program regulations that added no value relative to the risk to public dollars. We added a new lens to the process used by government and used student power to develop and implement survey techniques that purposely represented the diverse business population of California. Our focus was again on the small-business sector of the community, consistent with the program focus of the OCE. We were able to foster a win-win situation for the students in terms of interactive, real-world learning experiences; the state agency gained by significantly improving use of its program by small-business owners; and the small-business community gained by significantly increasing its use of public funds to improve specific competitiveness.

Mini Case Number 3: Electronic Benefit Transfer Project

The Electronic Benefits Transfer (EBT) program replaced food stamps across the country a few years ago. EBT is an ATM-like account to which recipients' food stipends are electronically transferred and from which they can draw at supermarkets and grocery stores. An interagency agreement between SFSU and the Health and Human Services Data Center of the State of California included a set of activities designed to help assess client satisfaction and acceptance of the new EBT delivery system.

Included in this assessment were the identification and surveying of clients of the two pilot counties of Yolo and Alameda. Additionally, the SFSU project team interviewed community-based organizations (CBOs) and a selected set of large and medium retailers (primary handlers of retail transactions for clients of EBT) in the pilot counties. A final major set of activities included surveying a selected set of small retailers, including those that have not responded to the EBT changeover, those that have declined, or ethnic retailers that may not have received sufficient outreach to encourage their participation.

A series of interviews, surveys, and key informants were used to evaluate the impact on the new delivery system on overall market acceptance. A particular focus again was on the client population of the California Department of Social Services, which is the sponsoring agency, and the small-business community, which is the targeted constituency of the OCE conversion. The EBT system relies on a technology that has been in the marketplace for more than two decades. Thus, the survey goal was not to focus on the technology per se, but rather to see how that technology was being understood and used by the targeted clients. Each faculty member assembled a cross-disciplinary team of four to eight students representing at some level the diversity within the client population of the EBT system.

The program enhanced efficiency and accountability of the food stamp program. The OCE team's study of the program in the pilot counties found that (a) the recipients like it because it increases their dignity when they shop, (b) the merchants have learned to adapt to it (though it changes some of the under-the-counter exchanges for alcohol and cigarettes that used to occur regularly), and (c) it led to a recommended change of putting a picture ID on the card to make it more difficult for ex-spouses to misappropriate funds. In addition to the general findings above, the OCE effort also found the following noteworthy: (d) most clients (about three out of four after the first two months with the new EBT delivery system) are satisfied and understand the EBT system. Some clients, however, do have difficulty making the initial transition. The loci of the difficulties are noticeable in the Asian and Hispanic client subpopulations. In addition to the impact on the clients themselves, client transition problems have a material impact on the counties, CBOs, and retailers; (e) after successfully obtaining a card and personal identification number, some clients have difficulty with specific issues related to understanding the process of the successful and efficient use of EBT; and (f) CBOs play an important role in reaching clients who have difficulty receiving or understanding routine communication materials.

Summary and Lessons Learned

Our primary goal in this chapter was to share projects that illustrate how community service learning can be used to affect political entities that have a shared interest in a component of our community. In these examples, we looked at the small-business community as a shared constituency that could benefit from leveraging public sector resources to assist in the potential long-term success of this constituency. We framed these efforts as examples of social entrepreneurship practiced by an element of the university, the OCE. Importantly, the OCE is only used as an exemplar. We strongly suggest that almost all universities can engage in this new type of partnership that targets social improvement by using traditional business tools, applied by faculty and managed by motivated students, to assist important issues in support of a common constituency. One avenue by which a university can assume community leadership is to assist the government in finding solutions to social issues.

In summary, the lessons learned as we review the examples discussed above include:

- the essential role of a visionary individual and institutional support for involving students in the community. This vision is facilitated by a mission statement that captures within its core value a clear commitment to community involvement. This adds to the timeliness of the concept of a public/public partnership that is at the heart of the relationship described in this chapter.
- the often overlooked value of civic participation and social cohesiveness that accrues to the participating students and faculty is brought to the foreground when the experience is viewed through the lens of community service learning.
- the need for an appreciation of experimentation and entrepreneurial thinking (i.e., creative thinking and innovative action) to help address

social problems with traditional business tools. The brutal truth of the marketplace is that perhaps only 1 in 100 ideas truly is successful. It is the nature of entrepreneurs, including social entrepreneurs, to suggest approaches that are unique and unorthodox. The public entity partner must be patient and diligent to admit some experimentation while keeping a watchful eye on progress toward its often statutory mission.

- an understanding of the need for flexibility and responsiveness to the unique attributes of the partners. Students (and faculty) are most often driven by the fixed time dimensions of traditional academic years in terms of semesters; activities must be planned around these general restrictions that are largely irrelevant to public agencies. Similarly, public agencies are typically bureaucratic in movement and decision making; students must adjust their expectations to coincide with this often less than desired pace, or certainly less than is dictated by the normal pace of business decision making. The planning process that brings the long-term perspective of public agencies in concord with the short-term student focus on semesters must include benchmarks and measurable impact analyses that can give the students a sense of accomplishment.

- artificial barriers tend to inhibit the partnering between business schools and public entities. The sciences and teacher training components of most universities have a long and cherished history of partnering with public sector entities; we see untapped potential to expand this tradition to the so-called professional schools of business, engineering, and computer science.

- the time horizon for working in the community is not to think of events but process. The role of community service learning and social entrepreneurship, as those terms are used in this chapter, is continuous and ever changing as the community is dynamic and ever changing. Each effort, each project, is merely a piece of the whole that it takes to help support a community, or more modestly, the small-business component of a community.

The final point to be emphasized is to recognize the role of the faculty as key drivers of the social mission in combination with requisite business expertise. Kramer (2004) suggests that the individual faculty member must accept the reality that his or her efforts in working with the community rarely reach a finale. The targeted needs of the community tend to be so complex and interwoven with other issues that resolution is rarely possible. Progress is the desired goal as work with the OCE constituency, namely, the small-business community, is compounded by myriad governmental regulations that affect that performance. Kramer captured this opportunity for frustration well when he noted that social entrepreneurs take 5 to 10 years to get their ideas to take shape and have the anticipated impact on the community. "Even then, ideas must constantly be simplified and modified, overcoming unanticipated obstacles along the way, only to hit more obstacles, and then more. . . . somewhere there must be a person of indomitable will, unshakeable dedication and considerable charisma" (p.2).

Perhaps the key for the OCE and others that choose to interact in the community with a business model is to have an attitude of continuous adaptation as new challenges emerge and old challenges represent themselves in a different configuration. In summary, it is useful to remember that few things happen without individual initiative, but very few things last without institutions. The role of the social entrepreneur, at the individual or institutional level, requires exceptional patience, persistence, and flexibility. It is not a task for the easily frustrated or rigid professional.

Note

1. In a speech titled "Bridges to Human Dignity," which was broadcast nationwide on CBS radio on April 25, 1968, Republican presidential candidate Nixon said, "What most of the militants are asking for is not separation but to be included in, to have a share of the wealth and a piece of the action. And this is precisely what the central target of the new approach ought to be. It ought to be oriented toward more black ownership, for from this can flow the rest: black pride, black jobs, and yes, Black Power—in the best sense of that often misapplied term. . . . The ghettos of our cities will be remade when the people in them have the will, the power, the resources and the skills to remake them. They won't be remade by Government billions. We have to get private enterprise into the ghetto. But at the same time, we have to get the people of the ghetto into private enterprise" (Nixon on Racial Accommodation, 1968).

In the interest of full disclosure, coauthor Richard L. McCline joined the Black Republicans in 1970 in an effort to capitalize on the opportunities that existed. These opportunities led to what at one time was one of the largest food retail stores in the Midwest.

References

Bahls, J. E. (1994, June). Seeing red. *Inc.*, 104–109.

Baron, R., & Shane, S. (2005). *Entrepreneurship: A process perspective.* Mason, OH: Thomson/South-Western.

Chao, E. L. (2007, December 11). Workforce competiveness in a global economy. Speech presented to the Chamber of Commerce Uruguay-USA, Montevideo, Uruguay. Retrieved from http://www.dol.gov/_sec/media/speeches/20071211_uruguay.htm

Cole, J., & Robinson, J. (2002). Internet use and sociability in the UCLA data: A simplified MCA analysis. *IT and Society, 1*(1), 202–218.

Cornwall, J. R. (1998). The entrepreneur as a building block for community. *Journal of Developmental Entrepreneurship, 3*(2), 141–149.

Dennis, W. J. (2004). *The public reviews small business.* Washington, DC: National Federation of Independent Business Research Foundation.

Edgcomb, E. L., & Klein, J. A. (2005). *Opening opportunities, building ownership: Fulfilling the promise of microenterprise in the United States.* Washington, DC: Aspen Institute.

Etzioni, A. (1993). *The spirit of community: The reinvention of American society.* New York: Simon and Schuster.

Gibb, A. A. (1994). Do we really teach small business the way we should? *Journal of Small Business and Entrepreneurship, 11*(2), 11–28.

Gray, J. (1998). *False dawn: The delusion of global capitalism.* New York: New Press.

Hemingway, C. A. (2005). Personal values as a catalyst for corporate social entrepreneurship. *Journal of Business Ethics, 60*(3), 33.

Kim, W. C., & Mauborgne, R. (2005). *Blue ocean strategy: How to create uncontested market space and make the competition irrelevant.* Boston: Harvard Business School Press.

Kramer, M. R. (2004). How to change the world: Social entrepreneurs and the power of new ideas. *Stanford Social Innovation Review, 2*(1), 77–78.

Kuratko, D. F., Hornsby, J. S., & Naffziger, D. W. (1999). The adverse impact of public policy on micro enterprises: An exploratory study of owners' perceptions. *Journal of Developmental Entrepreneurship, 4*(1), 81–94.

Moini, A. H. (1998). Small firms exporting: How effective are government export assistance programs? *Journal of Small Business Management, 36*(1), 1–15.

National Telecommunications and Information Administration and the Economics and Statistics Administration. (2002, February). *A nation online: How Americans are expanding their use of the Internet.* Washington, DC: Author. Retrieved from http://www.ntia.doc.gov/ntiahome/dn/nationonline_020502.htm

Nixon on racial accommodation. (1968, May 3). *Time.* Retrieved from http://www.time.com/time/magazine/article/0,9171,841235-1,00.html

Roper, J., & Cheney, G. (2005). Leadership, learning and human resource management: The meanings of social entrepreneurship today. *Corporate Governance, 5*(3), 95–105.

Sagawa, S., & Segal, E. (2000). Common interest, common good: Creating value through business and social sector partnerships. *California Management Review, 42*(2), 105–122.

Scranton, P. (1997) Beyond the broker state: Federal policies toward small businesses, 1936–1961. *Small Business History, 71*(1), 121–123.

Timmons, J., & Spinelli, S. (2006). *New venture creation: Entrepreneurship in the 21st Century.* Homewood, IL: McGraw-Hill/Irwin.

U.S. Small Business Administration Office of Advocacy. (2001a). Minorities in business, 2001. Washington, DC: U.S. Small Business Administration. Retrieved from http: www.sba.gov/advo/stats/min01.pdf

U.S. Small Business Administration Office of Advocacy. (2001b). Women in business, 2001. Washington, DC: U.S. Small Business Administration. Retrieved from http://www. sba.gov/advo/stats/wib01.pdf

U.S. Small Business Administration Office of Advocacy. (2006). Small business profile: California. Washington, DC: U.S. Small Business Administration. Retrieved from http://www.sba.gov/advo/research/profiles/06ca.pdf

What did Richard Nixon have to do with today's black middle class? (2005, June 9–15) *Jacksonville Free Press,* p. 2.

Young, M. (2002). An examination of information sources and assistance programs available to minority-owned small businesses. *Journal of Developmental Entrepreneurship, 7*(4), 127–129

SECTION THREE

POLITICAL ENGAGEMENT
THROUGH SOCIAL ACTIVISM

7

COMMUNICATING
COMMUNITY

Engaging Silicon Valley Through Student Activism

Anne Marie Todd and Deanna L. Fassett

I am truly glad that I chose this organization for my project. I think many people will never think twice about the organization they chose once they turn their paper in; I on the other hand, will never forget it. It has made me realize that the life of an activist is not easy. . . . you want everyone to care about the cause as much as you do, and when they do not, you get kind of mad or disgusted (especially since this one is dealing with kids). It is rewarding though, when you do get a group of people, whether it is three, thirty-five, or sixty, you know you have done your part!

—Communication Studies 130 Student[1]

S ervice learning has enjoyed a long history in the field of communication studies (see Droge & Murphy, 1999, for example). The study of communication, with its focus on democratic participation and diversity, is uniquely situated to employ service-learning pedagogy. As a member of the California State University, San José State University (SJSU) has long been supportive of service learning, in part through its Center for Service Learning and its history of pedagogy development grants for faculty. The communication studies department at SJSU reflects the commitment of our field and our university to service learning and civic engagement. As faculty in an *engaged department* (defined at SJSU as a department that has multiple courses designated service learning), we enjoy opportunities to explore the role of service learning in student engagement and associated learning outcomes. As faculty facing increasing demands in education and documented disillusionment with politics, we seek ways to adapt existing service-learning channels to engage students in democratic participation and civic responsibility. In this chapter, we explicate one such adaptation, the course project in a Social Movement Communication class, which has demonstrated results along three learning outcomes: political knowledge, communication skills, and activist values. Assessment of this course project is instructive for understanding how service learning implicates notions of agency and ideology in our pedagogical philosophy and practice.

Local Context: On Being a Metropolitan University in Silicon Valley

The California State University is committed to service learning and civic engagement, and encourages campuses to engage their surrounding communities as sources of individuality and strength. Local factors facilitate and present barriers to engagement (Ostrander, 2004). At SJSU, our situation is largely shaped by our reputation as a commuter school (students are reputed to be on campus, outside of attending classes, an average of six minutes). Although our location is central—in downtown San José—most students commute from around the San Francisco Bay Area. What is "local" is broad and ambiguous because SJSU draws students from as far as 75 miles away; we face unique challenges to creating a student-centered campus and, in turn, a campus-centered community. Many students report that they do not have time for service. Building course assignments around service learning can make courses very unforgiving for students who are, for various reasons, unable to give the requisite volunteer time to the organization. As faculty, we are increasingly aware of the importance of involving students in the campus and its surroundings as a means of nurturing integrative, lifelong student learning. It is in the context of our commitment to be a community campus coupled with our distinctive commuter status that this chapter endeavors to present new curricular ways to engage students: through assignments that ask them to politically engage by being an activist.

Communicating Political Engagement: Service Learning Through Activism

In response to changing economic, political, and social forces, Marullo and Edwards (2000) advocate pedagogical initiatives that link students to the community through service learning. They find this to be the best way to enhance the students' learning experience, shaping them into self-motivated learners who become civic participants. Service learning is transformative as pedagogy aimed at the development of democratic values and critical citizen-ship (Anderson, Levis-Fitzerald, & Rhoads, 2003; Howard, 1998; Saltmarsh, 1996). In particular, service learning can have a positive impact on political engagement (Battistoni, 1997; Hillygus, 2005; Hunter & Brisbin, 2000; Mendel-Reyes, 1998; Walker, 2000). Community-based learning promotes students' awareness of community issues and involvement with the commu-nity and can significantly raise their political knowledge (Galston, 2001). Morgan and Streb (2001) found that students involved in service-learning projects in which they have a high degree of voice and ownership demon-strated improved self-confidence and political engagement. In developing teaching methods to communicate the importance of democratic participa-tion, and to politically engage students, we can "encourage [students] to en-vision themselves as actors or agents in political arenas" by building "models of citizenship that combine critical consciousness with action and reflection" (Bickford & Reynolds, 2002, p. 230). Such methods of civic engagement are rooted in political, activist learning.

By grounding political engagement in community, students can rely on their own experiences to frame course material. Locating the SJSU commu-nity centrally in curricula establishes the relevance of the field of study to students' broader knowledge of their (our) own world. In understanding the city of San José and the greater Silicon Valley as a community, it is important to engage notions of power in society: political, social, economic, and cultural.

> Activist experience gives [us] experiential understanding of the power of the state, repression, social change, agency, surprise in history, the distor-tions peddled by authority, and the depth of commitment of those with power to maintaining the standing order through their journalists, histori-ans, police, and law firms. Activism shows us how it is that people told that there is no alternative to the way things are can in fact invent new alterna-tives, particularly in the streets and on the picket lines. (Lemisch, 2003, p. 241)

Social activism is a fundamental part of democracy. Protests and social movements are examples of political engagement that offer students a sense of the potential for social change. As laboratories of democracy, courses devoted to the study of social movements are distinguished by their call for students to engage their political community.

Communication Studies 130: Social Movement Communication (COMM 130) is an elective course that is taught once a year and enrolls about thirty-five students. COMM 130 is focused on the "study of theoretical and historical documents that reveal how social movements and protests have shaped and fueled political and cultural communication both nationally and internationally" (SJSU Catalog, p. 140). As the syllabus notes, protests and social movements are permanent features of the contemporary international political landscape (see Appendix A). Studying how protests, social movements, and dissent have transformed global society can provide students with an understanding of democratic participation.

COMM 130's curriculum is premised on the idea that social activism is a part of the democratic process and thus incorporates historical and theoretical approaches, examining diverse perspectives of what constitutes a social movement, how movements organize, and what different tactics of protest are available to activists. Courses in communication studies offer natural ways to incorporate service learning into the curriculum through focus on oral tradition, interpersonal communication, and public campaigns, for example (see Droge & Murphy, 1999). Indeed, COMM 130's emphasis on rhetorical and discursive practices provides ample opportunities for students to integrate theory and practice in community settings. The goal of this course is to provide students with a comprehensive overview of social movement theory, which they apply to case studies through readings and their term projects. The course is organized into three units: in the first part of the semester, students become familiar with the theoretical basis of social movements communication such as organizational and media strategies. In the second part of the term, students examine primary documents of historical movements including women's suffrage, civil rights, Black Power, Queer Nation, and radical environmentalism. These historical movements provide students with an opportunity to understand how theories of social movement communication can account for the successes and failures of activism. The third part of the course involves a contemporary study of the anticorporate globalization movement in which students are asked to trace connections between historical predecessors and contemporary struggles for global justice.

While students study the theoretical concepts of social movement communication in a variety of ways, the course project for the semester assigns an in-depth exploration of activism related to a local community issue. In this semester-long assignment, students observe and analyze the activities of an advocacy group or organization of their choice (see Appendix B). Students are given a choice of two project options: a discourse analysis research paper, or community-based participant observation. These two project options are designed to meet the same learning outcomes and provide students with flexibility based on their particular interests and schedules. Each semester, the students participate equally in their choices for their projects. Both projects have garnered positive student responses and demonstrated their utility as culminating projects for students enrolled in a course on social movements.

The discourse analysis option is tailored for people who do not want (or do not have time outside typical school assignments) to commit energy to working with a community organization. For this project, students are asked to write a term paper that analyzes the persuasion tactics of an activist organization based on a portfolio of the group's communication materials. Students who choose the discourse analysis option focus on texts produced by an activist group and cite at least three scholarly (peer-reviewed) sources to critique the communication strategies of efforts of the organization. Students compile a portfolio of examples of the group's public discourse and evaluate the group's communication strategies, asking how and to what extent the group's communication efforts meet its stated goals, and how the group's public communication fits into the theoretical framework established by the course readings.

The participant observation option is an example of a unique permutation of service learning that has demonstrated effectiveness in engaging students. This option is designed for people who want (and have time) to get involved with a social or political organization. Students observe and participate in the activities of an activist group of their choice. While students participate in a variety of groups each semester, several types of organizations have been recurring choices: environmental groups such as Silicon Valley Toxics Coalition; student organizations such as Rise-Up, a campaign concerning student fees; local chapters of labor unions; and international human rights projects with local chapters such as Global Exchange and Amnesty

International. The participant observation assignment is structured to provide several areas of engagement and reflection in journals, portfolios, and
reflective papers. Students keep a personal journal of at least five entries in
which they document their experiences and explore the connections to
course learning. Students compile a portfolio of an array of materials related
to their service as examples of their group's public discourse and as a way
to contextualize their experience. Finally, students write an integrative and
analytical paper (five–six pages) in which they reflect upon their experience
with their activist organization and evaluate the effects of their participation.
(For specific mechanisms used to evaluate students see Appendix C: Grading
Rubric.) In what follows, we elucidate our assessment of the participant observation option of the course project based on these materials, and evaluate
activism as a way for students to engage.

Assessing Activist Learning

Scholarly research identifies two categories of learning outcomes in the service-learning curriculum: student outcomes related to intellectual skills and
student outcomes related to personal growth (Dasaratha, Ravenscroft, Wolcott, & Zlotkowski, 2000). Assessable learning outcomes include personal
and interpersonal development, understanding and application of subject-
matter learning, critical thinking, perspective transformation, and citizenship
skills and values (Eyler & Giles, 1999).[2] For our course, we examined stu-
dent-written comments in reflective essays and journals in order to determine the effectiveness of our approach in realizing three key learning
outcomes: enhanced political knowledge, improved communication skills,
and adoption of activist values.[3]

Political Knowledge

One of the common student responses to service learning is increased knowledge: an enhanced awareness of community needs. For many students, the
initial knowledge gain was a motivating factor in overcoming their inhibi-
tions to participate in nontraditional curricular activities. As one student
noted, "Once I learned about the cause I dropped some of my fear and decided to become active." Another student's response is typical: "I really enjoyed doing this project and I'm glad that this class gave me an opportunity
to research the [group] and learn about their campaign to help the world's

oceans." For these students, like others who participate in activist groups, the knowledge gained through participation is an essential first step to recognizing their own contribution to community activism.

Through grassroots organizing, students infer the value of the common person's experience. This type of experiential knowledge is vital to grassroots organization and is empowering for students to understand their role in society. One student described being part of a campus activist group as "very vital." She describes how gaining knowledge about the issues helped her contribute to the group's goal:

> As I learned more and more about the group and the current issue we would be fighting for I began to ask "What if?" Again, I didn't know what to expect, so I wanted to prepare myself for the worst, and I think everyone else was preparing for the worst, and figuring out how to avoid the worst. I was a great asset towards the group because people need outsiders to understand those who are not interested in the cause.

This student's response reveals the importance of students' awareness and comfort in creating ideal situations for engaging the community. As students gain an awareness of and confidence in their community, they report an improved comfort level for participation in activist situations. Furthermore, students who are novice activists interacting with social justice organizations for the first time reported gratification in recognition of the value of their ideas. The commitment to the common experience in activist groups is based in the fundamentals of grassroots organizing: incorporate a multiplicity of views and involve individuals in the group's action plan. As students exhibit enhanced awareness of community needs, they gain an understanding of the utility of alternative methods of communicating about social issues, and they can gain confidence in their own participation and understanding of how such methods can be persuasive to a public audience.

Communication Skills

Students who participate in communication-based social movement activities are exposed to grassroots methods of organizing and communication. One student noted that members of her group were "very supportive of each other, they never had arguments. When there were situations that were shaky, the group thought up other alternatives or compromised with each other." The study of social movement communication involves examination of activist organization: the inner workings of a grassroots community. In this case, students discovered how communication networks are critical to achieving clarity and consensus. They also learned to use alternative methods of communication to compromise and come to action plans entire groups can agree upon and enact.

From the perspective of the communication studies discipline, service learning is about communicating with the community about pressing issues, concerns, challenges, and opportunities, and understanding how these issues are, at a fundamental level, characterized by, and emergent in, communication. Students of communication learn skills that allow them to participate in activities and decisions in their communities. In the Social Movement Communication course, students quickly realize the communication strategies of activists are strikingly similar to those taught in the introductory communication courses such as Public Speaking, Persuasion, Interpersonal Communication, Small Group Communication, and Critical Thinking.

The course project in the class asks students to apply these skills in their involvement in an activist organization. Through practices of public communication, students are able to evaluate the extent to which they have been successful. One student described the role of communication in her activist work:

> After learning how to approach a student or make a classroom presentation, we focused a lot of our efforts to have as many students as we can to sign our petition that is in support of asking [administrators] to give back [their] raise. The day of the rally and walkout we figured that our voices may not always attract students, so we came to the conclusion that a good method to lure students is through live music, picket signs, and banners.

Student comments indicate that through evaluation and adaptation of communication skills to fit the situation, they were able to participate in group decision making and affect the group's message. Learning skills through activist participation gives students a sense of effecting change through their communication efforts. As one student noted:

> Being on that microphone and seeing people actually listening to me gave me such excitement. I really felt that I was making a difference because I was advocating about the current issues. And for the day of action, the

walkout, it was that same rush. Holding the bullhorn and leading chants, encouraging other students to join the protest, it was a different type of fun that is unexplainable. Though the group was disorganized and not following the schedule I still had fun and felt the message was out there. This group and these specific people have definitely drawn [me] into standing up for student rights. I hope to continue my new experience, and fight many more battles.

Student responses indicate that communicating to a public audience requires knowledge of current events and strategies for advocacy. Getting the message out is the primary goal for students involved in activist groups, one that requires them to apply concepts such as audience, persuasion, visual communication, and so on in a public real-world situation.[4] Developing communication strategies emphasizes individual action. Some students, like the student above, who indicated that she felt a rush, experience a feeling of excitement. Others simply thrive on the feeling of achievement: "I felt accomplished. It was only day two of my experiences with [my group] and I had already done so much." Perceiving the positive effects of their communication efforts teaches students the possibilities of change through individual action.

Activist groups use various types of outreach, which require communication: press releases, banners, speeches, rallies, and such; students learn these communication skills by applying them to these real-world situations. Service learning requires more investment than other lessons that keep students in the classroom. For those students willing to invest in the participant observation, many feel a sense of accomplishment. One student describes the time she invested in communicating about her event to her friends:

I sat down and braced myself for what I knew was going to be a long time at the computer. I sent comments to almost every one of my Myspace friends that attends San Jose State letting them know that tomorrow would be the big day. . . . The next day was huge! I had over 60 people show up for the screening. . . . and the best thing happened. . . . tons of people signed up!

This student's experience demonstrates the importance of communication in building support for a cause. For many students, successful activist communication was a positive experience: "I felt very proud at that moment, of all the people who really did commit." As students engage in political actions, they hone these communication skills and gain confidence in their communication abilities.

One aspect of this confidence for many students is the realization that individual actions can make a difference through development of their communication skills. In her reflection paper, one student recognizes the effects of her actions on the goals of her activist organization. Her perceivable positive effect in the group's efforts to achieve social justice gave her a sense of accomplishment.

> The role I feel I play in the group is both small and large at the same time. I am only one person and I really am in no way affiliated with the organization, but I have put a lot of time and effort into helping to accomplish their goals. I have brought exposure to the organization and have also gotten others involved in the organization's activities. I know people are talking about me too, because at the [event] multiple people came up to me and said that they heard about [the group] through a friend and that friend heard about [the group] through me. I have to admit, it felt good. It lets me know that I did help to make a difference.

This student reports a positive feeling about her participation in the group because as an individual, she used communication skills learned in the classroom to promote justice in the community. As she documents her reputation for getting things done, she communicates a feeling of pride in her actions. Student reflection papers and journals describe the support and commitment students give to activist organizations. For many students this support is mutual; as they work with other activists, they are motivated by the positive response their ideas and values receive in the context of grassroots organizing.

Activist Values

In addition to the knowledge and communication skills that activist learning projects can promote, students gain a sense of activist values. As students invest their time and effort in the activities of their group, they recognize their potential to effect social change. Describing a campus group she joined, one student noted, "[we are] a new group that is comprised of six students, counting myself. Though we are relatively small, we do have a lot of potential in growing." With this awareness of access to social systems, students understand the value of democratic participation and thus realize the potential of social change. The student continued, "With the right motivation and the right people on your side, small steps are taken that lead to forceful movement." As students make the connection between their activities, they realize the power of individuals acting together in concerted, targeted efforts. This assignment asks students to evaluate their actions according to a framework for social movement success. In this reflective assessment, students recognize the possibility and power of social change: "the ability to make a difference in communities nationwide." With an understanding of social power and the potential for individuals to make a difference, students report gaining a sense of social responsibility. Halfway through each semester, several students change their assignment from their original choice of a discourse analysis to a participant observation because they become so involved in the project. One such student explains why: "I had a lot of fun getting involved with [my group]. The first day I looked into the organization I signed up for their email list and immediately began receiving emails. I made [the group's Web site] my homepage as a constant reminder of the assignment I had ahead of me, *never realizing how much more than an assignment this whole thing would become*"[emphasis ours].

Indeed this is one of the benefits of positive community experiences. Simply offering the opportunity for students to learn about organizations they were interested in created a chance for them to improve their own involvement. "Everyday, I looked into the organization, and the more I looked, the more I wanted to be involved. . . . My experience has also caused me to take this cause to heart, like it is *my* cause." Students become invested in the community, and this becomes more than an assignment.

Based on the experience of students in the social movements course, students' enhanced sense of social responsibility can have a lasting impression. Many students continue with the organization after they have completed the requirements for the course project. One student who volunteered to take water samples from a beach near his home as part of a water-testing program noted, "I feel I can make a difference along with all the volunteers who participate in their programs." While students differ in their adoption of activist sensibilities (some students self-identify as activists, while others don't), participation in an activist group changes students' perspectives on community values. One student noted, "I still don't look at myself as an activist, just a person who wants my community to be enjoyed by anyone who travels here." This same student noted that "researching and taking part in the group's activities" gave him "new respect" for activism. This sense of individual responsibility combined with an invigorated feeling of social obligation is a common reaction among students who conduct their participant observation.

Improvement in student knowledge associated with participation in activist organizations is correlated to democratic participation. Students feel that they gained access to "the system," and thus are empowered to promote change. Students gain access to the system through political engagement. One student noted in her journal the value in seeing the effects of her group's actions:

> At the end of our rally we were all hanging out just talking, and I notice an elder gentleman walking towards me. I quickly turn my head and tell the other members that it was [an administrator] walking by. As he walked past the table he smiled and pointed to our banner to read it. He realized what the banner said and quickly turned around trying to finish [his] phone conversation. Our friend joked around with him by chasing him a bit with the hundreds of petitions. It was the highlight of our day, and at least we know [the administration] is aware of the situation.

This journal entry illustrates the profound effect that a rally can have on students. Students who previously may not have recognized the power they have as students to effect change within the university system were wowed by the approach of a high-level administrator. As this official acknowledged the signs of the students, they gained the knowledge that the administration was aware of their message. This type of knowledge is empowering for students who gain access to a previously inaccessible university bureaucracy and work toward positive social change. For teachers who strive to impart the value of democratic participation in students, activist learning opportunities provide a sense of the impact on individuals and communities. This knowledge is the basis for improved communication skills inherent in political participation.

Implications

The social movements communication course provides an opportunity to evaluate the activist potential of service learning. Activist learning combines critical consciousness with action and reflection. Activist learning is more than service, it is asking students to find their own mode of active civic and political engagement. This is an alternative to requiring students to go out in the community, perform an act of service that benefits the less privileged, and then return to the classroom for regular learning, perhaps turning in a reflection paper. This study of activist learning reveals important implications of positive learning outcomes.

The activist turn is realizing that we are making those choices for our students and that we need to make them with our students. This idea of choice occurs at the start: in the framing of the learning objectives. Faculty must consider in what ways learning objectives are always ideological directives. If learning objectives are, choice becomes very important to students' sense of agency and action. Students must consider the role of this community work in their lives. They make the connection by being active participants. If students are to actively engage democratic society as part of the course requirements, flexibility is crucial to a successful project. Assignments have to include flexible, supple ways for students to engage, particularly at SJSU.

Choice is key in the positive response to this project. While research has focused on service learning's effectiveness as civic education, as with any teaching strategy, service learning's value depends on its implementation. For faculty who seek ways to get students to engage, whether to require participation is an important question (Parker-Gwin & Mabry, 1998). That the participant observation was an option of choice was significant in two ways: (a) students who initiated the project as a participant observation who were not having luck finding ways to participate in their chosen organization moved to a discourse analysis without feeling as though they had wasted the semester. And, (b) students who initiated the project as a discourse analysis and received an overwhelmingly positive response could change to a participant observation and take advantage of these encouraging forays into communication.

As we consider the meaning of choice in understanding our learning outcomes, we acknowledge the ideological nature of activist learning. At a basic level, a decision to send students into community-based organizations is inherently ideological. Even a course assignment that asks students to choose their own issues to rally around is ideological in its promotion of activist values and the importance of communicating for social change. Suggesting to students that they had the choice to be ideological promoted diverse knowledge and positive individual learning experiences. Students assessed what group they would be interested in participating with and analyzing. This required them to assess their own interests. In this course, we recognized the ideological nature of learning outcomes. Social responsibility has values instilled in it. As a political activity, it is a way to explore the potential of responsible citizenship in a way that students can understand what it means to be globally active. As we ask how best to engage students, engaged projects help us to understand the power of reaching outside the classroom to create a different type of pedagogical agenda.

Finally, the notions of agency and ideology impart understanding of community that embraces the unique location and situation of SJSU. In activist learning projects, difference is recognized in diversity as sameness is recognized in common situations. Activism argues for relationships based on connection. In their time with the project, students make provisional alliances, some of which outlast the course as the responses indicate. By engaging the community, students and faculty connect learning to "real world" contexts. We want students to establish roots in the community; we seek ways to draw students into the community and see SJSU as a place where they live and work.

Continuing to improve curriculum-based service-learning opportunities is important. This type of scholarship of engagement has a dual meaning: (a) connecting the university's resources to the most pressing social, civic, political, and ethical problems; and (b) creating a climate in which academic and civic cultures communicate more continuously and creatively (Boyer, 1996). By evaluating activist learning projects, we hope to continue to promote best practices in ways to communicate the importance of community and continue to engage the students of Silicon Valley.

Notes

1. Names and identifying information of individuals and organizations have been removed. Student comments were taken from journals and reflective essays.

2. For further resources on assessment of learning and activism in the field of communication studies see http://www.natcom.org/Instruction/sl-new/AssessmentResources.htm

3. See Howard (2001) for a discussion of knowledge, value, and skills as part of service-learning assessment.

4. We use the term *real world* to problemize its use to distinguish between classroom lessons and off-campus reality. We see engaging students through community-based learning projects as a way to combat this insular view of higher education.

References

Anderson, J. L., Levis-Fitzerald, M. R., & Rhoads, R. A. (2003). Democratic learning and global citizenship: The contribution of one-unit seminars. *The Journal of General Education, 52*(2), 84–107.

Battistoni, R. M. (1997, Summer). Service-learning and democratic citizenship. *Theory Into Practice, 36*(3), 150–156.

Bickford, D. M., & Reynolds, N. (2002). Activism and service-learning: Reframing volunteerism as acts of dissent. *Pedagogy: Critical Approaches to Teaching Literature, Language, Composition, and Culture, 2*(2), 229–252.

Boyer, E. L. (1996, Spring). The scholarship of engagement. *Journal of Public Service & Outreach, 1*(1), 11–20.

Dasaratha, V. R., Ravenscroft, S. P., Wolcott, S. K., & Zlotkowski, E. (November 2000). Service learning outcomes: Guidelines for educators and researchers. *Issues in Accounting Education, 15*(4), 657–692.

Droge, D., & Murphy, B. O. (Eds.). (1999). *Voices of strong democracy: Concepts and models for service-learning in communication studies.* Sterling, VA: Stylus Publishing.

Eyler, J., & Giles, Jr., D. E. (1999). *Where's the service in service-learning?* San Francisco: Jossey-Bass.

Galston, W. A. (2001, June). Political knowledge, political engagement, and civic education. *Annual Review of Political Science, 4*(1), 217–234.

Hillygus, D. S. (2005). The missing link: Exploring the relationship between higher education and political engagement. *Political Behavior, 27*(1), 25.

Howard, J. (2001, Summer). *Service-learning course design workbook.* Ann Arbor, MI: OCSL Press.

Howard, J. P. F. (1998). Academic service learning: A counternormative pedagogy. *New Directions for Teaching and Learning, 73*, 21–29.

Hunter, S., & Brisbin, Jr., R. A. (2000, September). The impact of service learning on democratic and civic values. *PS: Political Science and Politics, 33*(3), 623–626

Lemisch, J. (2003, Winter). 2.5 cheers for bridging the gap between activism and the academy. Or, stay and fight. *Radical History Review, 85*, 239–248.

Marullo, S., & Edwards, B. (2000). Service-learning pedagogy as universities' response to troubled times. *American Behavioral Scientist, 43*(5), 746–755.

Mendel-Reyes, M. (1998). A pedagogy for citizenship: Service learning and democratic education. *New Directions for Teaching and Learning, 73,* 31–38.

Morgan, W., & Streb, M. (2001, March). Building citizenship: How student voice in service-learning develops civic values. *Social Science Quarterly, 82*(1), 154–169.

Ostrander, S. A. (2004, March 1). Democracy, civic participation, and the university: A comparative study of civic engagement on five campuses. *Nonprofit and Voluntary Sector Quarterly, 33*(1), 74–93.

Parker-Gwin, R., & Mabry, J. B. (1998, October). Service learning as pedagogy and civic education: Comparing outcomes for three models. *Teaching Sociology, 26*(4), 276–291.

Saltmarsh, J. (1996, Fall). Education for critical citizenship: John Dewey's contribution to the pedagogy of community service learning. *Michigan Journal of Community Service Learning, 3,* 13–21.

San José State University. (2006). *Catalog.* Retrieved from http://info.sjsu.edu/home/catalog.html

Walker, T. (2000, September). The service/politics split: Rethinking service to teach political engagement. *PS: Political Science and Politics, 33*(3), 646–649.

Appendix A
COMM 130: Social Movement Communication Syllabus

Course Objectives:

Social activism and political revolutions are a fundamental part of the evolution of democracy. Protests and social movements are permanent features of the contemporary international political landscape. This course explores how protests, social movements, and dissent have transformed global society. We will study historical and theoretical approaches, examining diverse perspectives of what constitutes a social movement, how movements organize, and different tactics of protest. Throughout the course, we will analyze media coverage of protest and dissent, which will help to frame questions of movement success.

The goal of this course is to provide students with a comprehensive overview of social movement theory, which you will be asked to apply to case studies, through class discussions, assignments, and your term project. In the first part of the semester, we will read theoretical studies of social movements to understand what social movements are and how they operate. Then we will examine primary documents of historical social movements. The last part of the semester will entail a contemporary study of the anticorporate globalization movement. Throughout the semester, you will put together a portfolio of activist discourse on an advocacy group of your choice.

Required Texts:

- Course Reader. Available: Maple Press, 481 E. San Carlos St, 408.297.1000
- Prokosch, M., & Raymond, L. (2002). *The Global Activist's Manual.* New York: Thunder's Mouth Press/Nation Books. (GAM in syllabus)

Assignments and Grading: Students are responsible for class discussions and assignments, and otherwise come prepared to class. *I do not accept late work; I do not allow makeup quizzes or exams.* I do not accept e-mailed work.

Academic integrity statement: Your own commitment to learning, as evidenced by your enrollment at San José State University and the university's Academic Integrity Policy requires you to be honest in all your academic course work. Faculty are required to report all infractions to the Office of Judicial Affairs. The policy on academic integrity can be found at http://www2.sjsu.edu/senate/S04–12.pdf

Campus policy in compliance with the Americans With Disabilities Act: If you need course adaptations or accommodations because of a disability, or if you need special arrangements in case the building must be evacuated, please make an appointment with me as soon as possible, or see me during office hours. Presidential Directive 97–03 requires that students with disabilities register with DRC to establish a record of their disability.

Reading Quizzes/Response Essays: (40%, 400 points): 8 times during the semester, you will be quizzed on the course readings. Quizzes will either be unannounced in class, or assigned as take-home response essays of 1–2 pages. Each quiz is worth 50 points.

Participation: (15%, 150 points): This is not a lecture course. Students are asked to do the reading and participate in class discussions.

Final: (15%, 150 points): Multiple choice, fill in the blank, short answer, and essay.

Course Project: (30%, 300 points): Your project for the semester is to observe and analyze the activities of an advocacy group or organization of your choice. Your level of participation in this group can be tailored to your particular interests (and schedule), but should include a comprehensive survey of the communication strategies of the organization. You have 2 options:

Participant observation: This project option is designed for people who want (and have time) to get involved with a social or political organization. You are asked to observe and participate in the activities of an activist group of your choice, accepting all responsibility for your actions. You will keep a notebook describing your experiences and compile a portfolio of materials that represent the public communication efforts of that organization. For this assignment, you will write a 5–6 page paper that reflects upon your experiences with the group or organization, and evaluates the effects of your actions.

Proposal: 5%, 50 points
Portfolio/Notebook: 10%, 100 points
Paper: 15%, 150 points

Discourse Analysis: This project option is tailored for people who do not want (or do not have time outside typical school assignments) to commit energy to working with a community organization. You are asked to write a

7- to 8-page term paper that analyzes the group or organization and evaluates its persuasion tactics. You should gather a portfolio of communication materials of this group and apply social movement theory to critique the efforts of the organization. Your paper should cite at least 3 academic sources in addition to the primary sources you are analyzing. You should include suggestions for further action based on theories and historical examples of social movements we study.

Proposal: 5%, 50 points

Portfolio: 5%, 50 points

Paper: 20%, 200 points

Therefore your grade will be assigned according to the following point scale:

A	925–1000 points	C	725–764 points
A−	895–924 points	C−	695–724 points
B+	865–894 points	D+	665–694 points
B	825–864 points	D	625–664 points
B−	795–824 points	D−	595–624 points
C+	765–794 points	F	0–594 points

Schedule (subject to change):

Week 1:
Jan. 26: Introduction to the course

Week 2: What is a social movement?
Jan. 31: What is Advocacy? *Reading: Goldman (Handout)
Feb. 2: The '60s: Emerging Patterns of Resistance
Reading: Morgan, "The Sixties," Screening: *Protest in the 1960s*

Week 3: Organization/Infrastructure
Feb. 7: Leaders and the Vanguard: Historical Organization of Movements
Reading: Euchner, "Organization Matters"
Feb. 9: New Technology and Social Movements
Reading: Protest.net, IGC.org, http://www.conservativeusa.org *[Online]

Week 4: Tactics
Feb. 14: The Whole World is Watching
Reading: Euchner, "Tactics of Activists," Screening: *TreeSit*
Feb. 16: Community Mobilization
Reading: Epstein, "The Clamshell Alliance," ***Hand out term project**

Week 5: Civil Rights
Feb. 21: The Women's Suffrage Movement
Reading: Kraditor, "The History of Suffrage Organization," and "Political Parties and Suffragist Tactics," Screening: *Iron Jawed Angels*
Feb. 23: Civil Rights
Reading: King, "I've Been to the Mountaintop," Screening: *King's Legacy*

Week 6: Black Power
Feb. 28: Malcolm X
Reading: Malcolm X, "1965"
March 2: Black Panthers
Reading: Carmichael, "Black Power," Cleaver, "A Letter From Jail"
Screening: *Fists of Freedom*

Week 7: GLBT Rights
March 7: Stonewall
Reading: "Police Raid" & "Sick No More," Screening: *After Stonewall*
March 9: Sexuality in the Media
Reading: "Glamorization" & "Homicidal" Screening: *Homer's Phobia*

Week 8: Environmental Movements
March 14: Mainstream vs. Radical
Reading: Foreman, "Monkeywrenching," Screening: *Dirt First!*
March 16: Global Environmentalism
Reading: Revkin, "Chico Mendes," Screening: *Decade of Destruction*

Week 9: Globalization and Its Movement
March 21: Intro to Globalization *Project Proposals Due
March 23: What is this movement?
Reading: GAM, pp. 1–10, Screening: *30 Frames a Second*

SPRING BREAK: March 27–March 31

Week 10: Global Justice Movements
April 4: Crossing Borders
Reading: GAM, pp. 11–46
April 6: Building Coalitions
Reading: GAM, pp. 47–78, Screening: *Showdown in Seattle*

Week 11: Global Justice Movements
April 11: Power and Authority

Reading: GAM, pp. 78–100
April 13: Building Today's Global Movement
Reading: GAM, pp. 101–127, Screening: *Dissent*

Week 12: Global Justice Movements
April 18: Direct Action
Reading: GAM, pp. 128–169
April 20: Taking on Corporations
Reading: GAM, pp. 170–188, Screening: *TimberGap*

Week 13: Global Justice Movements
April 25: Mobilizing Consumers
Reading: GAM, pp. 189–226, Screening: *Adbusters-Culture Jamming*
April 27: Changing Rules of the Global Economy
Reading: GAM, pp. 227–242, Screening: *Secrets of Silicon Valley*

Week 14: Community Activism
May 2: Practical Tips
Reading: GAM, pp. 243–283
May 4: Project Work

Week 15: Community Activism
May 9: Student Debriefings
May 11: Student Debriefings ***Term Projects Due, Final Review**

Week 16: Review
May 16: Last day of class, Final Review

Final Exam (cumulative): Monday, May 22, 9:45 a.m.–12:00 p.m.

Appendix B

Project assignment

Course Project Assignment
30%, 300 points

Option 1: Participant Observation

Your project for the semester is to observe and analyze the activities of an advocacy group or organization of your choice and to write a comprehensive survey of activist communication strategies. This project option is designed for people who want (and have time) to get involved with a social or political organization. You are asked to observe and participate in the activities of an activist group of your choice, accepting all responsibility for your actions. As a participant observer, you seek insight that you derive from an activist community's values, dynamics, internal relationships, structures, and conflicts.

Proposal: 5%, 50 points. Due March 21
Write a 1–2 page proposal (typed) that covers the following 5 areas:
  1) Identify and describe the organization and its goals.
  2) Describe the strategies/tactics of the group.
  3) What constitutes the group's public rhetoric?
  4) Describe your plan of involvement for this project.
  5) What are some initial questions/issues you see as important?

Portfolio/Notebook: 10%, 100 points. Due May 11
You should keep a notebook describing your experiences and compile a portfolio of materials that represent the public communication efforts of that organization. You should compile a folder or notebook that includes at least 5 journal entries describing your experiences with the group and its activities, and 5 examples of the group's public rhetoric. You should participate in at least 2 different types of movement activities (one of which is a face-to-face interaction) and gather at least 2 different kinds of public rhetoric (i.e., print media, Web site, or speech). You will turn in this notebook with your final paper.

Paper: 15%, 150 points. Due May 11
For this assignment, you should write a 5–6 page paper that reflects upon your experiences with the group or organization and evaluates the effects of your actions. In your paper, you should address the following questions:

- Describe the organization including its goals, methods, tactics, and actions (50 points)
- Describe your experience with this group's activities. How do individuals relate to the group? How do members of the group work together? What are the goals and outcomes of its activities? (50 points)
- Evaluate how and to what extent the group meets its stated goals. Offer a conclusive evaluation of your role in the group and reflect upon your experiences as an activist. How did your experience affect your perspective about the group, its specific cause(s), and activism in general? (50 points)

Course Project Assignment
30%, 300 points

Option 2: Discourse Analysis

Your project for the semester is to observe and analyze the activities of an advocacy group or organization of your choice and to write a comprehensive survey of activist communication strategies. This project option is tailored for people who do not want (or do not have time outside typical school assignments) to commit energy to working with a community organization. Discourse analysis is concerned with language use in social context. Discourses are interrelated sets of texts that embody and enact certain ideas and ideologies. You are asked to analyze an activist group's public texts within a local, regional, national, and/or global context and evaluate the effectiveness of this discourse.

Proposal: 5%, 50 points. Due March 21
Write a 1–2 page proposal (typed) that covers the following 5 areas:
1) Identify and describe the organization and its goals.
2) Describe the strategies/tactics of the group.
3) What constitutes the group's public rhetoric?
4) Identify 2 theoretical sources that you might use for this paper.
5) Describe your plan for this paper.

Portfolio: 5%, 50 points. Due May 11
You should gather a portfolio of communication materials of this group. You should include 3 different types of the group's public discourse (i.e., print media, Web site, or speech). You should turn in at least 5 examples of public discourse (texts) with your paper.

Paper: 20%, 200 points. Due May 11

You are asked to write a 7–8 page research paper that analyzes the discourse of an activist group by applying social movement theory to your portfolio to critique the group's public communication efforts. Your paper should cite at least 3 academic sources in addition to the primary sources you are analyzing. You should include suggestions for further action based on theories and historical examples of social movements we study. Your paper should address the following questions:

- Describe the organization including its goals, methods, and tactics. (30 points)
- Introduce and explain the theoretical ideas in your 3 sources. Do not just summarize the articles, but explain how the ideas in these articles are useful for analyzing this particular activist group. (60 points)
- Evaluate the group's public discourse. How and to what extent does its communication efforts meet its stated goals? How does the group's public communication fit in to a larger movement framework supported by your sources? (60 points)
- Conclude with suggestions for how the group might improve its public communication efforts. Go into detail based on your discourse analysis. How can other movements' experiences inform the tactics of these activists? (50 points)

Appendix C

Grading Rubric

Grading Rubric

COMM 130   Name _____
Prof. Todd
Course Project Evaluation: Participant Observation (250 points)

Portfolio: 100 points
5 journal entries (2 activities)5 examples of the group's public rhetoric (2 types)

Paper: 150 points (5–6 pages)
Organization's goals, methods, tactics, actions (50 points)

Describe your experience. How do individuals relate to the group? How do members of the group work together? Describe the goals and outcomes of group activities. (50 points)

Does the group meet its stated goals? Evaluate your role. How did your experience affect your perspective about the group, specific cause, activism in general? (50 points)

8

THE POLITICS OF SERVICE LEARNING IN INTRODUCTION TO WOMEN'S STUDIES

Addressing Social Injustices Through Activism

Natalie Wilson

Although an emphasis on formal service-learning courses is relatively new within the academy, feminist pedagogy has a long and fruitful history implementing a broad conception of service learning. In particular, the critique of the banking model of education and the authoritative professor/passive student model examined in the field of critical pedagogy has wide circulation within feminist critiques of education, notably in the emphasis on the classroom as a community, professors as facilitators or collaborators, and students as engaged learners. Moreover, the feminist theoretical emphasis on *praxis*, or putting theory into practice in real-life contexts, and on extending what happens inside the classroom into all areas of life outside the classroom, constructs feminist disciplines as extremely conducive, if not dependent on, a service-learning, community-based model of education.

In this chapter I focus on service-learning pedagogy within the Introduction to Women's Studies (WMST 101) course I teach at California State University, San Marcos (CSUSM). This course broadly uses service learning in various ways; however, I focus in particular on the Student Discussion Leader program and the Activism Project in order to illustrate that successful models for service learning promoting active citizenship must incorporate appropriate pedagogical practices *and* what I term *engaged assignments*.

In relation to pedagogical practices that promote active citizenship, the first way WMST 101 at CSUSM emphasizes the classroom as a community of learners and activists is via the use of Student Discussion Leaders (SDLs). These SDLs team teach the course with me. SDLs assist me with course design and class planning. In class, we alternately lead interactive group discussions, facilitate class activities, and work with students in small groups. This format has the benefit not only of introducing students to a variety of teaching styles and approaches to the material, but also imparts the message that their peers, as SDLs, are as valuable as traditional instructors/professors in imparting knowledge. Thus, *collaborative learning* or *horizontal learning* is put into practice in the course. Students, serving as discussion leaders, help concretize the message of egalitarian, rather than top-down learning. Moreover, using SDLs helps to further break down the walls between the classroom and the outside world as it conveys that students are not just students but also teachers, activists, and citizens, and that the classroom is not just a classroom but a microcosm of the world. Further, using SDLs puts the *theory* of collaborative learning into *practice*, conveying that being a student of WMST is not necessarily limited to a semester but, for many, is a lifelong pursuit. As Manual C., who plans on serving as an SDL in the future, notes, "I truly believe that the changes that WMST has had on my life will last forever."[1]

While serving as an SDL is not defined by the university as meeting service-learning criteria, I would argue that the SDL model meets one of the main criteria of service learning, namely, that it is mutually beneficial to the student and the community. WMST 101 students undoubtedly benefit from seeing their peers in leadership roles, and faculty members benefit from serving as mentors, from enacting collaborative teaching endeavors, and from working with dedicated, passionate, and excited young scholars. Those who serve as SDLs benefit through their collaborative efforts with professors, each other, and the students. They garner a valuable teaching experience, and because many who serve as SDLs plan to go to graduate school to become educators, they are given a valuable taste of their future career. Finally, the wider community benefits as SDLs are active, engaged citizens and foster engaged citizenship among their peers. For example, in the spring 2006 semester, one SDL coordinated with a number of WMST 101 students and community organizations to organize an immigrants rights rally on campus. Other SDLs were instrumental in bringing the women's center to campus and worked with WMST 101 students to address how the new center could most effectively serve the campus and the wider community. As the following comment by Didi L., who served as an SDL for two semesters and who is the cofounder of the women's center reveals, students are prompted to become active via the living activist examples their SDLs embody:

> I realized that much of our citizenry is not well informed about current political issues (including racism, sexual harassment, abortion, sexism, etc). This further encouraged me to become more involved in educating people, which I see as the key to mobilizing both the activists and the masses. Teaching the 101 class also demonstrated the importance of grassroots organization. I could see the change I made in people's lives directly as the students participated in more activist events and engagements.

Similarly, Tasha I. reveals that she benefited from being an SDL by motivating other students to follow in her path and become SDLs themselves:

> When I see former students teaching and becoming active, I feel like I have succeeded. The most rewarding thing in life to me right now is knowing that what I said or what I did was inspirational or motivational to someone else. I believe that motivating others is the most important aspect of being a leader.

As the WMST 101 courses are comprised in the main of lower division students, many of whom are freshman who have never taken women's studies courses before and come into the classroom with preconceived notions of what college classrooms are or should be like, one of the first tasks is encouraging meaningful participation from all students. As with attempting to encourage participatory democratic practices from all citizens, this is not an easy task. For many, it is their first semester in college and they expect to be lectured to while dutifully taking notes. For others, their cultural differences and/or race/class/sexual/embodied social identities obfuscate the willingness and/or confidence to fully participate. Each semester, SDLs and myself have to battle against this reluctance to engage through a variety of means. However, in the end, this battle is well worth it, as the track record of WMST 101 students and SDLs who go on to a life of political engagement and active citizenship attests.

I turn now to a more specific discussion of course content and the emphasis on engaged assignments. However, before I begin, as a scholar schooled in post-structuralism and as a feminist schooled in the necessity of examining language, I would like to first consider the terms that circulate in the title of this chapter specifically, and the theory of service-learning pedagogy more generally. For example, how are we defining *service*, what is *activism*, and what constitutes *political engagement*?

Service seems to be a particularly thorny term from a feminist perspective, as women, as well as other marginalized groups such as people of color, immigrants, and those below the so-called poverty line, have long been the servers, or even the servants of society. Women have, in multiple and overlapping ways, served various others as caregivers, nursemaids, teachers, domestic laborers, sexual commodities, as mothers, partners, daughters, and sisters. They have served institutions via their unpaid volunteer work, via their nurturing role both within and outside the walls of power, via their often sexualized and domesticated labor. People of color, the poor, and immigrants also share an unfair burden of service via their unpaid or underpaid labor; via their sometimes willing, sometimes unwilling reproduction of existing power structures; via, literally and figuratively, their flesh and blood. Thus, from a feminist perspective, service must be reenvisioned in a more equitable, mutually beneficial way for those serving as well as for those being served. In regard to service learning, this reclamation involves serving the very people who were and are disenfranchised by dominant patriarchal, capitalistic conceptions of service. Moreover, the service should be beneficial to an integrated conception of community in which "community" does not privilege certain types of citizens and should be grounded within a framework that accounts for (and tries to dismantle) social stratifications in relation to gender, race, class, sexuality, ability, age, and so forth. However, as Cynthia Moulds (2004) argues in "Feminist Approaches to Social Justice," service learning as an academic practice does not necessarily consider "power relations and social location as factors" (p. 112). For, while the term *service* "carries the connotation of providing service to those less fortunate, a missionary expedition if you will . . . [it] does not ask the question 'How and why are most of these people less fortunate than I?'" (p. 112). Yet, one can easily incorporate such questions into service-learning courses. In my own course, for example, students complete a Social Identity Project in which they are asked to consider their own social positioning in relation to race, class, gender, and other factors of social identity. As described in the syllabus, the aim of this project is to locate yourself in relation to larger socio-cultural groups and issues. Considering the "complexities of oppression and privilege," ask yourself "How and why am I privileged/oppressed in certain aspects and why? How might I use my privileges to benefit others? How might I dismantle oppression, both individually and institutionally, to help not only myself but the wider community?"

This project, which requires a written and presentation component, serves as a bridge to the further work students will undertake in the semester-long Activism Project, discussed later in the chapter. For now, though, I would like to reiterate that service and service learning can be very conducive to feminist aims if one makes a point of examining power relations, social positioning, and concepts such as citizenship, engagement, and activism through a feminist lens.

Promoting good citizens who provide service to the community is of course a core goal of service learning. However, "citizenship" is a very broad concept, one not without deleterious hierarchical undertones that hold up certain binaries where the citizen is seen as superior to the immigrant, the outsider, the other. Citizenship entails the notion that citizens are entitled to certain rights, privileges, and protections and owe a certain allegiance to the nation or state they are members of. However, the concept of American citizenship is problematically embroiled within a history marked by imperialism and a society still colored by racism, sexism, classism, and homophobia. Taking these matters on board, one must admit that certain citizens are presented as truer or more valuable to America. Additionally, the concept of citizenry itself is problematic in that it often shores up uncritical nationalistic zeal and patriotic fervor of the type witnessed post-9/11. Also problematic in regard to citizenship is that the term favors the public over the private, a power-laden dichotomy fruitfully critiqued in feminist thought as a doctrine in which the public is associated with the "male world" of politics, institutions, and power, and the private is associated with the "women's world" of the home and family. Thus, one of the aims of the course is to reimagine the meanings and possibilities of citizenship through an emphasis on the basic dictionary definition of citizenship: membership in a community. As comments from students attest, WMST 101 helps remind students they are not the isolated, self-sufficient individuals American society prompts them to be, but are part of an interdependent society. For example, as student Jessica D. notes, "WMST gives individuals a feeling of cohesiveness, and real honest courage." This sense of courage is fostered by sharing experiences and realizing many people feel disempowered, silenced, and oppressed under the parameters of contemporary American society. As student Tasha I. relates, "When I first took the course I was ignorant to the fact that the issues I faced as a woman, and as a minority, were faced by many others. . . . After speaking up and finally finding my voice I then learned how to speak on the behalf of others and most importantly I learned how to listen." Speaking and listening about shared hardship often encourages further action. Student Angel J. says that WMST 101 "reignited my passion and got me back into the activist groove and out of my slump. It seemed there was no hope of things getting better in the world and Women's Studies reminded me I wasn't alone and together there was a chance to make a difference." Thus, the course fosters a sense of shared experiences, of community, and of the sense that together, as Angel J. puts it, we can make a difference. However, before taking WMST 101, many students do not envision themselves as part of a community of possible activists, let alone as important members of society able to initiate social or political change. In order to prompt such envisioning, I frequently call on students to reflect upon the ways in which they are already active. Do they belong to any campus or community organizations? Do they participate in any forms of boycott or protest? Do they fire off politicized e-mails or participate in activist blogging? Thus, the course aims to empower them to see themselves as active citizens able to change the society and the world they live in through political engagement.

This brings me to the next term I would like to consider, political engagement. Political engagement has historically envisioned (White) men as the primary actors and the primary beneficiaries of politics. As the work of Moira Gatens (1997) reveals, politics has long been associated with very particular types of citizens. As Gatens argues,

> From its classical articulation in Greek philosophy, only a body deemed capable of reason and sacrifice can be admitted into the political body as an active member. . . . At different times, different kinds of beings have been excluded from the pact, often simply by virtue of their corporeal specificity. Slaves, foreigners, women, the conquered, children, the working classes, have all been excluded from political participation. (p. 83)

Thus, as with citizenship, the notion of political engagement is laden with very particular dynamics of power that privilege certain groups and disenfranchise others. However, rather than throwing out these terms in a defeatist fashion, I aim to redefine them, and find that this very act of redefining is a useful way to begin the process of promoting broader and more productive conceptions of active citizenship and political engagement among students. Granted, each batch of students must work to come to new, expanded definitions of citizenship, definitions that engage the idea of a global citizenry rather than a citizenry tied to a nation-state, and new definitions of political engagement that invariably expand what is meant by the term *political* and the term *engagement*. The redefining of political seems particularly imperative, for, as Jordy Rocheleau (2004) posits in "Theoretical Roots of Service Learning," "The word *political* itself has come to have a negative connotation so that to call a speech, piece of writing, or action political is to accuse it of empty rhetorical strategy in a struggle for self-interest and unjustified power" (p. 15). In the current climate, to call a course, mode of study, or academic discipline political, is construed as an insult. Thus, in the course, I ask students to reflect on the famous feminist mantra, the personal is political. I ask them how and why does this phrase resonate (or does not) in their own lives? While students tend not to see that what they do in their personal lives has ramifications for the whole of society, it does not take too much prompting to get them to politicize the personal (for example, realizing that who is *expected* to do the dishes in their household is shaped by gender politics). Then, I ask them to turn the phrase on its head and consider the following: How is the political also personal? How do political decisions, acts, laws, and so on affect them each and every day? These reflections help students to begin to see themselves as part of the complex web of societal relations, rather than as atomized individuals.

Other issues regarding political engagement in the classroom are the stumbling blocks of apathy, cynicism, and defeatism. Repeatedly I hear comments such as, "This class is so depressing. It makes me just want to curl up and die" or "All this class does is complain about what's wrong with the world. Why can't we focus on what's right?" However, as I try to convey to students, the very act of "complaining about the world," as some would call it, is a crucial step toward change; we must first identity the problems and their root causes before we can begin to think about solving them. For some,

WMST 101 serves as an inspiration to not only think about solutions, but to become self-proclaimed activists. As one student notes:

> I know WMST 101 changed me as a person. Ever since I finished the course I feel more driven, like I (as in alone) can change the world, instead of feeling like I (as a singular person) was insignificant. I always felt like I HAD to have a group of supporters, BEFORE I could start my activism, but now I know, I can start out on a run across the country and watch my supporters follow suit. . . . Who knows, maybe one day, we'll all be running for [the] same thing, freedom and equality.

Or, as another student relates,

> my eyes began seeing other issues that affected others that went beyond what a classroom atmosphere could address and take a hold of. I began to reach out and grab other opportunities that involved my passion for constructive change. After one becomes committed, it becomes a lifestyle.

This lifestyle change the student refers to is one of the implicit goals of service leaning—namely, to encourage students to live a life that incorporates a sense of service (or activism) as part of daily life. However, in regard to service leaning, it seems necessary to question some of the rules of the game. Most literature on the subject outlines very specific criteria for what service learning is, namely, that it must involve an organized service activity with a community partner or agency, that the service must be integrated into the academic course work, that the service must meet a community-identified need, and that the community and the students must benefit from the service. Coming from a discipline that tends to question rules, I am prompted to consider the limitations of these parameters, especially of the first. While working with community partners and agencies is no doubt beneficial, I suggest that students can enact political engagement and active citizenship in much more varied ways. Stipulating that students *must* work with certain groups or agencies, in my view, limits the potential types of political engagement, and while this model is certainly appropriate for certain courses, I find a more open-ended approach to service learning is the most useful in my course as it allows for a more varied conception of service that can include participating in school governance, in Associated Students Incorporated groups, in action committees, in social networks with specified political goals, in political campaigns, or in local activist groups. Moreover, the stipulation that service must meet a community identified need begs the question of who is defining these needs. On my campus, for example, students worked tirelessly to bring about a campus women's center. However, in their struggle, they were invariably met with resistance and an attitude that the campus community did not *need* a women's center. Similarly, the stipulation that both the community and the student must benefit from the service learning prompts a questioning of how we are defining benefit. To stick with the example of the women's center, many on campus were resistant to the center because they felt it would not be a benefit to all students. Segments of the university population do not see the center, or the women's studies program more broadly, as a benefit; rather, by many, we seem to be construed as a thorn in the side, as a program that does not institute beneficial change on campus or in the wider community.

However, I would argue that women's studies courses benefit all involved, from the students taking them to the faculty teaching them to the university as a whole to the wider community. By exploring existing power structures and examining how certain subjects differentially marked by gender, race, class, sexuality, ability, and many other markers of difference are privileged and/or oppressed along multiple axis and from various ideologies and institutions, women's studies *benefits* those who study it (and those who teach it) through its revisioning of the world and its sustained emphasis on social justice. As Jane Kenway and Helen Modra (1992) observe in "Feminist Pedagogy and Emancipatory Possibilities," "feminism is . . . driven by a vision of a world which might be otherwise" (p. 139). This vision of a better world, as lofty as it sounds, is certainly at the core of critical feminism, and while a more equitable world may mean that those who have long *benefited* from unexamined privilege (for example, those who are White, male, wealthy, heterosexual, and/or able-bodied) may lose some of their unearned advantage, a more equitable world would certainly benefit the majority—the majority who have so often been construed as the other, the inferior, the *minority*.

Further, as scholar Peggy McIntosh (2006) tells us, we must begin to value the making and mending of the fabric of everyday life if we are to envision the world otherwise. Our current "iceberg structure" of society, in which a very small percentage of people are above water and control the majority of wealth and power as well as shape the world for those below water, must be revised to contain expanded models of politics, power, and citizenry that include the majority of people. This iceberg structure is of course enmeshed with some of our most sacred myths, the myth of individualism and meritocracy, for example, wherein those above water *deserve* to be there. This dog-eat-dog individualism must be examined if one is to promote the betterment of the world that service learning calls for. For in order to demonstrate the value and necessity of service outside oneself, the individualist ethos needs to be revealed as one that maintains certain power structures and discourages notions of a mutually beneficial community model. Women's studies seems particularly conducive to the dismantling of such an ethos specifically, and to the implementation of service-learning components that promote political engagement more generally. As Pat Washington (2004) wrote in "Community-Based Service Learning,"

> While community-based service learning is an effective tool for enhancing student learning in any setting, it is particularly useful for challenging entrenched cultural values and beliefs about the homeless, welfare recipients, lesbians and gays, feminist organizations, and other socially and politically marginalized groups. (p. 227)

As Washington's statement suggests, service learning has many of the same goals of feminism and critical pedagogy. And, while Cynthia Moulds (2004) reminds us that service learning is *not necessarily* feminist, she offers readers a wonderful blueprint of how to make it so in "Feminist Approaches to Social Justice."

In terms of pedagogy, it is imperative that those who wish to envision the world otherwise also envision the classroom otherwise, as feminist scholar bell hooks (1994, 2003) so cogently explores in *Teaching to Transgress* and *Teaching Community*. The banking model of education critiqued by Freire (1968/2003) in *Pedagogy of the Oppressed* where professors impart their knowledge to empty student vessels and then students regurgitate this knowledge is certainly not the most conducive way to promote active citizenship. In place of the traditional hierarchical classroom structure where professors talk and students listen, a collaborative classroom constituted of an engaged community of learners must be enacted. In my courses, this is achieved by means of emphasizing participation from all students by weighting it heavily in their grade, by requiring participation logs, and by creating a communal atmosphere in which all are encouraged to speak and listen.

This community atmosphere, students report, has a strong impact that prompts a sense of shared experiences and a communal ground from which to initiate change. This type of classroom environment encourages students to find their voice and to speak out. As student Manuel C. shares, "During the classroom sessions we would all speak our minds and argue certain controversial issues that we face on a daily basis. While expressing our thoughts, there was sense of comfort knowing that no one was going to be judging you." Student Lori W. found WMST 101 similarly empowering. She notes, "Women's Studies definitely helped me in being more confident in my political and social ideas. Before attending WMST 101 I felt unsure about women's, social, and political issues and my right to assert and act on those ideas and issues. I found my voice—that it had value and power."

In addition to creating a communal classroom atmosphere, the goals and objectives of those wishing to promote political engagement in their courses must be expanded beyond the traditional "mastery of the discipline" into much broader goals, such as enabling students to understand the connections between knowledge and social change, cultivating habits of civic engagement, demonstrating how academic knowledge can be concretely applied in addressing social ills, and unmasking power relations so that students see themselves as viable political agents able to enact real-world change. The WMST 101 course aims to achieve such goals by approaching service learning through the disciplinary perspective of feminist activism. Theoretically, this approach emphasizes the multiple and overlapping strands of privilege and oppression and focuses on various markers of social differences such as race, class, gender, sexuality, and so on. The design of the course reflects these perspectives through its inclusion of learning units that cover these categories of difference locally, globally, and historically. However, in order to keep in mind that the personal is political, students are regularly asked to reflect on how such issues affect them *personally* and what they can do about them *politically*. The course thus aims to demystify and redefine activism in ways that allow students to see themselves as already active and to formulate ideas about future actions they want to undertake. In order to prompt such analysis, students are regularly called upon to consider, verbally and in writing, how course concepts and texts affect them, what social issues under consideration *bother* them, and what *action* they might take to bring about change. By continually requiring students to analytically examine their responses, ideas, and plans of action, the course aims to introduce students to feminism as a social theory and a social movement, not just as a discipline but as a personal political practice that has to be *enacted*, not just studied.

I find this emphasis on action particularly imperative at this juncture because as Moulds (2004) and various other feminist scholars lament, "Women's studies seems to have marginalized activism in the classroom" (p. 110). In its earlier days as a discipline, women's studies was undoubtedly more political, radical, and actively engaged in envisioning the world otherwise. However, in today's climate, as noted earlier, politics is often perceived as a dirty word; hence, one must work actively (and carefully) to repoliticize the classroom. In the course, I endeavor to achieve this aim of promoting active, engaged citizenship by a simultaneous reenvisioning of what happens in the classroom with a combined emphasis on how the academic knowledge gained inside the classroom can be applied to the world outside the classroom.

By beginning to discuss active citizenship and political engagement from the very first day of class, and by requiring various assignments that require such engagement, such as the Social Identity Project and the Activism Project, students are continually encouraged to think beyond the classroom walls and to begin to see themselves as harbingers of action and change. The syllabus design of dividing the class into learning units, all of which introduce different social issues, also aids in engaging students. If eradicating poverty does not seem a concern for some, perhaps corporate control of the media will. If focusing on body image seems pointless to some, exploring global political activism or poverty in the United States may seem more pressing. While attempting to introduce many of the major ills of our world in a mere 15 weeks might seem like it would have the effect of fostering a defeatist attitude, I have found quite the contrary to be the case. While some students lament that the class is depressing and nothing will ever change, more tend to be spurred into action, especially given the wide range of community partners they are able to work with through our supportive campus Office of Community Service Learning. Many students leave WMST 101 with a renewed sense of purpose and an enduring dedication to bringing about social change. For example, as Lori W. said, "Since attending WMST 101 I have become a Women's Studies major, a committee member of our campus' first Women's Center, and been involved in demonstrations and protests on campus advocating social, political, and women's justice." Lori W. also raised funds to visit Camp Democracy in Washington, DC, in 2006. Other

WMST 101 students have gone on to graduate school, to work in local political campaigns, and to organize local rallies, marches, and events around issues relating to women's studies and social justice.

In the course, a key aspect of igniting the sparks that translate into becoming politically active is the incorporation of a number of engaged assignments throughout the semester. Now, *engage* has a number of connotations, but the ones I would like to emphasize here are the definitions of engage, such as "to hold the attention of," "to induce to participate, "to begin and carry on an enterprise or activity," "to participate at length," and "to come together." First, it is imperative to hold the attention of students, to get them interested, in order to prompt *them* to engage with the material. The course's emphasis on active learning inside the class as well as the requirements that students use what they learn inside class in a number of real-world settings serves as a transformational experience for many students and helps to bridge the gap between academic knowledge and everyday life that service learning calls for. One of the key assignments here is the Activism Project, a semester-long assignment that calls for a series of reflective assignments, engagements with the outer world, and progress reports shared with the entire class. To initiate the project, students must identify an issue or cause they would like to take action on or engage with. Students are then put into action groups according to their chosen projects. While the project report and presentations are not due until the end of the semester, students are encouraged to work on their projects throughout the semester, inside and outside class, and are required to report on their progress verbally and in writing. To monitor their work and provide feedback, I require that they each hand in a group project log about every other week that details their work, research, actions, reflections, and concerns.

The Activism Project is broken into three stages: research, action, and presentation. After researching their issue and cause and the best plan of action, students are required to take some form of action to bring about desired change. Students can work with campus organizations, specific community partners, or with nonprofit agencies for this project, and are encouraged to think about what social problems concern them most and what forms of activism would bring about the changes they desire. Part of the rationale for this more open-ended approach to promoting political engagement entails an understanding that students must come to a definition of social activism

and service that *fits them*. Hence, I try to avoid overtly proscriptive requirements, such as, "You must work such and such number of hours at such and
such institution." Often, their action involves working with select campus
groups or community partners. In other cases, students may organize a campus rally, a speak-out, a protest, or a poster campaign. To culminate the project, students are asked to present their project to the class, detailing their
issue or cause, their actions, their reflection, and how they plan to continue
to be active about their chosen cause in the future. In the written assignment,
students are asked to link the project to feminism and core course concepts—in effect to link the academic discipline to their personal political
practice.

While the overt aim of the Activism Project is to ask students what concrete actions they will take with the knowledge they have gained from
WMST 101, the implicit goals are first, to urge them to take action, and
second, to help them link theory with practice. In keeping with third-wave
feminism's emphasis on everyday activism, the project takes a broad conception of activism and is grounded in the belief that activism and effective engagement come in many forms. Overall, the project encourages students to
define a social ill that they want to change, and to go about changing it.
However, by requiring students to research their chosen cause, the various
institutions that address this cause, and the difficulties they are likely to encounter because of societal structures and institutions, they are prompted to
ground their planned activism in relation to their growing academic knowledge of women's studies. Also, by requiring students to query how the organizations or people they are working with identify *their* needs, students are
prompted to address their own aims in relation to the practical needs of the
community they aim to benefit. Moreover, by providing students with
ample opportunities for written and verbal reflections in which they share
their activism plans and experiences with the entire class, the course helps
students come to a definition of service and civic and political engagement
that relates to the course material. The process also introduces them to the
varied ways engagement can be enacted. When evaluating student's work in
the course, these multidimensional approaches and aims must be taken into
account. Thus, rather than basing their grade on exams or essays, grades are
based on participation—assessed by examining the Activism Project log, reflective reports, presentation, written report, as well as other verbal and written projects assigned throughout the semester. This form of grading allows

me to assess what the students have gained over the course of the semester, how much effort they have put in, and how their analytical and critical thinking skills have been used to master and reflect on core course concepts.

In conclusion, both WMST 101 and the SDL program promote active citizenship and civic engagement. Moreover, they do so not only for the duration of the semester or for the duration of the student's academic study. Rather, women's studies courses and the engaged learning they offer often spark a permanent change in students that leads them to continue to be more active citizens. For example, former students and SDLs have gone on to work with groups such as the Associated Students, Inc., the California Faculty Association, College Democrats, the National Latino Research Organization, the National Organization of Women, the League of Women Voters, the San Diego Budget Coalition, Action in Defense of Education, and the Center for Community Solutions. Additionally, many former WMST 101 students have gone on to serve as SDLs; to travel to Africa on peacekeeping missions; to work with orphanages in Tijuana, Mexico; to volunteer at local women's shelters or after-school programs; and to travel to the state capital of Sacramento to protest issues concerning students and faculty. Students consistently relate that their time in WMST 101 not only prompts "big" actions of civic engagement and service, but also affects their interactions in such a way that they become more politically engaged, active citizens in their daily lives. The emphasis on service and activism that WMST 101 offers not only sparks a dedication to continuing civic engagement in students, it also offers them concrete experience and knowledge of the politically transformative discipline that is women's studies, teaching them that "students in women's studies, and in academia at large, must turn questions of inequity into activist practice by allying feminist knowledge to social change in the community" (Moulds, 2004, p. 110). In so doing, the course promotes active citizenship and political engagement specifically focused on redressing social injustices and making the world a more equitable place for us all.

Note

1. Student comments included in this chapter are taken from assessment questionnaires. Names have not been changed.

References

Freire, P. (2003). *Pedagogy of the oppressed* (Myra Bergman Ramos, Trans.). New York: Continuum. (Original work published 1968)

Gatens, M. (1997). Corporeal representation in/and the body politic. In K. Conboy, N. Medina, & S. Stanbury (Eds.), *Writing on the body: Female embodiment and feminist theory* (pp. 80–89). New York: Columbia University Press.

hooks, b. (1994). *Teaching to transgress: Education as the practice of freedom*. New York: Routledge.

hooks, b. (2003). *Teaching community: A pedagogy of hope*. New York: Routledge.

Kenway, J., & Modra, H. (1992). Feminist pedagogy and emacipatory possibilities. In C. Luke & J. Gore (Eds.), *Feminisms and critical pedagogy* (pp. 138–166). New York: Routledge.

McIntosh, P. (2006, March). Keynote address at the Fourth Annual Women's Leadership Conference. University of San Diego.

Moulds, C. M. (2004). Feminist approaches to social justice: Activism and resistance in the women's studies classroom. In S. Weir & C. Faulkner (Eds.), *Voices of a new generation: A feminist anthology* (pp. 108–120). Boston: Pearson.

Rocheleau, J. (2004). Theoretical roots of service learning: Progressive education and the development of citizenship. In B. W. Speck & S. L. Hoppe (Eds.), *Service learning: History, theory, and issues* (pp. 3–21). Westport, CT: Praeger.

Washington, P. (2004). Community-based service learning: Actively engaging the other. In A. M. Johns, & M. Kelley (Eds.), *Diversity in college classrooms: Practices for today's campuses* (pp. 209–231). Ann Arbor: University of Michigan Press.

9

USING SERVICE LEARNING TO CHANGE SOCIAL STRUCTURE

The Gulf Coast Civic Works Project

Scott Myers-Lipton

I n fall 2003, I set out to see if it was possible to change social structure through service learning. I had been involved in the service-learning movement for almost 20 years. I had personally taken 20 student groups on domestic and international summer service-learning trips, taught over 30 service-learning courses, developed three service-learning leadership programs, and wrote my dissertation and six articles on service learning. I had dedicated my entire professional career to service learning; however, I began to have doubts about the effectiveness of service learning to change society.

Yes, I, and hundreds of others in the service-learning movement, had transformed individual lives. We had made our students more civically and intellectually engaged, more racially tolerant, and more globally concerned (Myers-Lipton, 2002, 1998, 1996a, 1996b). Based on all the research that has been done in the past 20 years, it is clear that service learning can transform individual lives. Yet, at the same time, we had not fulfilled the promise of service learning, which was to change society. Academe was basically running as it had before the service-learning movement. Yes, our universities used service learning to demonstrate their commitment to the community, but the movement had very little effect upon the culture of the campus, or the social structures in the larger society. In fact, we had gone backward on many of the issues (e.g., poverty rate) that service learning was supposed to address.

So several years ago, I set out to see if it was possible to bring about social transformation on my campus and in my community. The focus was not to be on individual change, even though this would still occur, but rather on changing social policy. I decided to develop a social action service-learning course in which the students would be on teams that would work on local and global issues, and would be designed to continue on after the class ended.

Sociology 164: Social Action

Sociology 164: Social Action is an action-oriented, solutions-based course on community activism. In this course, students explore issues such as community organizing, strategy, tactics, small-group skills (i.e., active listening skills, facilitation, consensus, group dynamics, and process), coalition building, and working with the media. Through interactive methods in the classroom, including group activities, small- and large-group discussion, videos, guest speakers, readings, and community service-learning projects, we explore the various issues surrounding community organizing.

What is unique about this course is that it is designed to actually *do social action*. Instead of just reading about it in a book, students learn how to bring about social change by *doing* it. Of course, students still use "book knowledge," but the hope is that this knowledge is challenged by the students' community experiences, and that they develop a more critical and deeper understanding of public issues and community change by integrating action and book knowledge. Practically, we spend about one-half of each class talking about the community action project and the other half talking about the text. Of course, we integrate praxis with text.

Over a two-year period, four viable student organizations were created from this social action course: the Student Homeless Alliance (SHA), Students Against Intimate Violence (SAIV), Students Advocating Global Education (SAGE), and a student chapter of the Worker's Right's Consortium (WRC). To support their work, I became the faculty advisor to these groups. In fact, the university recently awarded me a one-semester course release to continue to help these groups grow and develop strategy.

Critical Education Theory

Critical education theory, which is the perspective that guides my research and pedagogy, comes from critical social theory in the subdiscipline of the sociology of education. This perspective focuses on how dominant socioeconomic groups maintain power over the educational process, as well as how subordinate groups resist this domination. Critical education theory is interested in discovering the various types of curricula and pedagogy that allow teachers to become "transformative intellectuals," and students to become active, critical, and engaged learners (Giroux, 1988).

Critical education theory is best described as a perspective that has several common elements rather than a single shared theory. Influenced by macro conflict theory, interactionism, Antonio Gramsci, Paulo Freire, and the Frankfurt School, this perspective is unified by the objective "to empower the powerless and transform existing social inequalities and injustices. . . . to heal, repair, and transform the world" (McLaren 1989, 160).

Critical theory, as an overarching framework, is well suited for service learning because they share three key assumptions. First, critical theory and service learning are both interested in the development of a curriculum and pedagogy that transforms school into an agent of social change. Second, critical theorists and many service-learning educators share the assumption that students should actively question the power relationships in society and that through this questioning, transformational change of the student and society is possible. Third, critical education theory and service learning both make the assumption that humans are active agents of change. Because these two perspectives share these key assumptions, service learning can be grounded in critical education theory.

Creating Democratic Spaces

At the time I created this course focusing on institutional change, I simultaneously became involved in a student-led effort to build a statue for Tommie Smith and John Carlos, two San José State University (SJSU) student athletes. Tommie and John were students at SJSU in 1968; they were also gold and bronze medal winners that year in the 200-meter dash at the Mexico City Summer Olympics. However, their athletic feats were not the reason students wanted to honor them with 20-foot statues; it was what they did when they were on the Olympic podium, and that was to raise their fists in protest against racism and poverty in the United States.

I began to see this work with the students as part of a larger project to change social structure. If change was going to happen, students and faculty needed to have democratic space for them to meet and gather. After several years of hard work by the students, the statues were dedicated in spring 2006, and with Tommie and John present, 4,000 people were there to say thank-you for taking this courageous stand. These statues now serve as a focal point for student activism, and it was here that 40 student leaders gathered on election night 2006.

The students, many of whom had either taken or were taking the Social Action service-learning course, had gathered to protest the recently released U.S. Census Bureau report showing that Santa Clara County—home to Cisco, Adobe, and many other wealthy high-tech corporations—had become the Northern California county with the highest homeless population. The report stated that on any given night, over 7,600 people did not have a place to call home in Silicon Valley (Applied Survey Research, 2005).

The student protest was titled "Poverty Under the Stars." Accordingly, the students had put up signs around the statues stating such things as:

- 18 percent of all U.S. children live in poverty
- 37 million Americans live in poverty
- USA is number one in child poverty in the industrialized world
- 727,000 are homeless in America on any given night

The highlight of the evening was Spike Lee's film, *When the Levees Broke: A Four-Part Requiem*, a film that focused on the tragedy of Hurricane Katrina. A large screen had been set up directly in front of the statues. Each one-hour "act" of the film was shown, followed by a discussion.

The audience reflected America: Black, Latino, White, and Asian students were present. The students also represented a variety of groups: SHA, SAIV, SAGE, WRC, Hip Hop Congress, and several African American fraternities. But while they came from different ethnicities and groups, they had one thing in common—they were all Americans, and they had all come together to discuss poverty in America, and in particular what was happening on the Gulf Coast.

As a college professor, I felt it was a highlight event. Students had come together of their own volition to engage in dialogue and debate one of the most important events that had taken place in recent American history. Students said many important things. What I took away from the conversation was this: Students were upset, and even outraged, at what had taken place in

New Orleans. They couldn't understand how it was possible for the richest country on the planet to respond in such an ineffectual manner, both in the first week after the flood and in the year that followed.

The film started at 7 p.m., but with all the dialogue, the film ended around 1:30 a.m. The students then slept outside on campus (to show solidarity with the homeless). The students had asked me to camp out with them, and I felt obligated to stand with my students, so I spent the night outside with them. When they awoke, the students decided to march over to San José City Hall, which had recently been completed. Ironically, this one-half-billion-dollar building towers over both SJSU and the First Christian Church; the latter opens its doors each night to over 30 homeless adults and kids. Once at city hall, the students marched, drummed, and sang about the need to end poverty and homelessness in America.

Civic Work

After returning from city hall, I went to teach my morning class, which coincidentally happened to be focusing on the Civil Works Administration (CWA), the Works Progress Administration (WPA), and the Civilian Conservation Corps (CCC). These three programs were developed as a response to the social suffering caused by the Great Depression.

In class, I discussed how the CWA employed 4 million workers immediately in construction work (i.e., school repair, sanitation work, road building, etc.). Within two weeks of starting the project, 814,511 were on the payroll; within two months, 4.2 million were working. The Works Project Administration (WPA), which replaced the CWA, went on to employ a total of 8 million people in its 7-year history, and its accomplishments were many: the WPA built or improved 5,900 schools, 2,500 hospitals, and 13,000 playgrounds. And the CCC provided the opportunity for 500,000 young men (ages 18 to 25) to work on environmental conservation projects at 2,600 camps each year. The goal was to employ restless and discouraged young men, many of whom had previously roamed the nation looking for work (Myers-Lipton, 2006).

When I returned home from class, I was exhausted from lack of sleep from the previous night. I sat down and read the newspaper about the 2006 victory of the Democrats regaining control of the Congress. Interestingly, there was an article about a Green Party candidate who was winning her bid to become mayor of Richmond, California, a predominantly African American city. One of her main platforms had been the development of a public works project for 1,000 youths to combat poverty and crime.

Then, the idea came to me. What was needed in the Gulf Coast were living-wage jobs and the opportunity for residents to rebuild their community. I started to think that if the United States could put almost 1 million people to work in two weeks in 1935, we could put 100,000 people to work immediately today in the Gulf Coast. And if the Works Project Administration (WPA) employed 8 million people, and built or improved schools, hospitals, and playgrounds, we could rebuild New Orleans and the Gulf Coast today.

That is how the Gulf Coast Civic Works Project was born. The project was based on the research I had conducted for the book *Social Solutions to Poverty: America's Struggle to Build a Just Society* (Myers-Lipton, 2006). The general proposal for the Civic Works Project was to hire 100,000 Gulf Coast residents to rebuild New Orleans and the surrounding region. The residents would be given subsidized transportation to get back to their neighborhoods, where they would build and repair bridges, forests, hospitals, parks, public houses, roads, schools, and sewer pipes.

After I wrote the proposal, I e-mailed it to friends and colleagues. The response was overwhelmingly positive. One of my colleagues, who is a leading expert in the country on hunger, was so supportive of the proposal that he provided me with his contacts to key congressional lawmakers and promised to phone many of them personally. We also received early support from the NAACP Gulf Coast Advocacy Center.

The students were also equally positive. I presented it to a group of students in my Poverty, Wealth, and Privilege class, the same course that had been discussing the WPA, and five students were interested enough to start meeting outside class on how we could move forward with the Gulf Coast Civic Works Project. The students decided to join me at an upcoming conference in New Orleans, and in addition to attending the conference, we would spend our time discussing the project with citizens' groups in the region. At this point, another student asked if we could take some photographs while we were in New Orleans and uplink them to our Web site so that students at SJSU and at other campuses might be able to view what we were seeing. I told the student that rather than doing this, we should invite students from around the country to come with us to the Gulf Coast, and half jokingly said that we should call it "Louisiana Winter," in a reference to Mississippi Freedom Summer in 1964.

Later that night during my service-learning internship course, we discussed solutions to issues at the students' sites (e.g., at schools, antipoverty programs, and juvenile justice programs). I encouraged them to think big. After they had discussed their solutions, I told them, a bit sheepishly— because this idea was so big—about the idea for Louisiana Winter. After a brief discussion, I told them that if they were interested, they should stay after class, and we could discuss it further. I fully expected only 1 or 2 students to stay after, but I was surprised that 10 students stayed. I believe that the reason that the student interest was so high was that (a) everyone had seen the images of social suffering caused by Katrina, (b) many students had a relative or friend living on the Gulf Coast who had been affected, and (c) Katrina represented an American domestic failure, as Iraq represented an American international failure. This group of 10 students formed the core of what would become the Gulf Coast Civic Works Project.

From the very beginning, this project was focused on providing students with a firsthand experience of political engagement. The goal was to engage students politically by having them promote the idea for a specific piece of legislation. Throughout this political process, students would learn civic knowledge and skills by writing press releases, speaking to the press, facilitating meetings, developing strategy, fund-raising, and building coalitions with students from around the country. Through these real-life experiences, students would develop a civic ethic that was based on empowerment and engagement.

Louisiana Winter

Hurricane Katrina damaged or made uninhabitable more than 500,000 Gulf Coast homes. In addition, Katrina destroyed schools, hospitals, roads, community centers, bridges, parks, and forest lands. The government's response to this unprecedented disaster has been ineffective and weak. A year and a half after the storm, over 115,000 Louisianans applied for funds to rebuild, but only 3,000 had received funds. Today, almost two and one-half years later, 185,106 applications have been received, and 91,873 have been granted. Residents can do little to rebuild until these insurance companies come through. Today, the Gulf Coast is in crisis. There is an urgent need to jump-start the rebuilding process. What is needed is a rebuilding surge in New Orleans and southern Mississippi (Pelosi, 2007; Road Home Program, 2008).

In order to encourage Congress to develop and pass a bill based on the Gulf Coast Civic Works Project, a group of more than 100 college students from 15 universities traveled to New Orleans and Mississippi from January 14 to 20, 2007. As mentioned earlier, this week-long student campaign, Louisiana Winter, was inspired by a previous generation of college students who came to the Gulf Coast to register African American voters during Mississippi's Freedom Summer in 1964. Most students had heard about Louisiana Winter through our national call that we posted on the Internet.

Everywhere the Louisiana Winter students went, they were greeted warmly, whether it was in the New Orleans neighborhoods of Gentilly, Pontchartrain Park, the Lower Ninth Ward, or Uptown; or in St. Bernard Parish, east of New Orleans; or in Gulfport, Pass Christian, Long Beach, or Biloxi in Mississippi. And perhaps even more important, the idea for the Gulf Coast Civic Works Project was seen as a potential solution by almost everyone the students met.

In fact, support for the Civic Works Project cut across political orientation, as conservatives saw it as a "hand up and not a handout," and liberals appreciated the fact that the government would play an active role in relieving the social suffering. Importantly, both conservatives and liberals felt that the federal government had not lived up to its responsibility of taking care of its people, and overwhelmingly supported the Gulf Coast Civic Works Project as a way to rebuild their communities. Clearly, this was not a Democratic or Republican idea, but an American solution.

Louisiana Winter students traveled throughout the Gulf Coast, where they passed out 10,000 fliers; held two rallies; conducted two town hall meetings; gave multiple interviews to local, state, and international media; and perhaps most significantly, asked Gulf Coast residents for their opinions about what they wanted to see included in the Civic Works legislation. The residents' responses were carefully compiled, and now serve as a guideline for any future bill that comes out of Congress. The parameters for the Gulf Coast Civic Works Project are the following:

- The civic works jobs will be in the areas of construction, plumbing, electrical, masonry, air conditioning, etc.

- If workers do not have these skills, paid apprenticeships will be provided. These skilled jobs will soon become the backbone of the middle class.
- The civic works jobs will pay a living wage—no lower than $12 per hour, and preferably $15—so people can have enough money to feed, clothe, and house themselves.
- The civic workers will have the right to join unions.
- The local Gulf Coast residents and displaced citizens will have the first opportunity for the civic work jobs.
- The process to obtain a civic works job should be simple. A streamlined process will be conducted at county employment service offices and/or at faith-based and community initiatives connected to the White House.
- The communities affected by Hurricane Katrina (as well as Hurricane Rita) will decide which structures will be given priority to rebuild. Some communities may focus on housing, while others may focus on schools, hospitals, community centers, or parks.
- A Tennessee Valley Authority (TVA)-like agency will oversee the Gulf Coast Civic Works Project. This TVA-like agency will ensure transparency so that the American public knows exactly where the money is going.

We are proposing that the federal government, state governments, and insurance companies finance this $3.9 billion project. The projected cost is based on a ratio of labor to materials of 80:20—which was used during the New Deal—with a wage rate of $15 per hour. The projected cost of wages is $3.1 billion, while the cost of materials is $775 million. The amount of $3.9 billion is roughly one-half the cost of the war in Iraq ($8.6 billion) each month (Belasco, 2007). And while the Iraq War has been plagued with graft and corruption, similar large-scale public works projects have operated in the United States with little or no corruption.

The Gulf Coast Civic Works Project will not only rebuild homes, but it will also rebuild individual lives. What the students experienced in some of the Louisiana and Mississippi residents was a sense of hopelessness. Sadly, this lack of hope has already cost the lives of too many seniors, as the students were told firsthand stories about how some elders had lost the will to live in the face of such limited rebuilding.

The students also experienced the devastation on the youths, as they viewed many communities that had no place for children to play since the parks and community centers had been destroyed. By having Gulf Coast residents rebuild their own communities, the people will regain their sense of empowerment and hope, and see that a better future is possible.

The Gulf Coast Civic Works Project can also repair the frayed social compact between the government and citizen. As citizens, we have various responsibilities (e.g., pay taxes, sit on juries, and serve our country), while at the same time the government has responsibilities, and one of them is to respond effectively when its citizens are in crisis. Passing federal legislation to implement the Gulf Coast Civic Works Project will be a major step in repairing the social compact that is so badly damaged.

In January 2008, as this book goes to print, 19 SJSU students have just returned from Louisiana Winter 2. Students participated in community work with the local Association of Community Organizations for Reform Now (ACORN) office, met with the key staff members from Louisiana Recovery Authority, the Mayor's Workforce Investment Board, All Congregations Together, and Louisiana ACORN. The students also facilitated a meeting for 59 students from 10 colleges, who gathered at Loyola University to discuss how to promote the project on their campuses.

Engaging Students in Democracy

During April 9 to 14, 2007, students and faculty from 43 colleges, including Xavier, Tulane, Mississippi Gulf Coast Community College, Stanford, University of California at Berkeley, New York University, Princeton, Michigan, Howard, and SJSU, participated in a National Post-Katrina College Summit. The summit was a nationwide, week-long effort to raise awareness about the Gulf Coast through documentary screenings, lectures, spoken word, rallies, petition drives, and other events. The summit was an attempt to catapult New Orleans and the rest of the Gulf Coast back into the national consciousness and to promote federal legislation for a New Deal-style program for the Gulf Coast.

This movement is trying to generate as many ways as possible for students and the larger campus community to engage in democracy. In addition to participating in the summit, students also have taken action by gathering petition signatures, introducing resolutions to their city councils or state legislatures, and asking presidential candidates to focus their attention on the Gulf Coast. As part of the summit, we gathered over 5,000 signatures in support of the project. Students and faculty plan on hand delivering these petitions to Congress in the upcoming months.

Students and faculty are also approaching city council members and state legislators to ask them to introduce resolutions in support of the Gulf Coast Civic Works Project. The goal of these nonbinding resolutions is to put pressure on Congress and the president to enact a WPA-like project. This idea for city council and state legislature resolutions came from Jeanette Oxford, a representative in the Missouri State Legislature. Oxford contacted us in January 2007 and said she would like to introduce a resolution in the Missouri State Legislature in support of the Gulf Coast Civic Works Project. She, along with 21 cosponsors, introduced the resolution in late February 2007. Then, in March 2007, 10 students from SJSU and Stanford gave a presentation at a public hearing on post-Katrina conditions called by Sally Lieber, speaker pro tempore of the California State Assembly. At the hearing, the students asked Lieber to introduce a resolution in support of the project. On May 3, 2007, Lieber introduced Assembly Joint Resolution 22, which calls upon the California congressional delegation to support the passage of federal legislation based on the Gulf Coast Civic Works Project. Eight students were in the gallery of the California Assembly on that day as the state legislators took a moment to recognize the students' work on this project. Following this introduction, the students and Lieber held a press conference at the state capitol to promote the bill. Students and faculty returned to the state capitol to give a short presentation to the Jobs, Economic Development, and Economy Committee. The committee voted unanimously to support the motion. Then, on September 10, 2007, the California Assembly passed AJR 22, Assembly Joint Resolution 22 (AJR 22). AJR 22 urges California Congress members and the President to support the passage of House Resolution 4048: The Gulf Coast Civic Works Act.

Finally, we are engaging students in democracy by having them participate in the presidential campaigns. At first, we planned to create Presidential Candidate Dispatch Teams. The idea was to dispatch students and community members to ask questions of the presidential candidates from both political parties. Examples of questions included What is your plan to rebuild the Gulf Coast? What would you do differently from what is being currently done? If elected president of the United States, would you introduce legislation based on the Gulf Coast Civic Works Project? Do you support the idea of a WPA-like project to rebuild the Gulf Coast? Unfortunately, this idea was not very successful as the students couldn't get the information from the candidates about where they would be until a few days before an event. In fall 2007, project members and people allied to the project did have the opportunity to meet with Senator John Edwards and Senator Barack Obama.

The project has launched a major campaign on Facebook and Myspace titled "Bring the Debates to the Gulf." During the 12 Republican debates, the Gulf Coast was never mentioned, and in the Democratic debates, the Gulf Coast didn't do much better, with less than 1 percent air time devoted to discussing the rebuilding of the Gulf Coast. By having students post on Facebook and Myspace "walls" of the reporters embedded with the candidates, the project hopes to get questions about the Gulf Coast Civic Works Project into the debates.

At SJSU, about 75 students were involved in the Gulf Coast Civic Works Project during spring and fall 2007. About half of them were involved in the Social Action course, and the rest were from the Community Change concentration in Sociology and from the general student population. The students in the course who decided to work on the Civic Works Project were broken into four teams, focusing on petitions, resolutions, the presidential candidates, and the National College Summit. The students from the larger campus community met every Thursday night, and they planned the week-long summit for our campus. Events at SJSU included a concert, rally, documentary screenings, a solidarity dinner with the Katrina survivors, and reading the names of the over 1,800 known Katrina victims.

At campuses around the country, similar events took place. At the University of Michigan, events were held each night throughout the week. The highlight was when Lieutenant General Russel Honoré, the person New Orleans Mayor Ray Nagin credited with finally bringing in supplies to New Orleans, spoke to a packed room of students, faculty, and community members. At the University of North Carolina, students held a vigil for the Katrina victims and survivors. Mary Small, co-chairwoman of the campus group Extended Disaster Relief, was quoted in the *Daily Tar Heel* as saying that this vigil was different: "The ones in the past have been in memory of those who have died, but this one is to stand in solidarity for those still alive and struggling to survive." The article goes on to say that the goal of the summit was to obtain "signatures to petition the U.S. Congress to enact legislation that would create 100,000 jobs for Gulf Coast residents. And at Tulane University, students created a coffin and encouraged students to sign petitions with the theme being "Death to Apathy." The college newspapers from the various campuses covered all of the above events (Saraiva, 2007).

Fall 2007: Introduction of the Gulf Coast Civic Works Act (HR 4048)

Originally, the project had an early champion in Congressman Bennie Thompson of Mississippi, chair of the House of Representatives Committee on Homeland Security. Congressman Thompson became interested in the project when he was told about it by Congresswoman Zoe Lofgren. Lofgren had met with SJSU students and faculty a few weeks after the project was created, but she felt that Thompson, a southerner, rather than herself—a representative from California—would be the more appropriate person to introduce it, so she presented it to him.

In January 2007, in one of his first public addresses as chair of Homeland Security, Thompson announced that one of his three goals for the committee would be to develop a WPA-like project for the Gulf Coast, and he referenced our work. In fact, Thompson's staff told us that he considered the Gulf Coast Civic Works Project as a model for reconstruction. However, on May 15, 2007, the deputy director of the Committee on Homeland Security informed us that Thompson would not put forward a WPA-like initiative, but rather something called the Department of Homeland Security Corps. The deputy director did not release any details, but from the sound of it, this new program appears to be similar to an AmeriCorps program, which would be nice, but it is not a massive public works program. Soon after, Lofgren decided to take action. On November 1, 2007, Lofgren introduced in Congress the Gulf Coast Civic Works Act (HR 4048), with Charlie Melancon of Louisiana and Gene Taylor of Mississippi cosponsoring the bill.

While the students took the lead in creating the bill and pushing it forward over the past year, it would not have been possible to get the support of these other congressional offices without the project's three most important allies: ACORN, the Robert F. Kennedy Center for Human Rights, and ColorofChange.

ACORN has become deeply involved with the Gulf Coast Civic Works Project. Steve Bradberry, the lead organizer for Louisiana ACORN, said that he wakes up and goes to bed excited about the Gulf Coast Civic Works Project. Importantly, Bradberry has been working to bring together a coalition of Gulf Coast community-based organizations to work on the bill. In February 2008, Bradberry is planning a meeting in New Orleans of Gulf Coast organizations, with two students representing the project, and together we will plan the national campaign to pass HR 4048.

In addition, we have received support from the Robert F. Kennedy Memorial Center for Human Rights. Jeffrey Buchanan, communication director for the center, has been extremely helpful in setting up and meeting with congressional staff members. He is also taking a leading role in the Bring the Gulf to the Debates campaign. Additionally, Buchanan wrote a guest article for the project's Web site stating that if the United States can create 40,000 public work jobs in Iraq, why can't it do the same for the Gulf Coast (Buchanan, 2007). Lastly, James Rucker from ColorofChange has provided crucial support for the project from its very inception.

I began this chapter by stating that the goal of this project was to bring about change in social structure. While this has yet to be accomplished, the project is well on its way. Furthermore, we have had a profound impact on the culture of the campus. The project was on the front page of the college paper eight times during the past year. We were also featured several times in the *San José Mercury News*, as well as on the major TV and radio stations in the Bay Area. Students feel a new sense of activism on the campus, as was noted by one of the Louisiana Winter students during his graduation speech in which he stated that student activism was up tenfold on the campus. In addition, we have engaged hundreds of college students in the political process, and they have learned firsthand the civic knowledge and skills of working with the media, facilitating meetings, developing strategy, fund-raising, and building coalitions.

Sixty-eight years ago, Langston Hughes said, "O, yes, I say it plain, America never was America to me, and yet I swear this oath—America will be." The students are on that path to make America be.

References

Applied Survey Research. (2005, April). The 2004 Santa Clara County Homeless Census and Survey. Retrieved from http://www.google.com/search?q=Ap

plied + Survey + research + ASR + 7646 + homeless&ie = utf-8&oe = utf-8&aq = t&rls = org.mozilla:en-US:official&client = firefox-a

Belasco, A. (2007, March). The cost of Iraq, Afghanistan, and other global war on terror operations since 9/11. Retrieved from http://www.fas.org/sgp/crs/natsec/RL33110.pdf

Buchanan, J. (2007). Human rights for displaced Iraqis but not displaced Americans? Retrieved from http://solvingpoverty.blogspot.com/2007_03_01_archive.html

Caldwell, A. (2007). Vigil held to support Gulf Coast residents: Event part of National Week. *The Daily Tar Heel.* Retrieved from http://media.www.dailytarheel .com/media/storage/paper885/news/2007/04/10/University/Vigil.Held.To.Support .Gulf.Coast.Residents-2831329.shtml

Giroux, H. (1988). *Teachers as intellectuals: Toward a critical pedagogy of learning.* New York: Bergin and Garvey.

McLaren, P. (1989). *Life in schools: An introduction to critical pedagogy in the foundations of education.* New York: Longman.

Myers-Lipton, S. (1996a). Effect of a comprehensive service learning program on college students' level of modern racism. *Michigan Journal of Community Service Learning, 3,* 44–54.

Myers-Lipton, S. (1996b). Effect of service learning on college students' attitudes toward international understanding. *Journal of College Student Development, 37*(6), 659–668.

Myers-Lipton, S. (1998). Effect of a comprehensive service learning program on college students' level of civic responsibility. *Teaching Sociology, 26*(4), 243–258.

Myers-Lipton, S. (2002). Service learning and success in sociology. In C. Berheide, J. Chin, & D. Rome (Eds.), *Included in sociology: Learning climates that cultivate racial and ethnic diversity* (pp. 197–212). Merrifield, VA: American Association of Higher Education and American Sociological Association.

Myers-Lipton, S. (Ed.). (2006). *Social solutions to poverty: America's struggle to build a just society.* Boulder, CO: Paradigm.

Pelosi, N. (2007). Katrina. Retrieved from http://speaker.house.gov/issues?id = 0011

Saraiva, Caterina (2007, April 9). Restaurants to raise funds for relief. *The Daily Tar Heel.* Retrieved from http://media.www.dailytarheel.com/media/storage/paper 885/news/2007/04/09/City/Restaurants.To.Raise.Funds.For.Relief-2829518.shtml

Shelly, B. (2007, March 9). Volunteers toil, but Gulf still a mess. *The Kansas City Star.* Retrieved from http://solvingpoverty.blogspot.com/2007/03/volunteers-toil-but-gulf-still-mess.htm.

The Road Home Program. (2008). Weekly detailed statistics as of January 14, 2008. Retrieved from http://www.road2la.org/newsroom/stats.htm

SECTION FOUR

TEACHING OTHERS THROUGH POLITICAL ENGAGEMENT

10

MEDIA MENTORS

Nurturing Democratic Ideals
Among High School Journalists

Linda Bowen

Ajournalism student in a beginning news reporting and writing course raised her hand and blithely asked: "Do you *really* have to be interested in current events to be a journalist?" The answer should have been obvious. Yet, several of her 18 classmates added their voices to her query, lamenting their own aversion to reading the newspaper, watching TV news, or accessing online information on a regular basis. What, they wondered, could *possibly* be the advantage of a newspaper subscription if all they wanted was to anchor the news on *Entertainment Tonight* or the sports report on *ESPN?*

Not long ago that student was launched into the real world, armed with a bachelor's degree in journalism and a professed desire to work in broadcast news. Obviously, fulfillment of her quest was dependent on having learned to pay attention to current events. But her story is not unique and it embodies a dilemma facing journalism educators in U.S. colleges and universities: how to teach journalism skills to students who are not regular consumers of news and information and, like so many Americans, are detached from civic life and the political process (Kurtz, Rosenthal, & Zukin, 2003).

For educators, this situation goes beyond the nuts and bolts of teaching the traditional who, what, when, where, why, and how: Despite the vast proliferation of news outlets and information resources, studies reveal a sizable number of young people (those under age 30) are going without any form of news on a daily basis, preferring weekly news magazines (Center for Information & Research on Civic Learning & Engagement [CIRCLE], 2007). For example, only 11 percent of high school students access the news every day, going to Google and Yahoo before national TV or local daily newspaper sites. They opt mainly for entertainment programming (Knight Foundation High School Initiative, 2006, pp. 4, 6, 8).

In fact, less than one-third of 18- to 29-year-olds reads a daily newspaper, while the percentage of those who say they obtain their news from television or online has remained static since 2000, despite the use of cell phones and other electronic devices to access news. Fewer than 10 percent are regular blog readers (Pew Research Center for the People and the Press, 2006). Nor are they voting in appreciable numbers, despite jumps in turnout rates in recent national elections. Recent studies show only about one-third of young Americans (under 25) are involved in political or civic activities, and most of them are ignorant about current events (CIRCLE, 2006).

The situation was symbolized when ratings showed that more young men cited *The Daily Show with Jon Stewart*, the irreverent cable comedy program that critiques political reporting, as their main source of news about the 2004 presidential election campaign (Pew Research Center for the People and the Press, 2005). Even so, journalism majors should be more tuned in than their peers, because, as one student put it: "Journalists . . . have a responsibility to cover government agencies and to uncover any wrongdoings. When people know about a wrongdoing, they may be prompted to do something about it."

So the disconnect is palpable when journalism students say they are not affected by September 11, 2001, or an extensively reported international story on U.S. involvement in an unpopular war on distant soil even as classmates recount intimate details of a pop idol's sex life or latest arrest for substance abuse. How could journalism students *not* be interested in topics so closely linked to the press's historic and democratic role in America? Consider this: In today's 24/7 supermediated world, popular culture has captivated the news audience and news purveyors in ways unmatched by the workings of the U.S. Congress, state legislatures, or local city councils—unless the politician is a celebrity, too. One survey showed far more people (52 percent of Americans) could identify at least two characters from *The Simpsons* television show than could name (1 in 1,000) the five components of the First Amendment (McCormick Tribune Freedom Museum, 2006). In fact, only

16 percent of Americans surveyed for an annual study recognized *freedom of the press* among basic First Amendment rights (First Amendment Center, 2006). News consumers' appetite for celebrity or entertainment news is reinforced by the *staggering growth* of new tabloid-style entertainment magazines, such as *OK!* or *In Touch* (Project for Excellence in Journalism [PEJ], 2006).

Yet, a gap in journalism students' news knowledge cannot be blamed entirely on a penchant for celebrity, sports, or other *soft* news stories. A growing number of Americans of all ages, but particularly those under 40, are doing other things with their spare time, including watching DVDs, reading magazines and books, and playing video games or exercising (Pew Research Center for the People and the Press, 2006). Indeed, journalists and journalism educators have for some time expressed concerns about what they see as Americans' disconnect from public life, so intrinsic to the democratic ideals on which this country was founded (McChesney, 1997; Mindich, 2005; Moyers, 2004).

After spending a year traveling around the United States and talking to people under 40, journalism professor and former CNN news producer David T. Z. Mindich (2005) discovered the declines in news readership parallel the drop in the number of young voters. Mindich, the journalism department chair at St. Michael's College in Vermont, noted in an earlier essay: "Students who do not pay attention to politics cede their political power to their elders and their more involved peers. And, without political power they are screwed" (2004, p. B5).

The circumstances, he asserts, foreshadows a "democracy on the brink of a crisis" (Mindich, 2005, p. 112). In fact, Mindich notes the generational shift in newspaper readership is so profound that few young people are picking up the habit of their elders: 80 percent of them do not read newspapers. Current studies show the same is happening in broadcast news: "Just 26 percent of people in their 30s and 40s regularly tune in to the nightly network news, far below the number of older Americans who regularly watch network evening news" (Pew Research Center for the People and the Press, 2005, p. 45).

Therefore, it should not be surprising that American high school students' attitudes about the First Amendment are often contradictory: Nearly half of those polled think this right "goes too far" in its guarantees, according to new study data that also reveal they are taking more classes in the subject. At the same time, more high school students favor protections for news media, including their own campus newspapers (Knight Foundation High School Initiative, 2006, pp. 4–7).

Originally, the high school students surveyed for the landmark 2004 Future of the First Amendment study showed an overall lack of knowledge and understanding of essential aspects of this constitutional right. Conducted by researchers at the University of Connecticut's Department of Public Policy, the study polled more than 100,000 students in grades 9 through 12, 8,000 teachers, and 500 administrators at 544 schools across the United States. More than one-third of students disagreed with the statement that "newspapers should be allowed to publish without government approval" (Knight Foundation High School Initiative, 2004, p. 79).

The initial results were partly attributed to dramatic declines in student media, such as newspapers. One-fifth of U.S. secondary schools have no student media, while a "substantial number" have eliminated newspapers within the last five years (Knight Foundation High School Initiative, 2004, p. 62). In addition, fewer high school teachers are requiring students to read or watch news as assignments (p. 15).

Meanwhile, 15 percent of high school students, primarily women and minorities, were involved in journalism courses and media programs (Knight Foundation High School Initiative, 2004), and 2 percent were considered "young journalists," defined as those who were participating in student-run news media and who were planning careers in journalism (The Next Generation of Journalists, 2005).

Yet, the news is not all bleak. One encouraging aspect of the Future of the First Amendment (Knight Foundation High School Initiative, 2004, 2006) study, considered the largest of its kind, suggested those who had participated in media-related endeavors, took classes in media, or learned about the First Amendment were more knowledgeable, supportive of First Amendment protections, and people's right to convey unpopular opinions (Knight Foundation High School Initiative, 2004, 2006). Furthermore, many other studies support reinstituting a civics curriculum in schools and advocate for educating the larger American society (Ammori, 2006; CIRCLE, 2006; Comber, 2003; Kurtz et al., 2003), because it "makes a difference in the attitudes, knowledge and engagement of young people" (Kurtz et al., 2003, p. 11). Yet, the opportunity to teach and learn about First Amendment protections, particularly press freedom and free speech, increasingly is stifled at high schools where journalism skills are not valued and administrators practice censorship in spite of laws that protect student expression (Student Press Law Center, 2000). The Future of the First Amendment study's latest update reveals teachers are not making "'a lot' of effort to promote First Amendment principles through school activities, conversations, and policies" (Knight Foundation High School Initiative, 2007, p. 4).

Maintaining the freedoms espoused in the First Amendment has always depended on an informed citizenry that values the democratic ideals fostered by vibrant public debate and dissent (Mindich, 2005). Paradoxically, the decline in news consumption and participation in civic life, particularly among young people, has occurred as the amount and choice of information has expanded dramatically (Mindich, 2005; PEJ, 2006; Pew Research Center for the People and the Press, 2005, 2006). But this detachment has far-reaching ramifications for all citizens, when as research indicates, 42 percent of Americans do not have the informational background necessary to monitor the news (Pew Research Center for the People and the Press, 2005).

The Education of Journalism Students

Meanwhile, journalism professors and professionals across the United States are wrangling with a series of interconnected issues. Scholars cite "a fundamental concern with 'news,' and a corresponding concern with the acquisition of complex methods of knowing, representation, and analysis" (Adam, 2001, p. 317). More than 100 years after the first journalism schools formed, the debate over journalism education persists to varying degrees of intensity but particularly in this era punctuated by changing attitudes among students, who, many educators believe

1. Do not regularly consume newspapers (in whatever form)—the time-honored foundation for understanding the profession, which constitutes the very "underpinnings of democracy" (Mindich, 2005, pp. 7, 111);
2. Prefer broadcast or public relations careers to print, and are not interested in informing the masses about government wrongdoing (*"Pressing the issue: The superficial and the scandalous: Are j-schools to blame?"*);[1]
3. Lack the requisite critical thinking and have woefully underdeveloped writing skills (Bollinger, 2002; Borges, 2004).

Thus, journalism graduates enter professional newsrooms across the country ill equipped to make meaning of stories they cover (Carnegie Corporation of New York, 2005; Ghiglione, 2001; Medsger, 2002). In 2002, Lee Bollinger, president of Columbia University and a First Amendment scholar, abruptly ended the search for a new dean for the acclaimed Graduate School of Journalism, founded by Joseph Pulitzer, so the "yawning gulf" (Bollinger, 2002, ¶ 1) in journalism education could be addressed. His desire to adjust the curriculum to accommodate a changing world was amplified and came to signify everything wrong with journalism and journalism schools: "We live in an age in which the system of communications is widely understood to be undergoing revolutionary changes, and, at the same time, is the critical element in forging democracies, markets, culture and the phenomenon of globalization" (Bollinger, 2002, ¶ 3).

Bollinger's (2002) challenge to the academy, then, was to determine how citizens would understand local, regional, national, and international social, political, economic, and cultural dynamics, if the journalists they have relied on for synthesizing and interpreting events do not. Bollinger's assessment was not universally embraced (Samuelson, 2003), but scores of professional journalists and journalism educators at undergraduate and graduate institutions large and small contributed to the debate (Romano, 2003) and have taken action. Among the projects is Rethinking Journalism Education 2.0, spearheaded in early 2006 by journalism educators in the California State University and Community College systems (http://www.rje2.wordpress.-com). Columbia's new master's program, unveiled in 2005, is heavy on liberal arts specializations, focusing on "conceptual themes" of identity, justice, and power in covering government (Jaschik, 2005, ¶ 10).

Columbia's president was not the first to raise the alarm. The Carnegie Corporation, the nonprofit foundation focused on education and strengthening American democracy, convened a forum of professionals and educators to contemplate the state of the free press and to share ideas on how to improve journalism. President Vartan Gregorian stated at the time:

> Journalism schools have to be not only guardians of the First Amendment, but also guardians of public institutions and public knowledge, charged with providing the critical distance, perspective and discernment of what is happening in our country in order to protect our democracy (*Carnegie Reporter*, 2002, ¶ 12).

Catalytic Connection: Journalism and Service Learning

Ask a room full of college journalism majors, "How many of you can recite the First Amendment verbatim?" Even if a prize is offered, it is likely that few, if any, are keen or able to properly answer the question. Thankfully, they do know that freedom of the press is among the protections provided by the First Amendment. Yet, as numerous studies reveal, they are as likely as most Americans to take the First Amendment for granted, or lack knowledge about its connection to the public interest and their basic rights under the U.S. Constitution (Ammori, 2006; Knight Foundation High School Initiative, 2004, 2006, 2007). One example: "About one in five say the right to own and raise pets and the right to drive a car are First Amendment rights as well" (McCormick Tribune Freedom Museum, 2006, p. 2).

This "exodus of informed citizenship" (Mindich, 2005, p. 5), although frightening in its prospects, is not an insurmountable obstacle, abundantly demonstrated by several studies advocating programs aimed at educating the public (Ammori, 2006) and, by extension, students (CIRCLE, 2006). The Future of the First Amendment (Knight Foundation High School Initiative, 2004, 2006, 2007) study suggests that journalism classes and student-run media programs are vital for teaching and learning about the First Amendment and the other core civic ideals valued by democratic society. At the same time, the study makes clear that civic education at the high school level is in trouble, and so are student-run media programs. This is particularly true in urban and financially strapped schools (Knight Foundation High School Initiative, 2004), such as those found in the San Fernando Valley region of Southern California, where the California State University, Northridge, (CSUN) journalism department outreach includes an annual high school writing competition and skills workshop cosponsored by the *Los Angeles Times*.

Journalism programs of some sort exist at the majority of the 77 schools invited to participate in the campus event, started in the early 1990s. About 125 high school journalism students and their advisers attend the one-day series of seminars and presentations by professional and college journalists. Aside from the informal peer networking opportunity, the event provides a place for formal presentations geared specifically to new advisers, training for veterans, and updates on the activities of scholastic journalism groups, such as the national and regional Journalism Education Association (JEA). Inevitably, the advisers use this forum for expressing frustration with their own inexperience, crowded classes, or nonsupportive administrators.

Despite the existence of JEA and many other teaching resources for scholastic journalism educators, such as the Web sites Highschooljournalism-.org, Jteacher.org, or the Student Press Law Center (http://www.splc.org) they face countless challenges that transcend the CSUN journalism department's outreach. For example, one high school adviser taught two journalism courses, including an award-winning newspaper class, plus four advanced placement American Literature classes. Another adviser grappled with closure after 20 years of his school's newspaper class. A few advisers have journalism backgrounds and lead well-financed programs; most do not. One adviser ran a journalism club as an extracurricular activity, others had to borrow computers and staff and an after-school venue to help students start a publication. All the advisers have an interest in the democratic concepts of a free and unfettered press, even if their primary job is to teach biology, algebra, or English to 40-student classes. Some have the unqualified First Amendment support of their principals, but many do not.

Clearly, these advisers needed more than a two-hour workshop. So, several were recruited to participate in a service-learning-inspired pilot project, launched in spring 2005 and staffed by senior journalism majors taking a required 1-unit tutorial just as the initial Future of the First Amendment (Knight Foundation High School Initiative, 2004) study was released. The project, called Media Mentors, raised an assortment of questions: Was this the right environment to integrate the service-learning model as a means of promoting political and civic engagement among high school students? Could college journalism majors put into practice what they had learned about news skills and First Amendment rights and privileges by helping students produce their newspapers or other student media? In so doing, would their instruction and interaction cultivate engagement, interest, and involvement in civic life? How would we know?

Conceptually, the service-learning model with its confluence of academic study, practical experience, and civic engagement is an appealing means of teaching and learning about community social issues and potential solutions. The model integrates meaningful community service with instruction and reflection to enrich the learning experience, teach civic responsibility, and strengthen communities, as defined by Learn and Serve America's

National Service Learning Clearinghouse, the official site for information and resources related to the service-learning movement (http://www.service learning.org/what_is_service-learning/index.php). In addition, service learning serves as the bridge to what proponents in the news profession identify as "civic sensibility" (Schaffer, 2003), embodied by the civic or public journalism movement that began in the late 1980s (Rosen, 2000; Witt, 2004), and is "about treating our audience as citizens rather than just consumers . . . trying to get citizens involved in the news-making process" (Witt, 2004, p. 4). Civic journalism, once controversial and resisted by journalists, has experienced a renaissance and is quickly morphing into the no less divisive but popular *citizen journalism*. Driven by technology advancements and often taking the form of blogs, it represents a power shift from traditional gatekeepers to new public involvement in gathering and disseminating information (Project for Excellence in Journalism, 2006, 2007).

Media Mentors: Teaching and Learning in the Community

In their roles as service-learning participants, the CSUN journalism majors were expected to fulfill three interrelated learning objectives:

1. Articulate their knowledge and understanding of the purpose and principles of journalism and its ethical values in the practice of news reporting and writing;
2. Explore what impact their knowledge might have on journalistic skills, particularly in the extracurricular and challenging arena of high school student-media programs;
3. Mentor and instruct high school students as they produce their newspapers, magazines, and/or other news media.

The Media Mentors' efforts toward meeting these objectives were measured using (a) written reflections contained in a weekly guided journal that detailed their experiences and observations, (b) classroom discussions based on their experiences, (c) final self-assessment and critiques of their dual roles as students and mentors (they were asked to make specific suggestions on how the advisers might improve their newspapers and media programs), and (d) feedback from formal evaluations by the advisers and the high school students.

In that inaugural semester, the emphasis was on meshing academic with practical experience. The majority of the eight participants cited honing and sharing "good writing and reporting habits" among their objectives. Several were using the tutorial as a trial run for possible teaching careers, while at least three had fond memories of high school journalism and wanted "to give something back." Civic engagement and the connection to the First Amendment existed only as an abstraction and not a formal journal or discussion topic, although the CSUN students were aware of its importance to the community and the larger society, demonstrated by this journal comment:

> The main thing I hope to impart to my students is a sense of awareness about the world around them, and the importance of being an informed citizen . . . to understand the value of genuine news reporting and the significant role journalists play in our society.

The CSUN seniors were dispatched to four area high schools, with fairly diverse student populations. However, as one CSUN student pointed out, "all of these schools seem to be relatively well-off financially." Indeed, the four institutions had secure student-run media programs with long-time advisers who also taught beginning journalism and other courses. The advisers were grateful for the CSUN students' assistance, exemplified by this comment: "Many students were able to get the one-on-one assistance I'm not usually able to give them." Generally, the advisers saw the experience as positive, especially in the skills area and in giving high school students what one adviser described as "a peek into their future." While several of the advisers liked the informality of the mentors' presence for help with last-minute details before newspapers were sent off for printing, a few sought more formal workshops on specific topics, such as how to write using the inverted pyramid, the basics of feature storytelling, or production of a radio news broadcast. The CSUN students accommodated the requests after developing lesson plans and studying teaching tips.

Feedback from the high school journalism students included comments about skills, such as "how to find a good lead" and "to improve the basic layout of our paper," and more general evaluations, including "journalists have a lot to deal with and excuses don't count for anything." In the end, the CSUN journalism majors placed value on having reached the high school journalism students, as noted in one student's reflection: "All the students wrote that they appreciated our help and learned something from us. They sounded like we really made a difference." Perhaps, more critical was the CSUN students' ability to qualify their own knowledge, indicated by this comment: "Overall, after this first experience, I feel like I really was able to apply what I have learned throughout college in a real setting."

In fact, the students had numerous and specific suggestions for improving the planning, communication, and interaction among the mentors, advisers, and high school students. From a teaching standpoint, this meant adjustments in several areas, including overt connections to journalism's civic responsibility and the implications of the Future of the First Amendment (Knight Foundation High School Initiative, 2004) study, altering the learning objectives, and clarifying expectations as the project moved into its second and third semesters in the 2005–2006 academic year. Again, the seniors (six in the fall and eight in the spring) worked in two-person teams for two hours each week at the San Fernando Valley schools.

But now, with fine-tuning, the CSUN students' experiences stretched beyond assisting the well-advised and adequately funded newspapers. Several teams were placed in relatively new schools in the charter reform movement where principals and teachers were eager to start or resurrect newspapers for their diverse student populations. The journalism majors contributed start-up advice and expertise in the programs located in urban, economically disadvantaged, and mostly Spanish-speaking neighborhoods. One was a charter-type college preparatory academy started less than four years ago; two included middle school students, and one offered the newspaper as an elective after-school activity, while another scheduled the project during the last period, "free-time." In all three cases, the mentors were engulfed by numerous and major challenges, including: advisers' lack of knowledge and guidance; student apathy; absence of basic equipment (computers and printers, for example), and lack of sustained administrative support. One CSUN student expressed the frustration early on by writing, "I was annoyed at how unprepared [the adviser] is in running this paper. I didn't have all of the answers. . . . but I at least knew where to start to make these things happen."

As they had done in the pilot, the CSUN students in the traditional programs divided their time, depending on their schedules, between beginning journalism classes and the more advanced newspaper or magazine production classes. They worked closely with on-site advisers, devising and presenting workshops on specific topics, such as how to write a basic news story or how the First Amendment relates to student publications. In addition, the mentors were asked to work with individuals to critique a page layout, help edit a feature, or offer advice on brainstorming story ideas. These assorted situations required resourcefulness and flexibility among the Media Mentors, who often had to adjust their plans and expectations, as demonstrated by this student comment: "You can't know what you're getting into until you're there. Working with students is going to require tremendous amounts of improvisation and creative thinking. Luckily, I have no problem with either area."

Improvisation and creative thinking took on new meaning at the charter school sites, where getting and keeping students' attention competed with several obstacles, including the aftermath of statewide examinations when the students were described by their teachers as "too tired" to participate, and either the advisers' absence or unannounced class cancellations for in-service days. In one case, computers did not arrive until the project's seventh week so the students did not have enough time to publish a newspaper. Ironically, a perfect opportunity to demonstrate the deep connection between the press and political engagement was lost when a Media Mentors' session was cancelled during attendance boycotts sparked by the 2006 immigration reform protests across the nation.

Despite what one mentor described as "nonexistent" communication with the advisers, the team refused to give up: "Next week," one student wrote in her journal, "the mentors are going to practice . . . how to interview someone, for the students to get more comfortable with going out, finding a source, and asking good questions."

Conversely, the advisers saw few shortcomings, exemplified by this comment from the first semester: "With 40 students in one class, it would be very helpful to have mentors come in more often during the week." Their criticisms suggested the mentors provide "a greater perspective on journalism options in and beyond college," or better coordination on workshop topics and presentations.

Data, Data Everywhere and What It All Might Mean

A crucial aspect of this project was a set of assumptions about the status of high school journalism in the community served by CSUN and the potential for meaningful interaction with college journalism majors. The suppositions included (a) the high school students, like their counterparts in the national Knight Foundation High School Initiative (2004) study, were deficient in understanding and appreciation of First Amendment rights and privileges; (b) the university students were academically competent in their major, which incorporates First Amendment instruction throughout the curriculum, and thereby knowledgeable about the profession's bond with citizens in promulgating the liberties associated with press freedoms; and perhaps most important, (c) the CSUN journalism majors' efforts at conveying this expertise to their high school counterparts would be observable and quantifiable through various research techniques.

To test these hypotheses and gauge the project's impact, data were collected using both qualitative and quantitative methods that evolved as the pilot semester gave way to the academic-year project. In all three semesters, the CSUN seniors completed weekly guided journals documenting their experiences in relation to the learning objectives, designed and administered feedback forms to the high school students and advisers, and completed culminating guided self-evaluations. In conjunction with these embedded assessment tools, a study was conducted to measure whether the college seniors had fostered civic engagement among the high school journalists. The CSUN students adapted the Future of the First Amendment (Knight Foundation High School Initiative, 2004) survey, which was carried out prior to and following First Amendment-focused workshops at the targeted schools.

The pre- and post-instrument contained 18 multiple-choice questions (instead of the original 60) and two short-answer queries based on questions in the 2004 original. It was administered to 61 journalism students at the two traditional high school programs, and to 37 nonjournalism (American Literature) 11th-grade students at one of those high schools. Because the American Literature classes were sampled as a control group, these students were not included in formal First Amendment workshops by the CSUN journalism majors or asked to complete evaluation forms. In addition, the First Amendment workshops, which were presented in fall 2005 and spring 2006, produced written reflections by the CSUN journalism majors and were evaluated (fall 2005) by the high school students.

The charter schools were excluded only from the First Amendment questionnaire primarily because of challenges previously described. However, one adviser specifically asked the mentors to conduct a First Amendment workshop. "We agreed to do it," wrote one of the mentors, who might have been thinking of his media law training about libel or invasion of privacy in his response: "The students could learn from this, but there are other priorities. The students need to learn the basic skills of journalism, writing, grammar, structure, inverted pyramid, leads, interviewing, and story ideas, before going into laws." In other cases, the CSUN seniors were dealing with middle school students. So, the main concern became getting the logistics down before presenting more advanced material contained in a First Amendment workshop. For example, "they want our commitment and they want to better themselves in certain areas, like spelling and grammar. It will definitely be a lot of work with teaching them how to write leads, issues concerning libel, First Amendment, and also just explaining some of the terms that we use."

By the end of semester three, in addition to the Future of the First Amendment (Knight Foundation High School Initiative, 2006, 2004) survey results, which included about 160 responses to the short-answer queries, the data filled several binders with more than 1,000 pages of weekly journal entries, plus formal assessments from the 22 students who had completed the tutorials. In addition, the records contained dozens of evaluative feedback forms from school advisers and their students.

Originally, this inquiry was motivated by the findings in the Future of the First Amendment (Knight Foundation High School Initiative, 2004) study. It provided a template for comparing local students to the national sample, but, more important, it was seen as a ready-made mechanism for measuring the mentors' influence on the high school students' learning about the First Amendment. The survey adaptation was a logical tool for assessing knowledge acquisition, and it provided useful information.

The local high school journalism students were more knowledgeable and had a deeper appreciation of First Amendment freedoms compared to their peers in the 2004 national study, as demonstrated by this example: More than 25 percent of the local students said that the American press has "too little freedom," in contrast to the 10 percent in the national study. But as much as the survey showed significant differences, several factors evolved that limited the efficacy of the results, including selection of the control group outside journalism; traditional, well-functioning journalism classes; number and choice of questions and vague short-answer questions; incomplete list of answers that altered the responses to one question, and balance of gender and ethnicity.

Thus, the question became: Was the adapted pre- and post-questionnaire survey the best way to establish a knowledge base and calculate change? The national study showed that students in media-related classes or activities are likelier to be more sophisticated and have a greater appreciation of citizens' rights and privileges related to freedom of the press and speech. That proved true for these students. In fact, the short-answer responses from the high school journalism students provided a clearer picture of their understanding, symbolized by this reply to a question about journalistic responsibility: "They [journalists] should tell the truth. Journalism is like a direct conversation with government."

Engaging Students: "The First Amendment Got Stuck More in My Head"

Despite its intent, the survey-based study itself was an imperfect source of evaluation in comparison to the far richer written reflections, evaluation forms, and the responses to the survey's short-answer questions. For example, even as the high school journalism students cited journalists' responsibility to the public, they were highly critical when asked to respond at the questionnaire's end to "the state of the news media today." In fact, they referred to government and corporate control of the news media, fixation on celebrity coverage, biased coverage, and nonethical journalists, as demonstrated in this comment: "Some publications concentrate too much on unimportant issues like where Lindsay Lohan shops. More worldly issues should be addressed, or things that not many people know about."

Indeed, some of the high school students, by their own admission, are not tuned in ("I don't really pay attention," one wrote), but, for the most part, their comments were thoughtful and knowledgeable, epitomized by this quote about journalists' responsibility: "Journalists need to present the public with true issues, despite what controversy may be created so people can take action." Action is a key element of political and civic engagement, and the students' understanding of this concept is evident in their comments. Also, it was manifest in the high school journalism classrooms, typified by First Amendment activities described in the CSUN students' journals.

"I used real experiences and scenarios that take place in high schools, such as being able to run stories about a birth control rally or drug use, and the students had actually faced similar scenarios so they had a lot to say," wrote one student. She began the discussion, her teammate added, by listing "situations that may or may not have been a violation of the First Amendment." The technique inspired students to tell the mentors about how their school principal tried to impose prior approval on their newspaper's content: "But we all knew we had the right to tell him no," they responded.

On the other hand, a few of the mentors strained to relate a clear self-understanding of the importance of press freedom, in lieu of the other First Amendment protections. For example, in devising their workshops, several would concentrate on the five fundamental freedoms, or discuss flag burning and present all-encompassing activities or lectures. Nonetheless, the high school students repeatedly cited the First Amendment in the evaluation forms. As one student put it: "the First Amendment got stuck more in my head." To be sure, the high school students also cited the mentors' clothes or "cute hair" as memorable, but those were the exceptions.

The mentors' solid impact came in the practical aspects, such as how to improve interviewing skills and learning *The Associated Press Stylebook* rules, but also in the abstract, including exposure to a wider view of the profession. "The one thing that stuck with me the most is the realization that the world of journalism is hectic," stated one high school student. Another commented, "It helped me to communicate my thoughts and ideas to the paper in writing."

Of course, students often *say* they have learned something. We know self-assessment may differ drastically from actually demonstrating competency. Certainly, feedback on evaluation forms must be considered in that context. Yet, these evaluations and the journal reflections coupled with the study, flawed or not, symbolize the powerful potential of Media Mentors to influence younger students to engage in their communities. This was particularly true among many of the charter school students, who, perhaps for the first time, were exposed to journalism and its core values. These students identified with the mentors as role models who taught them "better ways to express" their ideas and opinions.

The mentors' very presence in the classrooms cultivated a sense of engagement in each setting. In the long-standing programs, they served as adjunct advisers, reinforcing and supporting the advisers' instructions. In the charter schools, in effect, they were de facto advisers, teaching journalism to students as well as to teachers. The most important journalism values displayed by the mentors, one adviser wrote, were "appreciation for the profession, importance of good writing, and completion of an assignment."

But the road wasn't smooth and easy, as several mentors discovered, including one who wrote, "the school just put some of these kids in the class because they had nowhere else for them to go." The realization that some of them might not finish school, he continued, was "a horrible feeling," prompting his question, "How do you prepare a student for failure?" Nevertheless, he saw potential for enrichment. He advised students, "Always assume your story has the power to open one's eyes and make a difference."

These responsibilities affected the CSUN journalism majors in unexpected and enlightening ways. Most wanted to make a difference, and needed tangible—and immediate—evidence, preferably in the content of the student newspapers. But direct feedback was not forthcoming, as indicated by this comment: "The process doesn't always reap instant effects—but that doesn't mean you haven't made a difference." Also, they had to confront and make meaning of their own knowledge acquisition and articulation. In some cases, this, too, was discomforting. A few students became frustrated by the controlled chaos of deadlines and newspaper production in the high school settings where informality was the norm; others were overwhelmed by the tasks they faced in the charter schools where expectations exceeded reality.

Nevertheless, the CSUN journalism majors consistently evoked the teaching aspect of their roles ("The students make an impact on you, too"), and how that helped them gain confidence in their own communication skills. One student discovered, "Some elements of journalism are impossible to teach. Instincts and talent are a big part of how successful someone is. You either have these qualities or you don't." In fact, every mentor gained something meaningful, even if it was the realization that "you can't 'wing' teaching," which must be "extremely interactive." And, many cited deficiencies in *their* students: "Students do not know the importance of news" or "many people do not know about the First Amendment."

Conclusion: Redesign in the Offing

High school journalism as an act of civic engagement is not a new idea. Yet, purposefully matching college seniors studying journalism with their high school counterparts proved a compelling way to engage all the students, but especially those who have been deprived of a voice in the world. The service-learning model provided the appropriate connection and foundation for guiding this project, which is adaptable in a variety of other journalism and mass communication courses. The structured reflection journal entries, classroom discussions, and feedback reveal how the mentors' awareness and understanding of their discipline enriched the experience for the high school students. The mentors fostered engagement, interest, and involvement by interacting and teaching these skills in the journalism classes, even when a savvier level of appreciation existed for the First Amendment.

Indeed, their journals were filled with admonitions on the proper way to write a lead ("summarize in 35 words or less"), lay out a photograph, follow ethical behavior, or determine what constitutes news. That is heartening, but the journals also have exposed inadequacies in students' essential writing (structure, grammar, and punctuation) and critical thinking skills. Granted, many students see "journals" as informal documents, more diary than news construct.

However, journalism students are instructed in the critical thinking skills associated with reporting (research), writing, and editing. They have been immersed in the process, including, for many, simultaneously working in student media newsrooms while carrying a full load of classes and holding down outside jobs. Yet, they fail to convey thoughtful, clear analysis of their experiences, opting for a stenographic list of activities. Worse, several appear to lack style, grammar, and punctuation skills, exemplified by this critical conclusion reached by a mentor about students he deemed were "not serious enough." He wrote: "Having a silk tarp covering the room with no motivation to do anything, it's comforting to see some students struggling to better themselves."

Although the lack of skills among college seniors is deeply troubling, in reality the project's future hinges on intervention where the outcomes can be seen and felt beyond the students' words reflected in journals or evaluation forms. To truly increase interest and involvement in civic life among high school students, Media Mentors needs a more deliberate approach, targeting programs that lack resources and are conducted in unstructured settings. This might include a series of activities, dependent on funding and other support, such as:

1. Partnering exclusively with a charter school that is trying to establish a global communications academy. There, CSUN students would take on the creation and development of a newspaper or its online companion, teaching as they go;

2. Designing and presenting free-press-focused First Amendment workshops to middle and high school students in nonmedia-related classes, and documenting their efforts for the local daily news media;

3. Expanding the annual high school workshop into an all-comers "Saturday school" on the CSUN campus staffed by the Media Mentors, who might present workshops and one-on-one training for high school journalism students;

4. Producing a multimedia series of stories for publication in the college student newspaper and its online and Spanish-language editions as well as for broadcast on the campus TV and radio newscasts.

Ultimately, the mentors must be involved in the planning process so their own political and civic engagement extends beyond the course requirements. As the project began its second academic year, a new group of seniors was conducting a needs assessment among the various high school advisers so they could decide collectively how best to go forward. It is likely they will choose a school in an economically disadvantaged neighborhood. Shifting the focus does not make the long-standing traditional programs less worthy, considering the worrisome challenges facing student-run media across America, such as when news organizations reduce or eliminate student journalism outreach, or censorship is condoned. But those students already have a venue in which to speak out. The students in the nontraditional public school settings do not. To truly make a difference the Media Mentors must venture into uncharted territory, where they can share their knowledge and respect for the values and responsibilities inherent in the First Amendment.

Note

1. From author's notes on panel discussion on the future of journalism education. California State University, Los Angeles and Los Angeles Press Club, May 5, 2004.

References

Adam, G. S. (2001). The education of journalists. *Journalism, 2*(3), 315–339.

Ammori, M. (2006). *Public opinion and freedom of speech.* Retrieved from http://research.yale.edu/isp/papers/ISP_PublicOpinion_fos.pdf

Bollinger, L. C. (2002). Journalism task force statement. Retrieved from http://www.columbia.edu/cu/president/communications%20files/journalism.htm

Borges, R. (2004). J-school: Which way to go? *Presstime, 26*(8), 30–35.

Carnegie Reporter. (2002). *Carnegie Corporation holds a journalism forum.* Retrieved from http://www.carnegie.org/reporter/05/interview/journal_forum.html

Carnegie Corporation of New York. (2005, May). Carnegie-Knight initiative on the future of journalism education. *Improving the education of tomorrow's journalists.* Executive summary. New York: Author.

Center for Information & Research on Civic Learning & Engagement. (2006). *Civic and political health of the nation survey.* Retrieved from http://www.civicyouth.org/index.php?s = Civic + %26 + political + health + of + nation + survey

Center for Information & Research on Civic Learning & Engagement. (2007). *Media use among young people in 2006.* Retrieved from http://www.civicyouth.org/PopUps/FactSheets/FS_Civics_Curriculum_Skills.pdf

Comber, M. (2003). Civics curriculum and civics skills: Recent evidence. Retrieved from http://www.civicyouth.org/PopUps/FactSheets/FS_Civics_Curriculum_Skills.pdf

First Amendment Center. (2006). *State of the First Amendment 2005 annual report.* Retrieved from http://www.firstamendmentcenter.org/about.aspx?item = state_First_Amendment_2005

Ghiglione, L. (2001). The splendor of our failures. Symposium: Journalism and mass communication education at the crossroads. *Journalism & Mass Communication Educator, 56*(3), 14–16.

Jaschik, S. (2005, March 28). Columbia rethinks journalism education. *Inside Higher Ed.* Retrieved from http://www.insidehighered.com/news/2005/03/28/journalism

Knight Foundation High School Initiative. (2004). *Future of the First Amendment* (Executive summary and key findings). Retrieved from http://firstamendment.jideas.org/findings/findings.php

Knight Foundation High School Initiative. (2006). *Future of the First Amendment.* Follow-up survey (key findings). Retrieved from http://www.firstamendmentfuture.org/report91806.php

Knight Foundation High School Initiative. (2007). *Future of the First Amendment.* Follow-up survey (Key findings). Retrieved from http://www.firstamendmentfuture.org/FOFA2007Survey.pdf

Kurtz, T., Rosenthal, A., & Zukin, C. (2003). *Citizenship: A challenge for all generations.* Denver, CO: National Conference of State Legislatures.

McChesney, R. (1997). *Corporate media and the threat to democracy.* New York: Seven Stories Press.

McCormick Tribune Freedom Museum. (2006). *Americans' awareness of First Amendment freedoms.* Retrieved from http://www.forumforeducation.org/re sources/index.php?item = 137&page = 32

Medsger, B. (2002). Getting journalism education out of the way. *Zoned for Debate.* Retrieved from http://journalism.nyu.edu/pubzone/debate/forum.1.essay.meds ger.html

Mindich, D. (2004, October 8). Dude, where's your newspaper? *The Chronicle of Higher Education,* p. B5.

Mindich, D. (2005). *Tuned out: Why Americans under 40 don't follow the news.* New York: Oxford University Press.

Moyers, B. (2004, September). *Journalism under fire.* Speech delivered to Society of Professional Journalists Convention, New York. Retrieved from http://www .commondreams.org/views04/0917-02.htm

Pew Research Center for the People and the Press. (2005). Media: More voices, less credibility. In Pew Research Center for the People and the Press (Ed.), *Trends 2005.* Washington, DC: Author. Retrieved from http://pewresearch.org/assets/ files/trends2005-media.pdf

Pew Research Center for the People and the Press. (2006). *Maturing Internet news audiences—broader than deep. Online papers modestly boost newspaper readership.* Retrieved from http://people-press.org/reports/display.php3?ReportID = 282

Project for Excellence in Journalism. (2004). *The state of the news media 2004: An annual report on American journalism.* Retrieved from http://www.stateofthenews media.com/2004

Project for Excellence in Journalism. (2005). *The state of the news media 2005: An annual report on American journalism.* Retrieved from http://www.stateofthenews media.com/2005

Project for Excellence in Journalism. (2006). *The state of the news media 2006: An annual report on American journalism.* Retrieved from http://www.stateofthenews media.com/2006/narrative_magazines_audience.asp?cat = 3&media = 8

Project for Excellence in Journalism. (2007). *The state of the news media 2007: An annual report on American journalism.* Retrieved from http://www.stateofthenews media.com/2007/narrative_overview_eight.asp?cat = 2&media = 1

Pryor, L. (2006). Teaching the future of journalism. Educators turn a critical eye to the curricula of convergence: A report back from a Poynter Institute seminar. *Online Journalism Review.* Retrieved from http://www.ojr.org/ojr/stories/060 212pryor/

Romano, C. (2003, March 21). Get me rethink!—the role of journalism education. *The Chronicle of Higher Education,* p. 12. http://www.lexisnexis.com.libproxy.cs un.edu:2048/us/lnacademic/results/docview/docview.do?risb =

Rosen, J. (2000). How far in? How far out? Civic responsibility and the journalism educator. In T. Ehrlich (Ed.), *Civic responsibility and higher education* (pp. 164–173). Phoenix, AZ: Oryx Press.

Samuelson, R. (2003, April 23). Snob journalism. *The Washington Post*, p. A35.

Schaffer, J. (2003). Civic journalism. Retrieved from http://www.asne.org/index.cfm?id=4940

Student Press Law Center. (2000). *The Student Press Law Center's High School Top Ten List*. Retrieved from http://www.splc.org/legalresearch.asp?id=3

The next generation of journalists: Who are they likely to be? (2005). Retrieved from http://www.firstamendment.jideas.org/latestresearch/wp3_nexgen.php

Witt, L. (2004). *What we heard, what we learned: Exploring the fusion power of public and participatory journalism*. Retrieved from http://pjnet.org/wp-content/uploads/legacy/FusionPowerReport.pdf

AN UNCONVENTIONAL
APPROACH TO CIVIC SKILL
DEVELOPMENT AND
SERVICE LEARNING

Mary Kirlin

"So, what you're telling us is that democracy is hard . . . that we have to learn about the issues ahead of time, vote and then we still have to follow up after the election?" Such was the question put to me toward the end of an upper-division public policy and administration course. "Yes!" I said, thrilled with the conclusion. Democracy *is* hard and my students had learned it firsthand. More important, whether they were aware of it or not, they had increased their own stock of civic and political engagement skills, and thus their ability to participate in a democratic society. This chapter addresses the question of how to teach civic and political engagement skills through service learning or community-based classroom experiences. My approach is unconventional for two reasons: First, I am interested in the development of civic skills rather than the acquisition of knowledge or the development of values; second, my definition of service is quite expansive, broadly including work with others that aims to improve a community. The community can be as small as the classroom or campus community and the "improvement "is left to the students to determine.

Understanding the Place of Civic Skills in Service Learning and Civic Engagement

Most disciplines interested in civic and political engagement acknowledge that several factors converge to create engaged citizens. Most commonly cited by educators, political scientists, and developmental psychologists are knowledge (system structures, history, and current events), dispositions, motivation, values, network connections, and civic skills (Carnegie Corporation of New York and the Center for Information and Research on Civic Learning and Engagement [CIRCLE], 2003; Kirlin, 2003a). Among the most well-known research is Verba, Schlozman, and Brady's (1995) seminal work that surveyed nearly 1,500 adults about their life experiences. The authors' Political Participation Model ultimately argues that engaged adults are motivated to participate, they are connected to the network of decision makers, and they have the necessary civic skills to do something with the time or money they have to contribute. The absence of any one of the three factors makes participation either impossible or ineffective. Nearly everyone knows someone who is motivated enough to complain but does not do anything to improve the situation. Similarly an individual might have the skills and relationships necessary to participate but lacks the motivation to get involved. Verba et al. (1995) find that all three components—motivation, connections to the network, and civic skills—are necessary for adult political engagement.

The Political Participation Model has significant implications for educators in K–12 and higher education, and provides a distinctly different starting point from traditional civic education frameworks. The list of factors required for participation includes values or dispositions and knowledge, neither of which is included in the Political Participation Model. Most civic educators (Carnegie Corporation of New York and CIRCLE, 2003) and many models of service learning argue for the importance of values or dispositions. Similarly, knowledge is central to many model program designs and service-learning objectives.

The traditional addition of knowledge and values in curricular design and objectives is problematic to me. First, I would suggest that the values and dispositions related to civic and political engagement are developed after participation experiences, or at least in a simultaneous fashion, but not before participation. In other words, in order to value participation, one must have some experience with participation. Values are based on either an experience or a belief, and the types of participation values we seek are not conducive to simply believing that it is important. Most of our programs seek to create engaged participating citizens as a result of their work. Service learning research is full of examples of participants who change their attitudes (beliefs) but not their behaviors (Perry & Katula, 2001). Service-learning proponents suggest that reflection deepens the commitment and value of participation. While this may be true in some cases, the differences stemming from short- and longer-term service-learning experiences seem to support the notion that the process of internalizing and valuing something develops over time and with experience.

The second question, then, is what is the role of traditional knowledge acquisition? Ultimately knowledge and motivation are intricately related; knowledge about something can make you motivated to get involved, and caring about something can make you seek out more knowledge in order to participate more effectively. (At the risk of digressing, my neighbors who are fighting a development project did not begin their participation by learning abstractly about city planning rules. They were motivated to learn the intricacies of city planning because something affected them.) Perhaps because academics tend to enjoy learning for the sake of learning, and think about the world in conceptual terms, we project that approach onto our students. While many of them may indeed love more abstract knowledge acquisition about something new, many others benefit from a more experiential and personal entry into learning.

My approach is nested in experiential learning as a central mechanism for opening the doors of learning to our students. This fits nicely with the Political Participation Model, which emphasizes civic skills as a prerequisite for participation. My goal in the classroom is to use community-based experiential learning to develop the requisite civic skills. I trust that knowledge acquisition and motivation will work hand in hand and that ultimately (after many more experiences) the value of participation will be internalized. This chapter focuses on civic- and political-engagement skill acquisition in experiential and service-learning classrooms.

Defining Civic Skills

Kirlin (2003a) provides a comprehensive matrix of civic skills subsuming existing literature into previously defined skill areas: communication, organization, and critical thinking, and a fourth newly defined skill area, collective decision making. Each is considered a skill because it can be learned through practice and experience rather than study or memorization. Competence and mastery are a result of sufficient practice in executing the skill, not understanding how others practice the skill. For example, if someone wants to learn how to swim, we would not show the person tapes of proficient swimmers and ask him or her to read about swimming. We would expect the individual to get into the water and begin to learn, step by step, the skill of swimming. Some people will learn faster, some will be stronger or more coordinated, but eventually, nearly all of them will learn to swim at a level that keeps them safe in the water. Similarly, civic skills are learned by practice, not study alone.

Skills can also be transferred from one arena to another; for instance, swimming skills learned in a pool can be transferred to swimming in a lake or river. If one learns effective written communication skills, the skill can be used to write letters, opinion pieces, or memos. Similarly, if one becomes proficient in working with a group at church to accomplish a shared goal, it is likely that the skill can be transferred to the workplace or political settings. The notion of skill transfer is buttressed by the significant body of research demonstrating strong correlations between extracurricular and experiential activities (with implicit skill development) and civic engagement (Kirlin, 2002).

Civic skills appear to be acquired over time, with practice, in multiple settings. Service learning and other experiential-based education opportunities provide a perfect venue for teaching civic skills.

Communication skills are the most intuitive and well understood of the four groupings. Competency in oral and written communication is central for civic and political participation, whether expressing your own opinion or informing and persuading others. For many students, expressing their own opinion, especially if there is likely to be disagreement, is one of the more difficult tasks.

Organizing is the second skill area. By this I mean learning to organize others to accomplish a goal. The goal may be as simple as holding a meeting; this seemingly simple task involves organizing people to participate, securing space, providing an agenda, conducting a meeting in a way that achieves goals, and possibly acquiring additional resources such as money, supplies, or equipment. Organizing may eventually mean more conventional political organizing, but the skill of finding resources and organizing people and events can be acquired in multiple settings, including classrooms.

Critical thinking is the third skill area. In this area, educators generally include identifying and describing, analyzing and explaining, synthesizing, thinking critically and constructively, and formulating positions on issues. Most critical thinking skills focus on rational understanding of information so that citizens can make rational choices about policy issues. While a level of critical thinking capacity is certainly appropriate, a purely rational or cognitive approach can constrict discussions about issues that are value based or normative and personal in nature. My focus in this course is encouraging students to think more completely; that is, to use cognitive skills to improve one's ability to understand the complex, subtle, and fluid nature of public issues.

The final skill area, collective decision making, is the skill least practiced in educational environments. This skill, the heart of democratic decision making, involves an interrelated set of activities including expressing your own opinion, understanding other's preferences, and working toward a decision (sometimes involving some individual compromise) for the collective or common good. This is a skill because it is a learned behavior, not purely a cognitive exercise. Most of the research on activities correlated with adult civic and political engagement point to consequential small-group experiences during adolescence (Kirlin, 2003a, 2003b; Verba et al., 1995). Extracurricular activities, simulations, and active classrooms (where conversation of current events is encouraged) are all consistently correlated with high levels of civic engagement (Carnegie Corporation of New York, 2003). And many of these have a common structure involving participants in the give-and-take of decision making in groups.

Some important nuances are worth observing. First, expressing one's own opinion is clearly a communication skill, but in this skill set it presumes an individual is in a group setting where preferences may differ. Thus, expressing one's opinion becomes important for having voice in the group. Second, the ability to understand others' preferences involves significantly more than tolerance or respect for differences. Again, the nature of the collective decision-making function presumes that the understanding of preferences is not simply to understand someone else's perspective; rather, the perspectives of the group need to be understood to define a common good for the group. It is a much more sophisticated step to understand what some-one else's position is in order to incorporate it into a group decision than simply to "tolerate" someone else's right to have a different perspective. The former is action based while the latter can be simply lip service.

Teaching civic skills, then, is really not as much about teaching them as it is about structuring service learning and classroom experiences in a way that facilitates meaningful practice of civic skills; it becomes more about ped-agogical design and less about content. This is particularly beneficial given the broad range of disciplines using service learning; nearly any subject being taught can incorporate civic skill development. Clarity about the definitions of civic skills and intentionality about incorporating them are key.

The discussion below spends minimal time on syllabus structure and maximum time on the nuances of managing student progress. This is consis-tent with my general approach to teaching; for the most part, I try to facili-tate student learning by taking advantage of who the students are and the opportunities that arise rather than creating assignments for students I have never met. This makes the syllabus a bit tough to construct, which I speak about toward the end of the chapter.

Incorporating Civic Skills Into Your Course: The *Do*-Something Model

For better or for worse, I almost never include the idea of civic skills explic-itly in my syllabi. It doesn't seem to fit as a logical objective, and meaningful assessment remains a major challenge (more on that later). Having said that, it is central to almost every activity I structure. The following is one of my favorite projects and I modify it for different topics and sophistication levels. This example comes from the group project in my Introduction to Govern-ment course. "You mean we have to *do* something?" Such was the shocked question emanating from the back of the room; I don't believe I'd ever heard the student utter anything previously. He was sure that he had misunder-stood me as I described a group project that was most certainly not a passive report.

Essentially, the assignment goes something like this: Over the course of the semester, each student will become part of a group that is working on getting something done. The process will be to identify a problem the group is interested in investigating, identify others interested in the same issue, figure out who is responsible for providing oversight of the issue, decide how to effect positive change, and, finally, *do* something to make progress in the desired direction. (This is described in more detail below.) The end product will be a class presentation about the issue and the actions the group took and a portfolio containing evidence of the effort: letters, notes from meetings, agendas from meetings, newspaper articles, letters generated, and so on. The portfolio is a group effort. In addition, I ask each group member to write a two- to four-page confidential reflective piece describing the process, the group successes, the group struggles, and what individual students have learned.

The assignment is short on directions because each problem is unique. Part of the intentionality in the development of organization skills is that students must learn what to do by doing it themselves. The confusion sets in almost immediately, with the more assertive students asking a barrage of questions while the quieter ones wonder if they can still drop the class. I am quite transparent at this point, explaining that if I defined the exercise from start to finish, they would dutifully follow the example and probably not learn much. I trust they are all quite good at variations on grown-up copying. Instead I promise, we are going to learn together.

There are two benefits to this strategy. First, it immediately diffuses the idea that the teacher knows everything and that the students are simply there to absorb what I tell them. Second, I begin modeling inquiry, demonstrating that it is OK to not know something. I am often confronted with questions that I cannot answer; I make sure my students hear me responding, "I don't know" and thinking out loud about "how we might find the answer." My students have reported that the open-ended nature of the assignment, plus my clear willingness to admit when I do not know something, ultimately empowers them to come up with ideas, ask questions, and learn on their own rather than searching for "what the professor wants." It subtly shifts the balance of power away from the teacher.

Deciding on Topics

The first step for the students is to identify something they are interested in and would like to work on. I strongly suggest that they read the campus and community newspaper for a week or so, jot down ideas that are interesting to them, and bring in a list of possible topics. Another strategy for identifying a problem or topic is to ask students what bothers them, if they were in charge what would they fix? Reading the newspaper for the first time is a lot like tuning into a soap opera for the first time; you have no sense of the context, the history, the characters, or the story line. I do my best to assure students that this will be the case for nearly everyone in the class, and that I will certainly not be aware of every issue they identify. It only matters that they are interested.

On the day that I ask students to bring in ideas for the group project, you can sense the tension in the class. Rather than asking what interested them, I ask them to briefly describe what they have read and what questions might be interesting to explore. Since everyone is able to generate questions (which they have lots of) rather than explanations (which they have few of) this often turns into a lively class discussion about what we have heard or read and where to obtain further information. This also encourages asking questions and sharing information, communication skill development. I facilitate the conversation but try to let students drive it unless I know something is factually wrong. I use these opportunities to talk about the differences between fact and opinion and the importance of knowing your source, critical thinking skills. Another benefit of this structure is that it provides peer pressure on those who might otherwise opt out of doing assignments. If a student is not prepared, it is very public.

The discussion of interesting current events often lasts two class sessions. Eventually, we develop a list of sorts of possible ideas to pursue. Students are encouraged to suggest all possible ideas for group projects, even if they do not want to be in the group. In fact, we create an "I just want to learn about it" category.

I make it clear that ultimately students will need to pick something to work on that is of interest to them. My interest and positions on issues are not relevant, nor are those of their best friend. This requires that they define their own interest and find their voice, an important component well documented in service-learning literature (Morgan & Streb, 2001).

Forming Groups

The process of forming groups for this project is decidedly skill oriented. Once the list is complete I ask each class member to verbally identify one or two topics that is of interest to him or her. When the task is complete I ask the students to find the people they might want to work with. This is generally followed by blank stares. They often presume that I will put them into groups and that they do not really need to listen to their classmates. I then gently suggest that they know what they are interested in much better than I do and that in the real world they will need to *find* others with similar interests. We often start the process over again, with class members now paying attention to others' interests. When the discussion is over I release them to find each other, learn the names of team members, and discuss what they know about their chosen topics.

From a process standpoint, this is a fascinating activity to observe. Some students are very clear about what they are interested in and find their partners quickly. Others mill about, finally winding up in the "I don't really care" group, looking to me for a topic, a group, and a direction. I have come to understand that I need to be brutally straight with these students. They will not be well served by being in a group with several other "I don't really care" students. This usually causes quick dispersion. (Humor goes a long way in this process as does cajoling and encouragement.)

While getting the groups formed is ostensibly the rationale, it also offers everyone a chance to speak to everyone else, express some (very safe) preferences, and interact with classmates. Simply put, they have had a tiny dose of oral communication and collective decision-making skills (expressing your preference and finding others who share your interests). They also begin the process of organizing themselves into a working group, another civic skill. Finally, they are forced to review the news and begin to sort out questions that involve critical thinking skills.

Solidifying Groups and Topics

Solidifying groups is often a one- to two-week task. Once identified, a topic or idea needs to become a project that can be managed. For example, irritation with campus parking (a common complaint) is not likely a problem that can be addressed in a semester. Topics evolve into projects as students learn about the issue and consider what might be done to address the concern. Project ideas don't always come together neatly. In fact, I steer students away from projects that are not doable in a semester or seem too obscure. A few examples of group projects help to highlight the process. One group focused on campus gardeners mowing the lawns on bad-air-quality days. (The state would declare a bad-air day and ask the public not to mow lawns. The students would then come to campus and see university employees mowing as usual.) The idea was initiated with the question, "What bugs you?" The topic selected demonstrated good observation skills and, frankly, good critical thinking. Students were connecting the dots between what the state was asking and what state university employees were doing.

Another group had a more fundamental problem. When I asked what their topic was the members said, "We are doing the death penalty." When I asked, "Which side?" they said they hadn't decided yet. After I pointed out that, ideally, they would effect policy changes with their project, they decided (a) they should all agree on the side to take, and (b) they probably could not have an impact on policies about the death penalty in one semester. What was disturbing about this discussion was that students were clearly quite comfortable researching and even arguing for or against an important policy position without worrying about their own position.

A final example demonstrates the benefit of asking students to think about what bothers them. A female student in one class noted that a critical light was burned out on a heavily trafficked path running through a park adjacent to school. She used the path to walk to school and was concerned about safety. Several other students agreed that this was an important issue and the group's issue evolved into a campaign to get the light replaced. This seemingly simple task was not completed by the end of the semester— although not for lack of effort on the part of the students. The groups that have the best learning experience tend to identify projects that are either campus based or are evolving in the local community. State- and national-level issues rarely work; there simply isn't enough time to have an impact on those areas. Campus and community leaders are usually accessible and students can often have a positive impact even in a short period of time. Thus, part of my role is thinking ahead during topic selection to ensure that students will have a manageable project experience.

Plunging In

Once groups stabilize, they begin investigating their topic. Over the next month groups are asked to find information, frame their understanding, and continue research outside class. Next, groups are paired with another group. Each group shares what it has to date. This helps groups frame content and offers them practice in communicating their ideas, reinforcing critical thinking, and developing communication skills. Groups are asked to provide feedback to each other about what they have heard—what makes sense, what is confusing, what is left out, and so forth.

Taking Action or "Doing Something"

Because these are semester-long projects, there is little time for the action phase. I almost always have to aggressively push students out of the research phase (a comfort zone) and into the action phase by requesting a draft action plan. Each group must sort out who the decision makers are for their issue and how to approach them with a request for change. This stage seems to be especially unnerving for students, as they usually don't have any idea where to begin and have little experience with making phone calls and writing letters in the real world. Ideally this is where the group begins to support each member, but it can also be where the group falls apart. Making sure that the draft action plans have names attached and that all group members are doing something is an important faculty role.

The action phase is really about organization and communication skills. Once decision makers are identified, students must decide how and what to request. The group trying to fix the path light discovered that what looked like campus property was actually owned by the Army Corps of Engineers. This complicated matters considerably. They also found that, unfortunately, campus personnel were not particularly interested in helping solve the problem.

Another group, attempting to increase the number of recycling bins on campus, found out there was already an active campus group working on green issues. They were able to partner with the group but also realized there were many other issues on the table that took precedence over the recycling bins.

The faculty role at this point is largely supportive. Assistance includes proofreading letters to decision makers, listening to practice presentations, and assisting with brainstorming if glitches occur. I also spend time reassuring students that they really are entitled to make reasonable requests. When the "no mowing on bad-air days" group got its ideas rejected by the maintenance staff, I urged the members to contact the campus president. With much urging the students finally did. And suddenly senior management began to look at the issue.

Connections to the Curriculum

Because I teach courses in government and public policy, the curricular connections are quite easy. Student experiences provide opportunities to drive home the idea that public agencies are accountable to elected officials who govern them, and that citizens can and should contact their officials for help. We can easily identify public services as distinct from private or nonprofit. Conversations about why public problems are difficult to solve become much easier when students have tried to make something happen. Students encounter situations that illustrate the tensions inherent in a democratic society. They begin to appreciate that not everyone will agree all the time about solutions, priorities, or resource allocations. Most importantly, students learn that participation is not easy but it is possible.

Not every idea students come up with works well, but this also provides opportunities to reflect on the more theoretical course content. Students are both humbled and empowered as they learn more. They are often surprised at how much effort and work has already been invested in an issue. For better or worse they also learn a lot about bureaucracies and why public processes often take a long time to complete. These are good opportunities to discuss checks and balances and the tension between efficiency and accountability.

Reflection and Assessment

A key component of service learning is structured opportunities for reflection on the service and the course content. Students in my classes are asked to write a two- to four-page reflective paper that discusses the project. Students are encouraged to include observations about the group process as well as the group activity. Students are attentive to the challenges and the rewards of doing the work. Two themes arise: First they begin to realize how hard it is to work with other people, and second, the experiential portion of the project seems to increase feelings of efficacy. One student commented, "I always knew I was *supposed* to know how to be involved but I never really did, I thought it was for other people. Now I really know how to do something if I want to." This is logical given that skills appear to be acquired with practice. Simply knowing what one could do is different than having experience making it happen.

Reflection also allows students to express their frustrations and ideally guides them toward a learning experience. This is a delicate balance. Sometimes students need to see that they did not put their full effort into something; other times they need to develop a respect for the slow pace of change and the work that has been done before them. Fortunately, most classes have some success stories allowing the class to see that some change can occur. I work to see that students leave with a healthy sense of how difficult change is but with an increased skill set that will allow them to engage in community issues that matter to them.

Unconventional Service Learning

I began this chapter suggesting that my approach was unconventional. To be fair, it will not be unconventional for everyone. When I began this work the suggestion that student-led projects of this nature should be considered service was a bit out of the mainstream. As the service-learning movement has evolved nationally, we now see new types of civic and political engagement.

I do not use the language of service in the conventional sense, but I think my students are contributing to the community as they work to improve things like street lighting, accessibility of recycling facilities, and cleaner air. These activities are political, as they often require individuals to convince publicly responsible bodies to "do something." The activities they choose are important and create value for the community.

Importantly, the community receiving the service may never know why something has changed. If more recycling bins show up, most students will simply be happy to have a location to pitch a can. If lighting is better, people using a path may feel safer without giving thought to what changed. There is no community partner in the traditional sense, students work with outside entities, but these organizations are not always receptive to the student's perspective or requests.

Despite what we might like to believe, many people get involved in civic and political life because they want to change something they are experiencing. It is not uncommon for that experience to lead to a broader view of why changes need to be made in society and to a more comprehensive view of the common good (Campbell, 2006). The students in my class who succeeded in getting the mowing schedule changed have the satisfaction of knowing that they made a difference. They now know they can do something again if they so desire. And finally, they are more aware of all the other people who are working to improve their lives, incrementally, and in ways they may never see.

Self-conscious or intentional attention to civic and political skill development is hard work. It means letting go of control of the process, while being almost hyperattentive to teachable moments. Our students are desperate for activities that are consequential, that have meaning in the world, and that will make them better prepared for adulthood. The development of civic and political engagement skills has the benefit of preparing students for the everyday challenges of being an engaged citizen.

References

Campbell, D. (2006). *Why we vote: How schools and communities shape our civic life.* Princeton, NJ: Princeton University Press.

Carnegie Corporation of New York and the Center for Information and Research on Civic Learning and Engagement. (2003). *The civic mission of schools.* New York: Author.

Kirlin, M. (2002). *The role of adolescent extracurricular activities in adult political engagement.* College Park, MD: Center for Information & Research on Civic Learning & Engagement.

Kirlin, M. (2003a). *The role of civic skills in fostering civic engagement.* College Park, MD: Center for Information & Research on Civic Learning & Engagement.

Kirlin, M.. (2003b, November). *Acquiring civic skills: Towards a developmental model of civic skill acquisition in adolescents.* Paper presented at the International Conference on Civic Education Research, New Orleans, LA.

Morgan, W., & Streb, M. (2001). Building citizenship: How student voice in service learning develops civic values. *Social Science Quarterly, 82*(1), 154–169.

Perry, J., & Katula, M. C. (2001). Does service affect citizenship? *Administration and Society, 33,* 330–333.

Verba, S., Schlozman, K. L., & Brady, H. E. (1995). *Voice and equality: Civic voluntarism in American politics.* Boston: Harvard University Press.

12

DEVELOPING TEACHERS' ABILITY TO SHARE LEADERSHIP

Kristeen L. Pemberton

I think that the garden project was a learning experience for both the students and myself. We were able to study just about every subject through the garden activity. . . . It was great for me to be able to test out a generative topic and to give the students the opportunity to have such a strong voice in the direction we took. The students, in turn, were able to learn while doing something they enjoyed. They saw real applications of math, science, language arts. They also came to see one another in a different light, and this was possibly the most powerful thing to watch. Because the garden project required a different skill set than [the ones used] in class work, new students were able to excel. One student in particular got pulled out for math and language arts for his special needs. The students were never happy to have to work with him, saying that he couldn't do anything. In the garden, he became a leader. He is amazing with his hands, he was knowledgeable and other students went to him with questions. The classroom teacher and I saw this as an opportunity to value his work and for him to be successful in a way that he struggled with in the classroom. We began giving credit for the outdoor work and for participation, and he began to feel differently about himself as well. I incorporated art and health and the students responded in a very positive way. . . . I learned a lot as you can see.

Karen's story was written in an e-mail message to me a year after I'd completed an action research study on my first attempt to infuse service learning into teacher education courses at San José State

University.[1] In preparation for her upcoming job search, she had asked me for a letter of recommendation for her professional file. I looked forward to writing about Karen's many strengths for potential employers to read, and I wanted to include aspects of her preparation that would set her apart from other candidates. So, I asked her to remind me about her service-learning project from the year before.

Karen's message is a success story resulting from an assignment in a required social studies methods course in a teacher preparation program. It's a success because the experience has revealed to the student teacher and the cooperating teacher the power of service learning as a teaching strategy. The outcome of this credential candidate's service-learning project gave children opportunities to experience themselves, their peers, and their community members as resources, problem solvers, and decision makers. This experience of self-efficacy is a beginning step in helping children, our future citizens, to recognize that building partnerships with others who may be very different from themselves is possible. Karen and the other college students in the social studies class learned that through high-quality service-learning projects, children can develop the skills and motivation to bring about political and social change. Karen's story represents the outcomes envisioned for all the students in a social studies methods class offered to credential candidates at San José State University.

From Impassioned Students to Critical Teachers

Graduate students come to the teacher preparation program with many different understandings of what it means to be a teacher. But most of those notions are based on preunderstandings, unexamined assumptions that are the result of the school experiences of those who have spent much of their lives as students. There is a need to provide opportunities for teacher candidates to reflect on the changing contexts in which they will be teaching children unlike themselves. These changes and differences don't include just those that result from the passing of time, shifting demographics, increased access to research on how people learn, or technological innovations. The larger global context has undergone dramatic changes that affect everyone. Some incoming teacher candidates recognize the need to address the confusion and apathy that have resulted from ongoing political and social strife and to investigate their potential as teachers to become agents of change. So motivated, these graduates find their way to the Critical Research Academy, one of several options in the Multiple Subjects Teacher Credential Program in the College of Education at San José State University.

Prior to enrolling in the social studies course, students have been introduced to postmodern foundations of education and sociology. Critical theorists, such as Paulo Freire (1995) and William Doll (1993), and sociology of knowledge theory (Bowers, 1984; Bowers & Flinders, 1990) provide students with a framework within which they can view the paradigm we are all immersed in. The current worldview is one that is characterized by a focus on the progress of the individual, resulting in such values as competition and development of expert knowledge. In their theoretical foundations courses, students gain a new awareness of themselves as unconscious carriers of traditions that may no longer be appropriate to perpetuate. As a result they recognize the need to develop teaching strategies different from the ones they once thought would be suitable to use in their own classrooms. They learn that public school teachers have the responsibility to recognize the role they play in socializing their students. The way a teacher uses his or her power results in one of two outcomes. Either the teacher's pedagogy limits the student to the taken-for-granted beliefs of modern culture that convince us that we must rely on professionals to conduct political activity, or it expands the student's knowledge in a manner that makes informed choice a possibility (Bowers, 1984). Within the context of carefully structured (high-quality) service-learning projects, teachers can enable children to recognize—and act to change—the conditions of how and what they learn. Service-learning experiences provide participants with opportunities to reach new understandings by confronting some of the difficulties in social communication and knowledge transfer. With insight into what it means to be a contributing citizen, children can become adults who are empowered to oppose the current milieu of apathetic mistrust and to negotiate oppressive power relationships.

Objectives of the Social Studies Methods Course

One of three major service-learning-related objectives of the social studies course was to provide opportunities for students to apply their newly acquired theoretical knowledge. A second objective was to develop students' appreciation of service learning as an appropriate strategy for teaching a standards-based social studies curriculum. In order for the social studies students to embrace service learning as an instructional strategy, they need to understand not only that our nation's children must learn the skills, knowledge, and dispositions needed for full democratic participation; they also need to accept that it's the teacher's responsibility to teach these attributes along with subject matter content. Finally, I wanted cooperating teachers as well as student teachers to recognize the use of service learning as an effective way to promote political and civic engagement among project participants.

Theory Teachers Can Apply to Promote Change

In the social studies course, students were introduced to the state standards that designate what subject matter is taught at different grade levels. They also applied learning theory based on brain research as they designed resource units and planned and assessed lessons they taught. What pulled together the content and the pedagogy were the strategies that student teachers learned about and practiced in their classrooms. They designed and practiced empowering pedagogy, an antioppressive educational framework developed by the Brazilian educator and activist Paulo Freire (1968/1995) and interpreted for classroom teachers by Ira Shor (1992). Empowering students means enabling them to collectively identify and address situations that limit their ability to participate in changing untenable social and civil conditions. Teachers who use service learning as a strategy, and who have student empowerment as their goal, provide their students with experiences that can transform their social relationships and local conditions. I wanted the student teachers to recognize not only the efficacy but also the potentially transformative power of using service learning as a strategy for teaching social studies.

A major responsibility that must be undertaken by teachers using service learning is to make explicit the connection between academic and civic skill development. Not doing so promotes the pupils' bifurcated view of schoolwork and community life. Sociological critique helped the student teachers recognize misperceptions that they'd come to accept as normal. Application of critical theory allowed the student teachers to view some of the existing barriers to the implementation of the civic mission of education. Examinations of the cultural values that contribute to disengagement reveal examples, such as in the following description from the 2003 Wingspread College Conference Report:

> Youths are told to ingest large amounts of information that point to a concern, yet are often discouraged from acting on their knowledge and idealism until they have secured their own economic futures. This deferral, coupled with a belief in the primacy of one's rights, leads to a perception that disengagement and apathy are youthful character flaws, when they are more accurately flawed social norms. (Granicher, 2003)

I had noticed in the past that applications of critical theory helped reveal to teacher candidates the unrecognized and inappropriate socializing aspects of the educational system; however, it didn't provide them with a usable model for their practice. These college students have gained access to the graduate level of academic competency mostly by means of their social status, their ability to navigate the advocacy systems, and/or their political connections. Few have experienced the empowering pedagogy that would motivate or inform them to want to use it with their own students. In her chapter on "Reinventing Teaching," Deborah Meier (1995) reminds us that "we cannot pass on to a new generation that which we do not ourselves possess" (p. 146). For this reason I wanted to infuse service learning, *high-quality* service learning, into our teacher preparation program.

High-quality projects are those that provide participants with opportunities to recognize and identify with social and political inequities, to participate in planning and implementing ways to rectify them, and to demonstrate self-efficacy as a result of their political engagement with the community. My specific objective was to provide opportunities for future teachers to experience political engagement on both personal and professional levels. Teachers who have experienced success as political activists know the social and personal values their students can gain from similar experiences. Those who haven't can come to value it when they see their students' responses to participating in a student-centered service-learning project. The children get to experience authentic learning, the kind that allows for reciprocal connections to the world beyond the classroom. Teachers who make content accessible through service learning provide children with opportunities to apply their knowledge while they come to recognize the value of civic engagement.

Once children find success in identifying and solving problems, they are more likely to engage with others to participate in community life. Civic engagement has always been an important concept in public schooling. For 32 years, Americans have ranked "preparing people to become responsible citizens" as the number one purpose of the nation's schools. However, according to a Phi Delta Kappa/Gallup Poll, "there is alarming evidence that students are not getting the knowledge and skills they need to participate in civic, community, and political life" (National Alliance for Civic Education, 2002).

Methods Used to Teach Service Learning to Student Teachers in the Social Studies Course

Karen and her colleagues, 17 other graduate students, were each paired with veteran teachers in kindergarten through eighth grade classrooms in schools located in the vicinity of the university. They were required to plan, implement, assess, and reflect on a service-learning project in collaboration with their cooperating teachers and "borrowed" pupils. First, students were introduced to the seven qualities that must be present in service-learning projects (Service Learning 2000 Center, 1995). Class exercises provided opportunities to assess examples of projects and look for the following attributes: opportunities for *dialogue* on local issues, pupils giving *voice* to their interests and concerns, addressing an authentic *community need*, *collaboration* between community partner and pupils, *integration* of standards-based content, pupils engaging in *civic action*, and pupils discovering what they have learned through ongoing *reflection*. Students were instructed to use seven steps (not necessarily coinciding with the seven qualities listed above) described in the teacher's guide for *Voices of Hope* (Giraffe Heroes Project, 2004) to structure their projects:

1. Choose the problem
2. Research the problem
3. Decide on a project that addresses the problem
4. Create a vision of the results wanted
5. Make a plan
6. Take action
7. Reflect and celebrate.

Each step was to be guided by one or more of the empowering values provided by Shor (1992); that is, curriculum was to be situated, affective, democratic, participatory, dialogic, desocializing, interdisciplinary, multicultural, activist, and include problem posing and researching.

Students were required to begin their planning process with three considerations in mind: (a) the interests, issues, and concerns that were part of the everyday lives of their pupils, (b) the content standards that were to be taught at their grade levels, and (c) their own ideals for the classroom society and the community it was related to. Gathering data on their pupils' interests and concerns required good observation skills, opportunities to build relationships with the children, and time for conversations with the cooperating teachers. The grade-level content standards are available from the *History-Social Science Framework for CA Public Schools, K–12* (California Department of Education, 2005). What was most difficult for some students was designating personal passions and ideals. The students had trouble setting aside preconceived notions of what teachers were supposed to do and to be. They did not recognize the constraints inherent in the fact that teachers interpret material they teach, filtering it through their own traditions and linguistically mediated experiences (Gallagher, 1992). Without careful reflection and critique, teachers pass along unintended messages to their students, messages that implicitly carry their own unexamined assumptions (Bowers & Flinders, 1990). An example of this was made clear at one point when a student teacher was trying to engage his seventh- and eighth-grade pupils in a dialogue for the purpose of brainstorming problem-solving ideas. Listening in, the cooperating teacher "helpfully" pointed out the various reasons that each of the pupils' suggestions wouldn't work. His deeply ingrained belief that teachers should tell students what will and won't work undermined the student teacher's efforts to develop pupils' abilities to contribute their ideas, debate them, research them, and discover collective ways to solve problems.

It was necessary for student teachers to negotiate their planning with members of the communities involved, with the cooperating teachers' needs, and with their own highly structured schedules. These constraints often made it impossible for student teachers to carry out all seven of the elements of high-quality service learning. As long as the student teacher was able to designate what was missing and explain reasons for its omission, this was not seen as a problem. The goal was for the students to demonstrate that they knew how to carry out a high-quality service-learning project, even if they were unable to fully actualize it.

Once a problem was identified, the student teacher was directed to turn to Wiggins and McTighe's (1998) Universal Backward Design model for guidance in planning. The students learned that the outcome they were assessing was not a project, but rather an enduring understanding that they believed would have value beyond the classroom. It needed to involve "doing" a discipline and to allow pupils to see how knowledge is generated, tested, and used. Teaching an enduring understanding would provide opportunities for pupils to grasp difficult concepts and/or processes while also offering potential for engaging pupils by provoking, and connecting to, their interests.

Students' Assessment of Their Service-Learning Projects

To evaluate the success of their projects, students maintained journals throughout the semester, and then reflected on two levels. They assessed their ability to develop and carry out their projects, and they evaluated their outcomes in terms of the enduring understandings they had established as goals. They used Ira Shor's (1992) set of descriptors for analyzing their curriculum and the teaching/learning environment in which their pupils' projects emerged. In this way, they could test the quality of their projects with the values that promote authentic learning, critical thinking, self-efficacy, and civic engagement. In addition they took note of the presence or absence of the seven elements of high-quality service learning. They shared descriptions of their projects with each other in class and wrote final reflections[2] on the outcomes of their projects.

Analysis of the Data and the Findings

In their reflections, students described their successes and failures and what they would do differently, as well as what they learned about service learning as a strategy for teaching social studies. I analyzed students' final reflections by looking for what worked to promote student teachers' abilities to implement their projects and what barriers they encountered. In particular I looked for evidence of student teachers' recognition of pupils' behaviors that indicated civic engagement was an outcome of their projects.

Factors That Enabled Desired Outcomes of Service-Learning Projects

Good Understanding of the Nature of High-Quality Service Learning and How Pupils Learn

All but three of the students demonstrated a good grasp of what teachers needed to do to carry out high-quality projects. Those who were most successful took great care to use the generative approach. Joan, whose third- and fourth-grade pupils carried out a buddy project with kindergartners attributed the surprising level of responsibility that her pupils showed to the fact that "the idea for the project was student-generated." She explains, " This largely contributes to the sense of ownership that the students had in what we were doing. To my own credit, I consciously put all of the decision-making power with respect to what the project would actually be into the [pupils'] hands." Several students described times when they were tempted to take over their pupils' projects but knew to resist this natural tendency and were rewarded with the fact that they could trust the children to make appropriate and creative decisions.

Since much of the students' understanding of the benefits of teaching with service learning came during their final reflection process, they realized the importance of providing opportunities for their pupils to reflect, too. One student whose kindergartners engaged in a playground cleanup project wrote,

> In the future, I would like [my pupils' review of their efforts] to include more suggestion and evaluation of the future of the project. This was the major aspect that went missing, a fact I hadn't realized until I began to write my own cohesive thoughts. We were so proud of our clean playground that formal evaluation was lost in the celebration. It would have been wonderful to hear reactive suggestions from the people we welcomed to our celebration.

Coming to the strategy with an appropriate pedagogical theory provided the students with the scaffolding necessary to make the right decisions during the planning and implementation of their projects. One student noticed the integration of the two: "Service learning and Shor's values are so entwined that if you choose to follow one of these modes of teaching you are inevitably choosing the other as well."

Most of the student teachers recognized the importance of student voice in the planning of the project. Alice's class decided to raise funds needed to train seeing-eye dogs. She wrote, "Of foremost importance to me was why the students chose this specific community cause to address; I believe it was because they have a tangible relationship with two people affected by a physical challenge."

While student teachers were working as temporary members of their borrowed schools, some of them struggled to identify authentic community needs. Successful student teachers discovered the value of supporting existing conditions with their projects. For example, Tom said, "My project came from a goal that the school already has in a more broad sense," because teachers had formerly identified bullying as a schoolwide issue that needed to be addressed.

One of the major misunderstandings about service learning is that it's not an additional activity to be inserted into the already crowded curriculum; instead, it's a strategy for teaching standards-based content. Student teachers were required to integrate social studies and language arts content standards into their lessons; however, many of them found opportunities to include math, science, and visual and performing arts standards as well. Student teachers recognized the value resulting from this kind of integration. One noticed that, "Students were able to work on life skills as well as curricular skills." Another's remark describes authentic learning: "Service learning allowed me to integrate state standards while building students' social skills which can be taken out of the classroom into the 'real world.'"

What excited student teachers most, as exemplified in Karen's e-mail message at the beginning of this chapter, was their pupils' response to the action phase of their projects. Karen described the children's changing opinions of each other while seeing new skills emerge as a "powerful thing to watch." Brenda's pupils went through a daunting series of communication activities in their efforts to gain support for their plan to beautify their school grounds. She was glad she didn't intervene when difficulties arose, because she said, "Having the students write the letters instead of me was effective, because it gave them a sense of ownership and responsibility for their garden."

Finally, some student teachers demonstrated their understanding of the important role of reflection in high-quality service-learning projects. Providing ongoing opportunities for their pupils to reflect on their activities allowed the children to discover not only what they'd learned, but also the meaning it had for them. For example, one student teacher recognized the value of affect in creating responsible citizens: "I think that feeling happiness about helping others is a major first step in achieving civic responsibility."

Opportunities to Interact With Pupils in Different Contexts

Students were to approach the planning process by finding out the concerns, issues, and interests already present in their pupils' lives. In describing this process, one student recalls how she was able to integrate her project with grade-level requirements regarding pupils' understanding of their neighborhood and the work that goes on there:

> Because I wanted to avoid a teacher-centered syllabus as much as I could, I spent time listening to the kindergarten world. Fortunately, my kindergartners were engrossed in an event surrounding "jobs" close to the time my search [for a project idea] began. Because the language and experience was familiar to the students already, I decided to begin a pursuit of student knowledge/desires by problem-posing about "jobs." . . . There is nothing quite as honest as young children talking about something they are familiar with.

Opportunities to Integrate Curriculum

Students' reflections included many expressions of surprise at the ease with which they were able to incorporate required subjects into the process of conducting their service-learning projects. Integration happened in four different ways. Natural emergence was the form that caught students off guard. For example, Brenda's garden project "went along with the season and what [the third graders] were already doing with the class coursework." Another form of integration took shape as student teachers intentionally looked for ways to incorporate more areas of the curriculum. Because they had expected major challenges, students' reflections included comments such as, "Much to our surprise we were able to address at least 8 different content areas."

A third form of integration arose for several students who came to recognize how to use the social studies framework's broad goal of skills attainment and social participation. They realized they were integrating social studies with other curricula when they combined the teaching of study, thinking, and participation skills while presenting and practicing content in other subjects. Finally, there were a few students who found natural connections among curricular areas when the study of a comprehensive topic was at the heart of their project. One student described how the pupils' research on water quality and use integrated social studies with three other subjects: "We studied how California has changed as we studied how water has changed along with it. [We] also incorporated reading through homework [assignments] and science, because changing water affects the ecosystem; math was addressed with the calculation of the water usage and making of graphs."

Opportunities to Differentiate Learning

Rarely do student teachers reach the point in their professional development where they can successfully create lessons that meet the needs of diverse students. Therefore, it was surprising and gratifying to find that service learning enabled some of the students to address different learning styles in their projects. Like Karen, quoted in the beginning of this chapter, some students found that new contexts for learning the standards allowed previously disengaged pupils to function at the same level as everyone else.

Access to the Community

Students' community partners included people as close as the classroom next door, as well as those farther away, such as elderly shut-ins within walking distance of the school. Several students began class projects that at first involved the principal or the custodian and then spread to the rest of the school, allowing them to see the possibility of a larger influence than they first imagined. One student wrote, "Service learning is great because it helps integrate the community into the school and the [pupils] into the community." One student's project brought children and their parents together, because pupils told their parents and others about the class meetings they were having as part of their project. In several cases the schoolwide community was able to witness the impact pupils can have on community issues.

Support of the Collaborating Teacher and Principal

Interestingly, only one of the students wrote, "Having the support of my cooperating teacher was fantastic! . . . She helped me reflect and encouraged me to try different teaching techniques." It appears that most of the service-learning projects were well tolerated rather than nurtured. Nonetheless, comments in students' reflections indicated that, even though school personnel were not very helpful, they were not discouraging. For example, in her reflection on where the garden's produce might go once it was harvested, Karen wrote, "I would like to see the kids go to the shelter and interact with the people there. This will not happen before I leave the school, but my cooperating teacher is very enthusiastic about finishing this project."

Opportunities to Observe Positive Results

Even though students worked in their classrooms for just 12 weeks, most were able to see remarkable changes resulting from their service-learning projects. For example, one student teacher had been struggling for several weeks to unite pupils in a common goal. He found that once these middle school children realized he was serious about tapping into their authentic interests, he "could see the barriers that divide the class start to lift off." One student described how interacting with the community promoted pupils' self-efficacy: "Students were empowered by learning that they can make a real tangible difference in a community."

Factors That Limited Desired Outcomes of Service-Learning Projects

Some student teachers and their cooperating teachers described conditions they believed interfered with the success of the projects. A common problem was the lack of time for ongoing discussions, a necessary component inherent in the collaborative nature of community service learning. Another time-related limitation student teachers encountered was conflicts with school and district schedules associated with testing practice and administration, various week-long seasonal breaks, and grading periods. Often school personnel perceived the student teachers' required projects as additional curricula for which there was no time. If they had understood that the grade-level content standards were to be integrated into the context of the project, they would have been able to help the student teachers find the appropriate entry points to teach required subject matter.

Two more limitations surfaced in the analysis of the data: student teachers' initial misunderstanding of the process, and cooperating teachers' reticence to adjust to nontraditional forms of teaching. Students needed to explain the nature of high-quality service learning in order to gain the confidence and support of their cooperating teachers and principals. Since they were only beginning to apply the lessons learned in their social studies course to their work in the field, a few were unable to articulate a clear description of what they needed to do. This initial misunderstanding of the process undermined their ability to engage pupils in the problem-posing aspects of the strategy. Omission of pupils' voices in the project results in one developed through what Shor (1992) refers to as "teacher talk." If the teacher plans the project and tells the pupils what to do, the opportunity for children to experience mutual discussion is missing. Key to making the process critical and democratic, Shor tells us, is "balancing the teacher's authority and the students' input" (p. 85). Compounding these few student teachers' inability to carry out the problem-posing aspect of their projects was their cooperating teachers' instructional style. Mentors understandably focused their attention on helping their student teachers establish an authoritative presence in the classroom or didn't model dialogic and participatory methods of teaching. And even if they understood the student teachers' democratic agenda, they couldn't always go along with it because "teaching as telling is hard to dislodge" (Meier 1995, p. 143).

Even in the presence of limiting factors, most student teachers gained a working understanding of the two basic characteristics that result in high-quality projects: integrated learning and meeting authentic community needs discovered through collaboration. Most also came to recognize the importance of student voice in the project, the use of dialogic teaching methods to allow the emergence of that voice, and the role of reflection in allowing learning to emerge. Unlike the other six essential elements of service learning, political and civic engagement emerged more as a result of the process than as part of the student teacher's plan.

The Relationship of Empowerment to Civic Engagement

One of the seven essential elements to be included in service learning is civic responsibility. No particular emphasis was placed on promoting civic engagement with service-learning projects; yet, a few students' reflections indicated compelling levels of its presence, represented here by Joan's comment, "The strongest component of the project, in my opinion, was in how it fostered a sense of civic responsibility. I was really taken by the level of responsibility my students showed." This surprising result suggests the potential for this strategy to provide teachers with a means of developing what is generally deficient in our citizenry. Using service learning, teachers can engage children as active, responsible citizens. Ultimately this strategy allows teachers to

> encourage students to know, understand, and appreciate democratic history and process; understand how to engage in the democratic process and recognize when they are involved in it; and know how decision-making occurs in the development of public policy and participate in it in appropriate ways. (California Department of Education, 2003)

The Civic Responsibility Work Group (California Department of Education, 2003) suggests five sets of skills and dispositions needed by youths to be effective citizens. Although few students stated it directly, their reflections suggested that their service-learning projects provided opportunities for their pupils to develop the following five traits.

Interpersonal and Communication Skills

Mary's kindergarten class became much more cohesive as a result of the service-learning project. She wrote, "I was amazed to watch as the students addressed responsibility throughout this project, whether it was in or out of their garden. Students worked together to keep their garden looking beautiful, and have learned firsthand how their actions can impact their local environment." Another student wrote, "I couldn't go to all the community visits, so I had to rely on [pupils'] observations and reflections; within my classroom I noticed a better support system . . . reliance upon one another rather than on me."

Inquiry and Critical Thinking Skills

Reflecting on her pupils' dialogue about what to do with the produce grown in their garden, Karen noticed applications of their research and evaluative discussions in their postproject behaviors. She said,

> At first the students wanted to have a party in the classroom with our vegetables and invite some parents to join. However, after discussing service and community in greater depth, the students decided that it would actually be more helpful if we donated the food to people who don't have any. The fact that the students were able to come up with this idea tells me that they are better grasping the fact that civic responsibility is important and we need to help each other in the community.

Action

One student teacher compared a project in which she had made all the decisions to one that she said

> evolved so much from the students. I had attempted to lead students
> through another project earlier in the semester in which it was much more
> teacher-directed and it failed miserably. This project emerged naturally. . . .
> I had a vague idea of what the outcome would be, but did not care what
> course we took to get there. As a result, I was able to let the students take
> more control and choose what was important for them.

Several of the students were surprised and delighted at their pupils' ability to think of good ideas and carry them out with little assistance. About her first graders, one student teacher wrote, "I am confident that if we were to do a second service learning project, I probably could turn over more responsibility to them."

Dispositions/Self-Awareness

Joan's third graders developed a project in which they taught their kindergarten buddies how to make a healthy snack. She wrote,

> The students already had a relationship with the buddies. The service-
> learning project built upon this foundation in a way that helped to coalesce
> and more sharply define their relationship. This was incredibly important
> to me, and probably what I valued most about this project. This lesson in
> civic responsibility gave these students who are so used to feeling helpless
> a way to be in the teacher/organizer/mentor/decision-maker role.

Tools

Bernice's pupils "learned that in order for change to happen, they needed to 'use their words' in various mediums, such as letter writing and dialogic interactions with each other, their parents, and their community." Amy wrote of her kindergartners, "Student voice had opportunity to shine in recognizing the ideas I bridged the children's thinking toward. Their voices were also able to show through my planning in helping to coordinate ideas for concrete representations of our project (i.e. signs that would be posted on the playground and developing the celebration)."

Final Thoughts

In her e-mail message to me, Karen found it easy to find reasons for the successful outcome of her service-learning project. What is most important is her current news report; she is excited enough about the outcome of her initial endeavor to become involved in another service-learning project with an activist focus. Karen's engagement in the process assures me that she trusts its ability to contribute to her pupils' self-understanding and to the participatory climate in her future classes.

Along with curricular standards, textbooks, institutional norms, and relationships with colleagues and pupils, Meuwissen (2005) found that teacher education courses and teachers' personal beliefs are two powerful influences on their classroom decision making. This course has addressed what he refers to as the "disconnections between methods instruction and life in the classroom" (p. 253), and these data suggest that the social studies students recognize that.

The results of this study lead me to believe that the social studies students have become hooked on the use of service-learning pedagogy. In continuing to empower the children in their classrooms, they are developing the leadership qualities that can result in creating political and civic engagement as the natural attitude of democratic citizens. The next challenge for these new teachers may be to learn how to respond to the K–12 hiring processes that may not positively recognize service-learning competency (Anderson & Pickeral, 1997).

In an address at the 2006 Association for Supervision and Curriculum Development Annual Conference, Andy Hargreaves lists endurance as one of the characteristics for promoting lasting change. He said, "If you want continuity, you must distribute leadership to many" (as cited in Scherer, 2006, p. 7). By infusing high-quality service learning into teacher preparation through the social studies class, a small contribution to the promotion of education's civic mission has been made. Never mind small; civic engagement *is* the distribution of leadership, so change is in the wind.

Notes

1. Hereafter, comments by student teachers are direct quotations taken with permission from their reflections written at the completion of their service-learning projects.

2. Along with notes taken during exit conferences with cooperating teachers, these final reflections were the primary source of the researcher's data.

References

Anderson, J., & Pickeral, T. (1997). Challenges and strategies for success with service-learning in preservice teacher education. Retrieved from http://www.nationalserviceresources.org/filemanager/download/NatlServFellows/anderson andpickeral.pdf

Bowers, C. A. (1984). *The promise of theory: Education and the politics of cultural change.* New York: Teachers College Press.

Bowers, C. A., & Flinders, D. J. (1990). *Responsive teaching: An ecological approach to classroom patterns of language, culture, and thought.* New York: Teachers College Press.

California Department of Education. (2003). Linking service and civics through service learning: The report of the Civic Responsibility Work Group. Sacramento, CA. Retrieved from http://www.cde.ca.gov/ci/cr/st/linkservicecivics.asp

California Department of Education. (2005). *History-social science framework for CA public schools, K–12.* Retrieved from http://www.cde.ca.gov/re/pn/fd/documents/ hist-social-sci-frame.pdf

Doll, W. (1993). *A post-modern perspective on curriculum.* New York: Teachers College Press.

Freire, P. (1995). *Pedagogy of the oppressed* (Myra Bergman Ramos, Trans.). Rev. 20th ed. New York: Continuum Press. (Original work published 1968)

Gallagher, S. (1992) *Hermeneutics and education.* Albany: State University of New York Press.

Giraffe Heroes Project. (2004). *Voices of hope service learning guide.* Langley, WA.

Granicher, B. (2003). Linking service/civics through service-learning: The report from the Civic Responsibility Work Group. California Department of Education. Retrieved from http://www.cde.ca.gov/ci/cr/sl/linkservicecivics.asp

Meier, D. (1995). *The Power of their ideas: Lessons for America from a small school in Harlem.* Boston: Beacon.

Meuwissen, K. W. (2005). Maybe someday the twain shall meet. *Social Studies, 96*(6), 253–258.

National Alliance for Civic Education. (2002). *The importance of civic education.* Retrieved from http://www.cived.net/tioce.html

Scherer, M. (2006, May). Perspectives/the challenge to change. *Educational leadership, 63*(8), 7.

Service Learning 2000 Center. (2004, 1995). Service learning dipsticks: A project assessment tool. Retrieved from http://www.yscal.org/resources/assets/Dipsticks .pdf

Shor, I. (1992). *Empowering education: Critical teaching for social change.* Chicago: University of Chicago Press.

Wiggins, G., & McTighe, J. (1998). *Understanding by design.* Alexandria, VA: Association for Supervision and Curriculum Development.

13

SERVICE LEARNING THAT ENGAGES STUDENTS IN THE IMPLEMENTATION OF CHILDREN'S RIGHT TO PARTICIPATE IN COMMUNITY DECISION MAKING

Kim Knowles-Yánez

Children at Mission Middle School in Escondido, California, could easily list the deficiencies of the physical environment of their school: graffiti, old bathrooms, sweltering locker rooms, lack of landscaping, and unkempt playing fields and fences. The school is, after all, over 50 years old and shows all the expected signs of age. The school is located in an overcrowded and impoverished part of Escondido's urban area. Most staff, faculty, and administrators have their hands full dealing with the overcrowded student population. Indeed, the school was known as Grant Middle School up until it failed to meet the standards of the No Child Left Behind Act in 2005. The school is now being restructured at the same site with a new name: Mission Middle School. The students of the school have little power to change anything about the socioeconomic conditions of their neighborhood or the overcrowded and underachieving nature of Mission, but that does not mean they are unable to research, analyze, and problem solve to improve their school's physical environment and, in the process, learn valuable skills for participating in political and civic life. As the middle school students have learned through participatory action research projects with university students at California State University, San Marcos, they can engage in the political life of their school by activating citizenship skills, making a difference, and achieving positive changes in the physical environment of their school.

Adults rarely have the opportunity to enable the political engagement of children. In fact, our society is firmly structured to privilege the political power of adults over children. The opportunity to think about the political rights of children provokes self-examination of one's own political rights, which can lead to a deeper understanding of one's own opportunities and tools for political engagement. This chapter will introduce faculty to a service-learning practice that enables university students to work with children on environmental issues in any setting. Underlying the concrete task of improving the physical environment of children is the practice of genuine political engagement by the university students and the children. This concept is guided by the principle that every child has a right to participate in decisions that affect his or her life. As university students facilitate children's participation in environmental issues, both sets of learners are engaged in democratic processes and techniques that expose them to the value of civic participation. University-level students learn the value of activating children's rights and become more aware of their own right to participate as they work in the field with elementary and middle school children in a class titled Children and the Environment.

My disciplinary background is in urban and regional planning. I was hired by a liberal studies department to teach geography and geographic information systems classes. Most liberal studies students plan to become teachers. As my classes evolved, I developed an interest in my students as future K–8 teachers. I asked myself how my disciplinary background—urban and regional planning with a strong interest in community development and civic decision making—might help future teachers. My interest in planning has always stemmed from wanting to understand how members of communities make decisions about how community resources are used. Could I help future teachers develop ways of thinking about children as members of a community? In turn, could the process of helping children in civic participation lead students to a higher level of political engagement? First, I had to better understand what role children could play in community decision making. My interest in this area was piqued when I began to study the United

Nations 1989 Convention on the Rights of the Child (CRC) and the literature that evolved out of the CRC (UNICEF, 2006).

The CRC contains four guiding principles: nondiscrimination, best interests, survival and development, and participation. The latter guiding principle has spawned a whole body of literature that explores the child's right
to participate in decisions that affect his or her life (Knowles-Yánez, 2005). I
consider Chawla (2002), Driskell (2002), and Hart (1997), all of which are
excerpted in my Children and the Environment class reader and are described below, seminal works in the field of action research projects with
children.

Each author made key contributions. Hart (1997) identified the action
research technique as a way of activating the right of the child to participate
in decision making for his or her physical environment. Chawla (2002) and
Driskell (2002) expanded on this idea in the revival of a project called Growing Up in Cities (GUIC), which is sponsored by the United Nations. In this
project, researchers from around the world work with children in their local
communities, employing action research techniques that help children better
understand and solve problems for their communities. Through GUIC projects and the research techniques employed, children become politically engaged. Techniques include:

Informal observations and "Hanging Out"
Interviews
Drawings
Daily Activity Schedules
Family and Support Networks
Role-play, Drama, and Puppetry
Guided Tours
Photographs by Young People
Behavior Mapping
Questionnaires and Surveys
Focus Groups and Small-Group Discussion
Workshops and Community Events (Driskell, 2002)

Recognizing that children could be involved in decision making in engaging and age-appropriate ways helped me to better understand the role of

children in civic and political engagement. I realized that, not only do children have an authentic and engaged role to play in community decision making; it is in fact their right to take part in making decisions.

These two ideas led to the design of my class Children and the Environment, an upper-division interdisciplinary social science course that provides a creative, experiential, and meaningful approach to working with children in developing their own communities and learning lifelong political engagement skills. In this class, most students complete service-learning action research projects oriented toward community problem solving with children. I begin the semester by spending the first several weeks exploring the CRC and the types of action we can take to activate the underlying goal of the CRC: the child's right to participate in decisions that affect his or her life. The literature argues that children are not ready to participate in social problem decision making (Hart, 1997). For example, children cannot be expected to have the social and developmental tools nor the understanding to work on solving social problems such as poverty and disempowerment. However, children are able to understand physical (or environmental) issues such as the condition of the locker rooms at their school. And, on these types of physical environment issues, children are able to take action, learn more about the problem, and even provide guidance to adults on ways to improve the physical conditions of their environment. For example, in the GUIC project in Semilong, Northampton, United Kingdom, children worked with adults to come to a better understanding of the use of community spaces. In the GUIC project that took place in Boca-Barracas, Buenos Aires, Argentina, children worked with adults and used mapping and photography techniques to create a community action plan (Chawla, 2002). These activities involved age-appropriate data gathering and problem solving that gave children the tools to see that they are active participants and citizens of the world around them. These experiences become seminal examples and provide well-honed political and citizenship tools that others can emulate.

Action Research

Action research involves placing participants in a setting in which they, as active researchers, collect data and solve problems for their own environment (Hart, 1997). For example, many land-use planners use a workshop technique, sometimes called a *charrette*, in which participants describe the community they live in and collectively shape goals and ideas for the changes they would like to see in their community (Race and Torma 1998). This is action research because it involves people collecting data about their own experiences and systematically analyzing it to create new knowledge regarding the future of their community. Action research can include other techniques, such as participant observation, guided walks, the creation of photographic exhibits, and oral histories. These techniques have been adapted to address the CRC's call to involve children in community decision making. For example, Driskell's (2002) GUIC manual describes how to work with children to create maps and use photography that will allow the children to show others how they view their neighborhoods. The children of Boca-Barracas in Argentina "developed an exhibition of their photographs to express their perceptions and ideas to the larger community" (p. 133). Rights-based action research calls upon adults to facilitate children's participation in collecting data about their communities. This call to action represents a kind of political engagement rarely practiced by adults—the facilitation by adults of children's political engagement. By using action research, children learn more about their communities and, when they deem it necessary, plan actions to improve their communities.

Hart (1997) advocates the following action research process when working with children: problem identification, analysis, planning, action, evaluation and reflection, and more action and evaluation and reflection until a successful end to the project is reached. Political engagement and democratic ideals are embedded in this kind of action research. The literature has demonstrated that children's participation in decision making for their physical environment has the potential to ensure their rights to participate in decision making, to bolster their decision-making skills, and to teach them skills needed as citizens in a democracy. Chawla comments on several projects she has been involved with:

> For the children involved in the GUIC project, being listened to appeared to have a powerful effect. The South African chapter described how the children of Canaansland moved from initial shame over what they assumed to be the inadequacy of their words, drawings and ideas—having internalized a sense of inferiority as squatter children—to increased self-assurance after they learned that they and their ideas would be treated with respect. Similarly the children in Baybrook moved from an apathetic conviction that they and their views were unimportant, to enthusiastic creativity when

they had a chance to contribute to transforming their environment for the better. (p. 234)

Indeed, merely explaining to children that they have the right to participate in decisions that affect their lives can be empowering. All too often our schools teach about citizenship, voting, and democracy via textbook learning and testing. This has its purpose but is not the same as fostering genuine engagement by letting children research a problem that they care about and nurturing an environment where they can devise ways to address the problem. Letting children conduct action research gives them tools to act upon their citizenship and effect proactive change. In turn, having college students work with children who are in the process of learning how to implement their own right to participate reinforces the knowledge college students have about political engagement, democracy, and participation.

Class Organization and Design

The class covers a broad array of topics related to children and their environments, with a significant portion of the class devoted to discussion of children's rights and action research. The learning objectives of the class are for students to understand and appreciate children's rights, action research with children, development of environmental competence, childhood socioeconomic conditions, environmental health issues facing children, and land use planning and children. A complete list of readings can be found on the syllabus (see Appendix A).

During the first third of the semester, students are introduced to the research on children's rights. Several weeks are spent discussing how to employ action research with children. This includes a discussion of case studies and methods. The intent is to prepare the students as quickly as possible to work on their action research projects outside class time. This is necessary since it can sometimes take students awhile to develop a relationship with a group of children. Other topics covered include children and the environment, children and wild areas, children and urban areas, children in the U.S. family, and children and toxic chemicals. Midsemester, students give presentations on their action research projects. The last week of the class is dedicated to in-class presentations on the results of the action research projects. The final exam includes an essay question about these projects, which all students, even those who did not complete action research projects with children, must answer.

Conducting action research projects requires student flexibility. Students are asked to continually adjust as they progress. As the children they are working with, the students are learning by doing, which is at the heart of action research. Students have to decide what group of children they are going to work with, how they will facilitate group cohesion and problem identification, what techniques they will use to guide the children, and make adjustments in techniques and approaches as their work progresses.

Over the years, my students and the children they have worked with have chosen a variety of environmental projects to work on. Sample projects include beach garbage pickups, school improvement projects such as fence painting, and nature journals. The typical trajectory of a student project involves first finding a small group of children to work with followed by an icebreaker activity that engages the children and gets them to talk about their physical environment. For example, guided by class discussion and readings, especially the techniques suggested in Driskell (2002), many of my students initiate the process by having the children draw a map of their neighborhood or their school. Students then interview or question the children about what they have drawn on their map. A second activity might include walking with the children around their neighborhood or their school, asking them what they like and do not like about their surroundings. In the second meeting with the children, the college students are expected to adjust techniques and develop an understanding of the engagement they are trying to nurture. As one pair of students wrote in their final paper about their group's second meeting:

> Discussions [between the students and the children] were good, but [the children] still had no real grasp as to what they were really doing and why. To help keep motivation high, we asked [the children] to take us on a tour of the school's campus using a video camera to document the areas that were important to them and other areas that caused concerns (Driskell, 2002, p. 102). It was during the tour that some of the boys offered up some questions and problems that they had with the campus and wanted to discuss in more detail.

One of their concerns was the condition of the locker rooms at the school. From this point on, this group focused on the locker rooms as its project.

From these experiences, students come to see what the children appreciate about their neighborhoods and schools and what they see as problematic. The children, facilitated by my students, identify the issue or problem they wish to focus on. In the locker room project described above, this stage presented a challenge for my students, which underscored and tested their understanding of democratic decision making, again from this group's final paper:

> The consensus [of the children] was split between having more lockers added to the locker room and construction issues regarding making more space within the room by moving walls and enlarging entry ways. . . . As facilitators, this portion of the project presented some issues since we did not want to discourage the children in their identification of the problem. . . . Having an understanding that any attempt to try to convince a school board to knock out a wall to make five extra feet of space would not likely happen, it was difficult to dissuade the children from proceeding with this concept.

My students took this opportunity to step back and slow down the problem identification process so that they could facilitate the children becoming more informed about the situation. In fact, my students never forced the children to come to a consensus on which aspect of the locker room to focus. Rather, over the next few meetings, they slowed down the problem identification phase and guided the children toward collecting more data on the condition of the locker rooms, which the children eventually presented to the principal.

With the target issue in mind, the groups move on to collect data about the problem area. As Driskell (2002), Chawla (2002), and Hart (1997) suggest, this process may involve interviewing others, taking and classifying photos, or talking to experts. The data collection period can be lengthy.

The problem-solving phase, which can also take a long time, follows. Guidelines to the students make it clear that it is OK to spend most of the semester on problem identification, data collection, and planning actions. In fact, I make it clear that they are to emphasize process and engagement over product. I do not want students to feel that they have to rush the children toward a conclusion to the project. Rather, I want them to take the time necessary to complete any given step of the action research process, without undue concern about making it all the way through the process.

For children at Mission Middle School, our long-term study site, graffiti was often identified as something the children did not like to see at their school. Working with my university students, the children learned that they could do something about the problem by talking to their school principal. Over the course of a year, several groups of students visited the principal to talk about the graffiti, and after each conversation graffiti was removed. One group presented a historical overview of graffiti to the principal and other teachers as a way of demonstrating their research activities. The children learned that they can perform good citizenship in their school community and actively solve problems in their school. These service-learning projects served as powerful examples of how and why children should be involved in community problem solving.

All students in the class are taught and tested on the same action research literature. Additionally, all students involved in action research service-learning projects are required to present information about their projects to the class, first, at the beginning of their project, and again at the end of their project. This way, even those students who do not choose to complete an action research project are able to follow along with and learn from the students who do them. The final exam includes an essay question asking each student to describe implementation of the action research technique, using a class project as an example.

Logistics and the Service-Learning Setting

Teaching service-learning classes requires flexibility on the part of the faculty member. Because many of the students taking this class are also working, caring for family members, and taking other classes, not all students are able to take on the extra demands involved in meeting with small groups of children on a regular basis throughout the semester. Thus, while it would be ideal for every student to complete an action research project with children, I have adapted the final project to allow for other options. Students are given three options for completing the class project: (a) writing a rigorous literature-review-based research paper on a class topic developed in concert with the instructor (for example, previous students have written research papers on how toxins such as lead in the environment affect children, the impact of fetal alcohol syndrome on a child's development, and the effects of divorce on a child's education), (b) conducting action research with children they have organized (typically from church groups, their own neighborhood, or from their student teaching), or (c) participating in my long-term action research project with children at Mission Middle School.

As I mentioned earlier, flexibility is a useful characteristic to employ when teaching service learning. One of the ways I try to make action research with children accessible to my students is by giving them a choice of service-learning sites. They can work at the site of their choosing or at Mission Middle School. After several years of teaching this class, I found that focusing on one site best suited longitudinal research (Knowles-Yánez, 2005). I originally established a relationship with Mission Middle School because it was the primary educational institution in the most impoverished neighborhood in our community. The mission statement of California State University, San Marcos, declares that the university will nurture "sustained enrichment of the intellectual, civic, economic, and cultural life of our region." I incorporated this mission into my nascent project by reaching out to this middle school in spring 2005. Administrators were receptive to the idea of action research and I have been working with my Children and the Environment students at Mission Middle School ever since.

Students also choose their own service-learning setting for their action research project with children. Allowing students to chose their own setting means that they typically find one they feel comfortable in and anticipate having minimal startup issues.

Social Mobilization Versus Action Research

The learning objective of this class is for students to read, discuss, and write about the literature on participation, rights, and civic decision making and then apply what they have learned as they work with children and youths in action research projects. Thus, they learn how to involve children and youths in planning, decision making, and problem solving for their actual, lived-in communities. The outcomes of such an approach include increasing the political engagement of students, facilitating the development of children, and improving the well-being of communities.

The rights-based approach is based on the CRC, which asserts, as a guiding principle, the right of the child to participate in decisions that affect his or her life. Students in this course learn the importance of having children experience authentic participation, in which they, with adult guidance, set the agenda and decide what issue(s) they wish to study. According to Hart (1997), "The great value of participation over social mobilization . . . is that it fosters the long-term development of citizenship, and more specifically, a sense of local responsibility, rather than simply providing a short-term solution to a community problem through the use of free labour" (p. 15). When children decide for themselves that they want to contribute to improving their physical environment through garbage pickup or graffiti removal, this action has a more meaningful impact on them than when adults simply tell them to pick up trash or remove graffiti. While children could find the latter quite fun, it is not genuine political engagement.

In this project, students learn that to set the agenda for the children and provide too much guidance would lead to social mobilization, which would be an undesirable outcome (Hart, 1997). While students grasp the meaning of authentic participation rather easily, they often exhibit difficulty in employing the concept in the field. Asking future teachers to turn the tables on themselves by requiring that they let the children decide what issues they want to research is initially disorienting. As one student wrote in her final paper, "When I spoke to [the children] of having rights and the ability to present their point of view, it seemed as if I was speaking a foreign language since they did not comprehend the concept any more than I had in the beginning." Many students begin their projects and after the first meeting come to my office to discuss the feasibility of authentic participation. They are afraid that they will end up guiding the children too much and will never be able to move beyond social mobilization. I assure them that the action research technique requires that they put on a different hat. They learn to feel their way toward merely guiding and facilitating the children. As one student wrote in her final paper:

> The one problem I faced throughout the entire project was worrying too much about whether or not the project could be seen as a perfect example of authentic participation. I had a younger group and when they would state something like "we will have an adult take the donation to the Red Cross," I would record and validate that idea but at the same time let them know that their idea needed more information. For example, who is the adult? where is the Red Cross? and who will ask them to help? etc.

I identify the process that they are going through—the tension between the new (facilitating and engaging) and old (directing) way of dealing with the children—as one of the most important learning experiences of the class.

Overcoming Student Fears of Implementing Action Research

Allowing students to choose not to do the action research project eliminates some of the worry about how they will implement it. This can have unintended yet positive consequences. Several students decided early on to do the literature review research project instead of the action research, then found their own curiosity leading them back to the action research project. In a social setting, they observed children talking about their environment and mulled over in their minds what they were hearing about in class regarding action research with children. Suddenly they found themselves conducting an action research project. The fact that the project came to them rather than having them seek it out was exciting to the students and provided them with what they reported to be "fun and thoroughly enjoyable" learning environments.

For instance, one of my students unexpectedly found herself implementing action research with a "girls under age 12" soccer team that she coached. My student planned to do a research project rather than the action research project to fulfill class requirements, but as she was coaching her team, she found herself using skills she was learning in class to encourage her players to find out more about why the team practice schedules, field layouts, and equipment-use schedules were the way they were. This led team players to draw maps of the playing field, consult with the league director about the schedules, and devise a map of all the playing fields, which helped equal out playing time with the desired equipment. My student began to view the children she was coaching and herself as active participants in decision making within their community. Her players, in turn, learned another set of civic engagement skills from their soccer coach.

Time Constraints

A problem that crops up every semester is that the length of a semester is often too short for students to complete the projects they have started with the children. Since I emphasize process and engagement over product in the project outcome reports, whether or not they have "finished" a project with the children is not important in terms of their final grades. However, some students have a sincere desire to bring the project to a more natural end point for the children. This usually involves working with the children beyond the end point of the semester, after they have already turned in their final papers.

Fabrication and Oversight

One of the most disappointing moments of my academic career occurred while reading the student evaluations of this class the first year that I implemented action research as a requirement for all students. One of the evaluations pointed out something that I had not suspected—some of the students had fabricated their action research experience. I thought about this a great deal the following summer. I reasoned that I did not want to do away with the action research component of the class and that I would never be able to police the truth of each student's project given the many settings and meetings involved. I did believe that I could rein in the temptation to cheat by alleviating the pressure on all students to complete their own action research projects. This is the reason students are allowed to choose other options. If they simply cannot come up with a comfortable setting to work in with children on their own and do not want to participate in the Mission Middle School project, they have alternatives. However, the structure of the class ensures that even those who do not conduct action research learn a great deal about it via course discussions, reading material, exams, and class presentations.

Assessment

The change in students' understanding and ability to implement action research with children is tracked via mid- and end-of-semester presentations as well as their final report. In this report, students are required to compare the opinion they brought to the class (regarding participation and children's rights) with how they viewed these issues after taking the class. The point of the assignment is to determine whether their experience with rights-based action research changed their understanding of civic decision making, rights, planning, action, and participation. I grade each presentation and paper based on a preset rubric (see Appendix A). The intent of each rubric is to reinforce the directions provided for the assignment and reward or discount their work based on their overall quality of engagement with the project. This allows me to give proper credit to students who are enthusiastic in their approach to applying children's participation and to those who successfully explain (in writing or in oral presentation) the links between their service work and the theory studied in class.

Sometimes the change in students' perceptions during the course is dramatic. For example, one student wrote in her final class paper,

> Growing up, I always did what I was told. I never questioned authority because to do so is considered disrespectful in my culture. . . . You can imagine my surprise when I read the CRC and participated in action research for the first time. What an amazing tool for children that fosters knowledge, appreciation, and civic engagement towards the greater good. Having seen the change in some of the [children] from the beginning of the project to the end, I can see the power of implementing action research with [them] in order to empower children with knowledge about what it means to be an active citizen in a democratic society.

Many of the class discussions and readings emphasize how to recognize authentic participation, even as they are creating the setting for it themselves. Here is how one student wrote about coming to understand this in her final paper:

> Over the course of this project, my perception of children's participation has changed completely. Before the project, I was mainly familiar with social mobilization, where [children] carry out a predetermined agenda. To me, participation was participation and it didn't matter whether it was predetermined or not. I did not understand the effect that authentic participation has on children. . . . Instead of being told that they have rights, they were given the freedom to exercise them, which in return, caused them to take on greater responsibility than they would have otherwise. . . . The girls that I worked with were thinking on completely different levels than I ever imagined they could.

Since many of the students consider themselves future teachers, their reflections on what they have learned often allude to how what they have learned in this class will help them in their teaching practice. From another student's final paper:

> When I spoke to [the children] of having rights and the ability to present their point of view, it seemed as if I was speaking a foreign language since

they did not comprehend the concept any more than I had in the beginning. Having an understanding of rights and developing a voice through the democratic process, the [children] were able to identify a problem. This is a key concept for me as a future teacher. . . . this concept was an eye-opening experience for me as I watched the students' attitudes and understanding of their own environment change from week to week.

Of course, student writings and presentations on their projects are important and illuminating; however, some of the most rewarding feedback comes verbally from the students. In the beginning of the semester, many students in the class tell me how frustrated they are as they make the set of decisions for setting up their projects, talk to children, and devise activities for the projects. They frequently lament that they just don't get what I want them to do. I reassure them that this is the kind of project that they will only understand as they implement it, that feeling reticent and unsure is typical, and that it is impossible to fully understand action research by merely studying class materials. I coach them as best I can with their specific projects and then wait. Invariably, the same students will rush up to me before or after class to report on a breakthrough they have had with their children and tell me that the children are really excited to work on trash collection or a school improvement project. In these moments, and more formally in their presentations and written reports, students demonstrate understanding that the set of decisions they made for how to set up their meetings with children, how to facilitate the work with children, how to employ research techniques, and how to nurture the action research process, guided by the literature studied in class, led to a deepening of their knowledge and practice of political engagement, as well as that of the children they worked with.

Future Directions

Logistics are always the hardest part of service-learning efforts and I encourage faculty to work with their own campus service-learning and human subjects research offices on the details surrounding their projects. According to my university's human subjects' research board, it is not necessary to receive permission for each student to work in a setting of their choosing on their class action research project. However, with my long-term research site, Mission Middle School, I did want to set up a formal relationship. The advantage of working within an established relationship is that you can build on previous work. You do not have to start from scratch. Indeed, even while working at the same school site, I have experienced constant turnover of staff. Yet, while I have had to explain my project again to new staff at the beginning of each semester, I can refer them to other staff members who know my work at the school. Faculty can explore forming service-learning relationships with local school districts and/or individual schools in order to implement the action research projects discussed here. If their university is like mine, it has already established contractual service-learning relationships with local school districts. This means that instructors do not have to set up the service-learning contracts on their own. However, it was still necessary for the instructor to make and nurture the individual contacts to garner permission to work at the school. So far, my principal contacts have been with people who work in the after-school programs. However, it is likely that a civics or history instructor would be interested in introducing action research and civic engagement skill-building techniques to students.

Presenting students with a rarely used tool of political engagement such as facilitating the right of children to participate in decision making in their communities is a unique way of reinforcing student decision making and participation skills. Working with university students on participatory community action research has tremendous potential to reaffirm and create new knowledge of democratic practices for our university students. Perhaps, just as beneficial, is the legacy these projects have on the children our students serve. Through action research service-learning projects, our students nurture the seeds of democratic practice in children—the future adults of our communities.

References

Chawla, L. (2002). *Growing up in an urbanizing world.* London: Earthscan.

Driskell, D. (2002). *Creating better cities with children and youth: A manual for participation.* London: Earthscan.

Hart, R. A. (1997). *Children's participation: The theory and practice of involving young citizens in community development and environmental care.* London: UNICEF.

Knowles-Yánez, K. (2005). Approaches to children's participation in land use planning processes. *Journal of Planning Literature, 20*(1), 3–14.

Race, B., & Torma, C. (1998). *Youth planning charrettes: A manual for planners, teachers, and youth advocates.* Chicago: American Planning Association Planners Press.

UNICEF. (2006). *Convention on the rights of the child.* Retrieved from http://www.unicef.org/crc/

Appendix A

LBST 307: Sample Syllabus, Project Instructions, and Grading Rubrics

Syllabus:

Course Web site: http://courses.csusm.edu/lbst307kk/

Course Description
This course provides an interdisciplinary exploration of the environment and children. Students will engage in cross-disciplinary exploration of children's rights, the development of children, childhood and socioeconomic conditions in developed and developing countries, the particular environmental health issues facing children, planning and sustainability, and children's relation to wild and urban areas. Particularly useful for students who are parents, or who plan to be parents, and for those who wish to work as teachers, or with children in other professions.

Learning Objectives include student knowledge of and ability to write about and discuss:
- children's rights
- action research with children
- children's development of environmental competence
- childhood and socioeconomic conditions
- environmental health issues facing children
- land use planning and children
- natural areas and children

Students will complete an environmental action research project involving children or a research project based on course topics. These assignments are designed to fulfill the university-wide writing requirement.

Required Book: Sobel, David, *Children's Special Places: Exploring the Role of Forts, Dens, and Bush Houses in Middle Childhood*, Wayne State University Press, 2002.

Topic and Reading Schedule, based on two class meetings/week:
Introduction
Interdisciplinary Study, Democracy, and Children's Rights
Reading: UNICEF's Convention on the Rights of the Child

Research Projects
Reading: From class Web site, Directions for Children and Participation Action Research Project *and* Research Project

Children's Participation
Reading: Author: Hart, "Children's Participation Introduction," excerpt from *Children's Participation: The Theory and Practice of Involving Young Citizens in Community Development and Environmental Care*
Review: Author: Driskell, "Participation Toolkit" excerpt from *Creating Better Cities with Children and Youth* and "Interview 01 by Louise Chawla"

Children's Participation
Reading: Author: Driskell, "Young People's Participation," excerpt from *Creating Better Cities with Children and Youth*

Children's Participation
Reading: Children as Community Researchers: http://www.unicef.org/teachers/researchers/

Children's Development I

Children's Special Places I
Reading: Sobel, beginning to p. 74

Children's Special Places II
Reading: Sobel, pp. 77–161

Children's Development II
Reading: Author: Nabhan, excerpt from *The Geography of Childhood*, "The Scripture of Maps, the Names of Trees," Nabhan and Trimble
Author: Louv, excerpt from *Last Child in the Woods*

Academic Research
Class Meets in Library for Research Session

Planning and Children I (Land Use Planning)
Reading: Author: Bloom, "Viewpoint: Does Littleton Deserve the Blame?" *Planning*, July 1999
Author: Condomitti, "No Space Left to Play Ball" *North County Times*, October 30, 2002.

Planning and Children II
Reading: Author: Hersch, "Introduction" from *A Tribe Apart*

Author: Hamilton, "How Suburban Design Is Failing Teen-Agers," *New York Times*, May 6, 1999

Planning and Children III
Reading: Author: Chawla, Chapter 10—"Toward Better Cities for Youth and Children" from *Growing Up in an Urbanizing World.*

Children and Participation Project Oral Progress Reports
Research Project Prospectus Due
Hand out study guide for midterm exam

Making Connections: Review for Midterm
Midterm Exam

Children, War, and Terrorism I
Reading: Author: Crosette, "When War Steals a Parent, or a Childhood," *New York Times*, January 26, 2000.
Watch in class video: *Children and War*

Children, War, and Terrorism II
Finish watching *Children and War*

The Child in the U.S. Family I
Reading: Author: Kirn, "Should You Stay Together for the Kids," *Time*, September 25, 2000, Vol. 156, Issue 13
Watch in class video: *Vanishing Father*

The Child in the U.S. Family II
Reading: Author: Herbert, "When Strangers Become Family," *U.S. News and World Report*, November 29, 1999, Vol. 127, Issue 21
Finish watching in class video: *Vanishing Father*

Children and Health Issues in the Environment I
Reading: In Harm's Way: Toxic Threats to Child Development, Greater Boston Physicians for Social Responsibility

Project Presentations

Final Exam

Children and Participation Action Research Project Instructions (from http:// courses.csusm.edu/lbst307kk/):

Objective of your Children and Participation Action Research Project:

The objective of this project is for you to engage in an action research project involving children. The children in your group will drive the project; you will guide them in agreeing upon the physical environmental issue to be researched. This process will teach you a method for working with children and to research environmental issues that you may apply throughout your life and career; the same process will teach the children about citizenship, democracy, and participation. You will present your work in written and oral formats.

Forming your group of children:
Some specifications for the group of children you work with:
- The children should be between 5 and 15 years old.
- Your group should consist of 2–8 children.

Some good places to contact children who might be available to work with you: at church; within your own family; in your volunteer work; in your neighborhood; in a school you may work at; through your work; community organizations such as Cub Scouts, Girl Scouts, Boys and Girls Club, YMCA; and after-school programs such as the YMCA or those sponsored by public schools. Additionally, Professor Knowles-Yánez may be able to arrange for some of you to work at Mission Middle School (newly renamed from Grant Middle School) in Escondido.

It is important that you work with the same group of children throughout the duration of your project.

Some of the settings you may choose to work in may require a letter of introduction/ explanation. Please ask for help if you need assistance in writing this letter or ask me to provide you with such a letter should the need arise.

Setting up your Project: You have a lot of leeway in setting up your action research project, however, you must keep in mind that the actual design of the project will be determined by the children you work with.

Your project will follow the steps shown on p. 92, Figure 34, of Hart, and slightly modified below:

1. Group Formation.
2. Icebreaker. (Plan a mapping, walking, drawing, game, reading or camera activity as an icebreaker. Also, remember that children love

to eat and drink and usually have three meals and a midmorning and midafternoon snack. Make sure to provide snack breaks as needed.)

3. Problem Identification, p. 92. (Note that problem identification does not mean that children must identify a problematic issue in their environment; rather, it only means that children must identify an issue they want to research. They do not need to try to "solve a problem." Their research can be as simple as identifying and evaluating elements of their environment. For example, they can create an atlas that documents their physical environment or they can create poster boards that describe what they like or don't like about their school.)

4. Investigating the Study Site or Theme, p. 95.

5. Analyzing and Interpreting the Data, p. 96.

6. Planning Environmental Actions, p. 97.

7. The Actions, p.97.

8. Evaluation.

Your goal for this project should be to complete "Planning Environmental Actions," though you should keep later steps in mind and complete them where possible.

Methods: "Children as Community Researchers," Driskell's "Participation Toolkit," Chawla's interview instruments, and other class readings provide explanations of the kinds of participatory techniques you may use with your group. We will also discuss these techniques in class.

Keep the developmental level of the children you work with in mind. Revisit Hart's "Developmental levels of social perspective-taking" (p. 32), "Children's Developing Capacity" (p. 90), and "The development of children's capacity to make and use maps"(p. 166).

KEEP IT SIMPLE! *Do not become focused on creating a product at the end of your project.* If there is a product, great! But remember, the goals of this project are for you to learn how to conduct action research with children and to teach children about citizenship and participation. The process is the goal here.

Recording your activities: You should keep detailed notes of all your activities for this project, from inception to completion, because these notes will be crucial toward completion of your progress and final reports. Look at the directions below for your final report so that you can have a clear idea of the categories of information you will need in order to write your final report.

By all means, keep any of the written material your activities with the children generate so that you can share these with the class during your progress reports and final presentation.

Grading: Your grade on this project is based on:

1. Midsemester Oral Progress Report
2. Final Written Report
3. Final Oral Progress Report

Consult your class syllabus for due dates and for the percentage of your overall grade each part is worth.

Oral Progress Report

For the oral progress report, your goal should be to reach the stage of "Problem Identification."

In your talk:

- introduce your project to the class by explaining how it is an action research project.
- identify the setting and the group of children, include demographic information about the children and the setting; a good place to start to research this information is the U.S. Census Bureau Web site: http://factfinder.census.gov/home/saff/main.html
- provide an up-to-the-minute report of your progress in organizing and working with the group
- describe any problems you have encountered (do not focus on time and logistical issues.)
- indicate how you might conclude the project
- and elaborate on the participatory nature of your project **by describing what your research has to do with the CRC, children's rights, authentic participation, action research, and increased understanding of citizenship in a democracy.**
- if you use PowerPoint or some other graphics presentation tool, be sure to cite in writing or verbally any graphics or material you copy from another Web site

Before your presentation, review the grading rubric for the Oral Progress Report.

When you receive your graded oral progress report grading rubric back from me be sure to save it as you will need to turn it in again with your final paper. I will use the notes I make on your grading rubric to grade your final paper. Therefore, if you do not understand something I've written on your rubric, you must ask me to clarify.

Final Report: This will be your opportunity to present a complete description of your project, from inception to completion. Working from the detailed notes you have been taking while conducting the project, you should write a 10-page report that contains the following:

- A step by step description of your project, from inception to completion. This means that you must create a stand-alone report, one that will fully explain your project to someone who knows nothing about it. Be sure to describe your role in the activities and to provide a description of the children.
- Demographic information about your children and study site. Include demographic information about the children and the setting. The U.S. Census Bureau Web site, http://factfinder.census.gov/home/saff/main.html, is a good site to use for this.
- Description of problems you encountered.
- *A thorough explanation of what your project has to do with the CRC, children's rights, authentic participation, action research, and increased understanding of citizenship in a democracy.*
- Reflect on how your perceptions of children's participation, rights, citizenship and democracy have or have not changed during the course of the project
- Standard essay format: an introduction, a body, and a conclusion.
- Your paper must include citations and a list of references (bibliography). All material from another source must be cited. You may use any citation/reference/bibliographic format that you are familiar with; however, you must maintain consistent formatting throughout your paper. You must cite Hart for the action research technique and you must cite the CRC in your discussion of children's rights. See the CSUSM citation and bibliography guides.
- Attach your original, graded oral progress report grading rubric to your paper so that I will be able to use the notes I made on your rubric as I grade your final paper; I will check to make sure you followed through on my suggestions.

Edit your paper very carefully and check your spelling. Grammar, spelling, and syntactic variety will count toward your final grade. Review the grading rubric for the paper.

Please heed the following guidelines for all written work turned in for this class:

> Include an introduction, body, and conclusion in your essay
> Edit for style and grammar
> Spell-check
> Use 12-point type
> Double space
> Have 1-inch margins
> Follow the required page length
> Include only complete paragraphs with clear transitions
> Include a thesis statement in the introduction
> Include complete citations for all material (paraphrases and quotations)

Avoid plagiarism:
Long quotes (those over 4 lines in length) must be indented. You should not have more than one long quote per every 5 pages. All quotes must have quotation marks and citations. All paraphrased sections must have citations. All graphics taken from a Web site must be cited in writing. Review the complete discussion of plagiarism in your syllabus.

Oral Presentation of Final Report:

Describe your project and elaborate on the participatory nature of your project *by describing what your research has to do with the CRC, children's rights, authentic participation, action research, and increased understanding of citizenship in a democracy.*

Audiovisual aids are strongly encouraged. Review the grading rubric for the final presentation, which will also show you how your presentation should be formulated. (Note: Presentation schedules will be discussed in class, closer to the due date.)

Progress and Final Oral Report Grading Rubric

Name: _____

_____ (60) Baseline for doing presentation, with preparation evident

_____ (10) Introduction, which identifies project and children

_____ (10) Conclusion, which summarizes project

_____ (10) Communication of ideas; graphics and other material from other sources cited in writing or verbally in presentation

_____ (10) Overall Quality of Engagement With the Process

Comments:

OVERALL GRADE: _____ **(of 100)**

In your talk:

- introduce your project to the class by explaining how it is an action research project.
- identify the setting and the demographics of the group of children; include demographic information about the children and the setting. A good place to start to research this information is the U.S. Census Bureau Web site: http://factfinder.census.gov/home/saff/main.html
- provide an up-to-the-minute report of your progress in organizing and working with the group.
- describe any problems you have encountered. (Do not focus on time and logistical issues.)
- indicate how you might conclude the project.
- and elaborate on the participatory nature of your project by describing what your research has to do with the CRC, children's rights, authentic participation, action research, and increased understanding of citizenship in a democracy.
- if you use PowerPoint or some other graphics presentation tool, be sure to cite in writing or verbally any graphics or material you copy from another Web site.

Final Report and Analysis Grading Rubric

Name: _____

_____ (10) Introduction, which identifies project, children, and underlying concepts

_____ (20) grammar, spelling, syntax, proper use of citations, and format

_____ (25) quality of discussion of the underlying concepts: CRC, authentic participation, action research, and increased understanding of citizenship in a democracy

_____ (25) communication of ideas (Are the steps your project engaged in clearly examined? Does the reader have a good sense of who the children you worked with are and how they reacted to the progress of the project?)

_____ (10) Conclusion, which summarizes project and underlying concepts

_____ (10) Overall Quality of Engagement With the Process

_____ (5) Reference List

Minus 5/page for each page under 10 pages; minus 5 for not citing all sources in text; minus 20 for not citing any sources in text or not including a reference list; minus 10 for each day late.

OVERALL GRADE: _____ **(of 100)**

INDEX

ACORN. *See* Association of Community Organizations for Reform Now
action: civic skills projects and, 188, 193; teacher education and, 212
action research, 219–22; fabrication and, 228; project instructions for, 234–41; versus social mobilization, 225–26; student fears on, 227; in teacher education, 224–25
activism, 101–58; assessment and, 108–12; definition of, 132–33; emphasizing, 139; resources on, 116n2; students and, 130; values of, 112–14; women's studies and, 128–43
Activism Project, 140–42
administration, and politics, 7
advocacy: for children's decision making, 216–41; as civic skill, 6; communication studies and, 103–27; Gulf Coast Civic Works Project and, 144–58; small business and, 88; for undercounted populations, 53–67
African Americans, and small business, 83–85, 97n1
alternative voting systems, 12
Asen, Robert, 31
assessment: in communication studies, 108–12, 127; in economics, 81; in government course, 194–95; in journalism course, 169, 173–75; in social research course, 45–50; in teacher education, 204–10, 228–30, 237, 239–41; in women's studies, 141–42
Association of Community Organizations for Reform Now (ACORN), 153, 156–57

banking model of education, 137
Barajas, Manuel, 38–52
Bollinger, Lee, 166
Bowen, Linda, 161–82
Bradberry, Steve, 157

Buchanan, Jeffrey, 157
business: and political engagement, 69–99; service learning in, 82–99

California Employment Training Panel, 92–93
Carlos, John, 146–47
CCC. *See* Civilian Conservation Corps
census anxiety, 55
Census 2000 Complete Count Campaign, 56–57
census ignorance, 55
census studies, 53–67; background of, 54–55; community partner agencies, 66–67; objectives of, 55–58; organization and implementation of, 57–58; outcomes in, 58–60; recommendations for, 60–61
charrette, 219–20
children, and community decision making, 216–41
citizen journalism, 169
citizenship: informed, media mentors and, 161–82; student conceptions of, 8; women's studies on, 132–34
civic engagement: definition of, 6; empowerment and, 210–12; index of, 9; teacher education and, 197–215. *See also* political engagement
civic sensibility, 169
civic skills: definition of, 185–88; development of, 183–96; importance of, 184–85; teacher education and, 200–201, 211–12
Civilian Conservation Corps (CCC), 148
Civil Works Administration (CWA), 148
classroom: in Political Campaign Communication course, 25–28; in women's studies, 130, 137–38
collaborative learning, 129; in teacher education, 202, 208–9